Temples of the Earthbound Gods

Temples of

he Earthbound Gods

Stadiums in the
Cultural Landscapes
of Rio de Janeiro
and Buenos Aires

CHRISTOPHER THOMAS GAFFNEY

University of Texas Press ◆ Austin

Requests for permission to reproduce material from this work should be sent to:
    Permissions
    University of Texas Press
    P.O. Box 7819
    Austin, TX 78713-7819
    www.utexas.edu/utpress/about/bpermission.html

∞ The paper used in this book meets the minimum requirements of ANSI/NISO Z39.
48-1992 (R1997) (Permanence of Paper).

Library of Congress Cataloging-in-Publication Data

Gaffney, Christopher Thomas.
    Temples of the earthbound gods : stadiums in the cultural landscapes of Rio de
Janeiro and Buenos Aires / Christopher Thomas Gaffney. — 1st ed.
        p.   cm.
    Includes bibliographical references and index.
    ISBN 978-0-292-72165-4; 0-292-72165-X
    1. Stadiums—Social aspects—Brazil—Rio de Janeiro. 2. Stadiums—Social aspects—
Argentina—Buenos Aires. I. Title.
    GV415.G32 2008
    725'.827098—dc22   2008018452

To all those who have lost their lives in the stadium

Contents

Foreword

JOHN BALE

The stadium is a significant feature of places ranging from metropolitan centers to small towns and villages. The stadium, like the church, is a place of congregation—and, some would say, worship. In addition to the church, several other metaphors seek to essentialize the stadium—a garden, a theatre, and a prison. On the one hand, it is a much-loved place that folks often want to retain as a community focus and as a site that stimulates a sense of pride. On the other, it is arguably the most secure building in the city; hence, it has historically been used as a site of incarceration for criminals, immigrants, and "others." Consequently, over time it has become meaningless to name a stadium after its sport. A baseball "field" or a "football ground" can be turned into a convention center, almost at the switch of a button. Instead of being a much-loved site, the stadium has become a multi-purpose facility, typified by domed arenas with their artificial lighting and plastic greensward.

Stadiums vary in size, function, and design. It is often felt that stadium architecture is becoming more standardized, moving toward the concrete bowl (after Le Corbusier) as a machine for making sport. Unarguably, the rules and regulations, manifested in the layout of the "playing" area with its predictable lines, zones, and limits *are* being standardized. In the stadium are found predictable geometries. The "sameness" that characterizes the sports site makes it a global phenomenon. A soccer pitch has to have the same dimensions in London, England as in London, Ontario. Geography has to give way to geometry.

The stadium is a melding of horticulture and architecture. I find it interesting that while rules and regulations govern the traditional layout of the horticulture (i.e. the playing "field"), the surrounding architecture is given free reign in terms of design. Difference can be found in the architecture that is required to contain the sporting action and to provide for spectators. Compare, for example, the postmodern exterior of the Beijing Olympic stadium with the gothic, granite facade of the 1912 Olympic stadium at Stockholm.

There are few sports whose immediate milieu has not been written about in some form, and written works on the stadium cover a vast spectrum in subject matter and approach. Many relate to the summer sports of baseball and cricket. Others allude to football stadiums, hockey arenas, and swimming pools. A single stadium can take up a book. The famous rugby ground in my home city of Cardiff, for example, has been eulogized in *Taff's Acre: A History and Celebration of Cardiff Arms Park*. Also on my bookshelf I have William Jasperson's *The Ballpark*, a paean to Fenway Park in Boston. From France, *Les Yeux du Stade* is an insightful text on Colombes, the stadium in Paris that is dubbed *Temple du Sport Français*. Other books take a broader view. For example, Philip J. Lowry's *Green Cathedrals* celebrates the 271 Major and Negro League ballparks past and present. Similarly, Simon Inglis has surveyed *The Football Grounds of Europe*. Each of these are valuable and informative works, but they tend towards the less scholarly end of the spectrum; therefore they are often snobbishly labeled "coffee table" books.

At the other end of the spectrum a substantial amount of writing is the result of heavier "academic" work, scripted by those among us who are paid to study sport. *Stadion: Geschichte, Architektur, Politik, Ökonomie* is a stunning 450 page tome published in Austria and essayed by an interdisciplinary group of scholars from several nations. I co-edited a similar kind of multi-authored publication, *The Stadium and the City*. Other "heavyweight" texts are scattered among journal articles and monographs. They deal with such subjects as the costs and benefits of stadium relocation and the economic impact of a stadium on its surrounding community. They command a relatively small audience despite the burgeoning field of sports studies.

In the representation of the homes of sport the "popular" and the "academic" sometimes come together. Novelists allude to the stadium in ways that inform our senses as well as supplying the "facts." Philip Roth is a case in point. In two of his early works he reveals the place and "meaning" of the baseball stadium in the life of the troubled Alex Portnoy, while in *Goodbye Columbus*, he deconstructs the sport-spaces (swimming pools, basketball courts, high school running tracks) of suburban New Jersey. But also take, for example, the delightful little book by A. Bartlett Giamatti (a renaissance scholar and former President of Yale University and Commissioner of Major League Baseball) titled *Take Time for Paradise*. In this work the baseball stadium is more than a "temple"—it is paradise itself. Also in a more humanistic vein, Christian Bromberger, in *Le Match de Football*, has analyzed the ritual dimensions found in stadiums in Marseille, Naples, and Turin through the eyes of an anthropologist and ethnologist.

To these highly selective studies must now be added the work of Chris Gaffney. In the pages that follow he supplies a novel and wide-ranging view of the world game of soccer, or football as Europeans insist on calling it. His work is wide-ranging but also narrowly focused on two major soccer cities in South America—Buenos Aires and Rio de Janeiro. He is not the first to study soccer in these cities; Eduardo Archetti has researched the former while the latter was the focus of the pioneering study by Janet Lever. Each of these eminent scholars was an anthropologist. Gaffney was trained as a geographer, however, and has applied the geographer's broad gaze to a wide field. He works through a variety of scales—from murals and monuments to rituals and records. He paints views of what it is like to be in the stadiums of these two giant cities, teasing out examples of "sense of place" and *genius loci*. At a different scale he explores the global football scene, including of soccer's history and its diffusion to, and adoption in, Latin America.

My view is that this book, with its lavish collection of photographs, maps, and diagrams, and its clear and lively writing, deserves to be read and digested by readers in all disciplines. Unquestionably, it makes a major contribution to geographical studies of sport but it has much to tell students and teachers in cognate fields. It will also satisfy the Latin Americanist and the informed sports fan.

Preface

It is often said of writers that their first book is autobiographical. This book is no exception. I spent my adolescence somewhere between Dallas and Fort Worth working at an all-you-can-eat catfish restaurant on the Interstate 30 frontage road that zipped past Arlington Stadium, home of Major League Baseball's Texas Rangers. During the summers, the stadium set the rhythm of work and I would listen to the radio broadcast of the game with my fellow busboys and dishwashers. Occasionally, a famous ballplayer would come into the restaurant and we would queue up for autographs. One year, my brothers and I managed to get hold of a home plate from the stadium, installed it in our backyard, and built an outfield fence of pilfered plywood. Whenever I had to explain where I was from I would answer, "Arlington, you know, where the Rangers play." That satisfied some people. My high school buddies and their families worked at Arlington Stadium in a variety of capacities: ticket vendors, parking lot attendants, ushers, grounds crew, concessions. Even though the Rangers were never very good, in the 1980s "Metroplex," Arlington Stadium and a pair of amusement parks put us on the map as the "Entertainment Capital of Texas"—an early lesson in the geography of the banal.

When the 1994 World Cup came to Dallas, what happened in and around the Cotton Bowl was a revelation. Nigerians, Mexicans, Bulgarians, Argentines, Koreans, Germans, Brazilians, Dutch, even U.S. Americans all gathered in the same place to celebrate the same thing: Football! ¡Fútbol! Fußall! Futebol! Soccer! Having played and watched the game for most of my life, I thought I wouldn't be surprised by the power of it, but seeing and feeling people from all over the world celebrate together was simply fantastic. Partying outside the stadium, saying the names of famous players over and over again, remembering wonderful goals, expressing a collective sense of justice and injustice was enough to make friends from all over the world.

Before the World Cup, I had joined a soccer team in Austin run by Irish and English, populated by Euro-Americans of various stripes. My life as itinerant carpenter was quite literally punctured, and I made the transition to moving furniture and hanging curtains. After several months of scrimping, I quit my various mundane jobs, sold my things, and bought a one-way ticket to Costa Rica. I had no idea what would happen, but I knew that my soccer shoes were going to be more useful for communicating than my two years of high school Spanish. Six months and a functional second language later, I traveled from Costa Rica through Nicaragua, Honduras, Guatemala, and Mexico—playing soccer nearly all the way. Even when there wasn't soccer, there was baseball, and I had my ideas of stadium normalcy turned on their head when I bought a pint of rum and a Cuban cigar in Managua's Estadio Dennis Martinez while dancing out of the way of fireworks thrown in the aisle. Dennis Martinez! Hadn't he come into the restaurant after a Rangers-Orioles game? I couldn't be sure, but it made for a good story.

After learning enough Spanish to be a danger to myself and playing with locals in both beautiful and terrible places, I went to Taiwan to teach English. While there I found a team run by English and Irish and populated with Europeans, U.S. Americans, and Taiwanese. The league comprised teams divided along ethnic, national, and occupational lines: expat Brits/Scots/Irish/Yanks (one team of teachers, another of rapacious capitalists), South Koreans, Cantonese, Taiwanese, Mainland Chinese, Japanese, Filipinos. There were plenty of fights on the way to winning the league championship on a rainy day in front of 400 fans in the 25,000-seat Chungshan Soccer Stadium. Our team traveled to tournaments around Southeast Asia where we played against ex-pat and local teams from Kuala Lumpur, Hanoi, Jakarta, Manila, Phnom Phen, Hong Kong, and other places. Yet again, football was the glue that established bonds between very different people.

I returned to the United States to take a job as a soccer coach and language teacher at Suffield Academy in Connecticut. Switching from player to coach opened up new ways of understanding the game. My first summer vacation, I joined five friends and rented a twenty-five-foot recreational vehicle for the 1998 World Cup. France '98 confirmed and expanded on everything that I had discovered in USA '94, and subsequent trips to Europe, Latin America, and the Caribbean proved time and time again that participating in, going to, or talking about sport is the easiest way to remove linguistic and cultural barriers while entering preexisting social networks. After reading a few good books on the subject, it seemed plausible to give it a go myself. However, I wanted a more sophisticated framework than that of the flaneur and opted for geography at UMass-Amherst, where the first question from my future adviser and mentor, Dick Wilkie, was, "What is your philosophy of travel?" I had found an intellectual home and began working toward this book.

As I pursued my graduate studies at UMass-Amherst and UT-Austin, teaching courses in geography and anthropology, the stadium became of greater interest to me. Part of the reason was that deciphering space and place became a gripping philosophical endeavor, allowing me to connect my education and lived experience with theoretical frameworks that made intuitive sense. I became absorbed by figuring out how to understand, interpret, share, and connect with the deep cultural meanings associated with stadiums. Why did these places mean so much to so many over such broad reaches of time and space? How could I come to understand similarities and differences between and among vastly different cultures through a common medium? What were the geographic and historical circumstances that spread stadiums to every corner of the globe?

My studies also gave me a legitimate excuse to explore the inner workings of stadiums and to think about their historical and contemporary impact on people and cultures at multiple scales. Of course, being on the field at World Cup Qualifiers, top-level professional games, and third division nail biters wasn't bad either. Some years later, I have been to hundreds of stadiums and seen (counted like Romario's goals) a thousand stadium games in twenty-odd countries on four continents.

To my delight, the more I went to the stadium, the easier it was to get in. And since my playing career had been shortened by multiple and repeated injuries, this was a great good. The more I explored stadiums, the larger they became and the more I found. Unfortunately, I can no longer experience them unconsciously, and after reading this book neither will you. A stadium, even a very small one, is an incredibly complex "thing"—nearly impossible to describe its entirety, each one requiring a deep reading of the cultural landscape.

My travels and studies have taught me that everyone experiences the stadium differently, can tell a different story about it, and uses different language to do it. The complexities of the stadium extend well beyond geographic inquiry into the realms of imagination, city planning, governance and taxation, architecture, environmental studies, transportation infrastructure, sewage, electricity, horticulture, security and surveillance, ticketing, marketing, player migration patterns, international trade agreements, citizens' rights groups, eminent domain law, global capital, local, regional, national and cultural identities, gender performance, geopolitical conflicts, and global mega-events, to name more than a few.

Part of the problem of examining stadiums is their mind-boggling complexity. They can be understood from so many disciplinary, historical, geographic, experiential, and methodological perspectives that a totalizing view is impossible. On the other hand, this complexity allows for nearly everyone to connect with them. If you are reading this, you have been to a stadium and have your own story to tell, your own connections to make. The stadium contains and radiates power, holds and creates memory and meaning, permitting everyone, even those who never go there, to experience it in some form or other.

In writing this book for both academic and general audiences, I allowed stadiums to tell their own stories. Of course, these stories were colored by my experience, abilities, interests, predispositions, and interpretations. As an urban and cultural geographer in a most-modern moment (since postmodernity is apparently behind us), this book is steeped in the traditions of humanistic, cultural, and critical geography, oriented to landscape studies, influenced by cultural anthropology, conditioned by comparative urbanism, and shaped by three languages and minimalist travel. As a meeting ground for multiple and overlapping academic disciplines, geography is a good fit for stadiums, allowing us to identify connections that fit within our particular theoretical and methodological frameworks.

Because this book is based in geographic traditions, there are no clear paths to the goal for those who may wish to discuss it in terms of theoretical models. In some senses, the theoretical grounding of this book is the methodology. By laying out a way to conceptualize stadiums and then getting out and looking at them, I am suggesting direct links between theory and fieldwork in Latin America. I strongly believe in direct and total immersion in the field as a way of coming to grips with an alternative reality. Reflective distance from intensely lived experiences is also a critical element of interpretation.

In other ways, the methodology is the book. The stadiums of these two cities each merits its own tome, but their comparative compression into one book allows us to see larger patterns and processes that would not otherwise be as visible. Comparative urbanism is a blossoming area of investigation, yet the units of analysis are amorphous. By comparing the stadiums of Rio de Janeiro and Buenos Aires, I am also suggesting that this particular spatial form allows us to effectively compare any two urban areas (of similar characteristics) and that through the stadium we can better understand how cities and their sporting cultures function.

In allowing the stadiums of Rio de Janeiro and Buenos Aires to tell their own stories, there developed some rather awkward methodological choices that resulted in a book that gives equal yet unparallel coverage. Each city is treated over two chapters, one historical and one contemporary. In Rio de Janeiro I use four case studies to examine social and political trajectories, whereas in Buenos Aires I use a historically grounded, generalist approach to understand contemporary culture. The reason for this methodological choice is in part that the incredibly high number of stadiums in Buenos Aires makes micro-level investigation problematic as the whole is much more than the sum of its parts. In Rio de Janeiro the coexistence of stadiums with strong national and global symbolism alongside relatively obscure stadiums (even on the local level) within a limited geographic area argued for a micro-level analysis.

One of the most obvious contradictions that resulted from these choices is that in Rio de Janeiro I deal with issues of race and national identity but not gender and sexuality, whereas in Buenos Aires I examine gender and sexuality but not issues of race and national identity. This is not to suggest that race and national identity are not important issues in Argentina or that issues of gender and sexuality are not present in Brazilian stadiums. My intention in choosing unparallel investigative paths was threefold: first, to show that stadiums allow us to navigate through urban and cultural realms in very different ways; second, to deviate from a proscriptive model of cultural analysis; and third, to use stadiums to explore as many different issues as possible. In another person's reading, gender could be a central theme in Rio and race in Buenos Aires but would result in a very different book. I have taken what I believe are the most salient issues from the stadiums of each city and connected them to larger frameworks that I hope will make methodological (and good) sense to the reader. In the event that they do not, I bridge some of the methodological gaps in the conclusion.

That said, this book takes a fairly straightforward approach, moving from the general to the specific and back again. Chapter One outlines a general theory of stadiums, explaining some of their histories, contradictions, complexities, and peculiarities. By developing a theoretical model for understanding *any* stadium, I hope to impress on the reader the idea that *any* stadium tells you more than you can think about all at once. By picking it apart, turning over each constituent element, and putting it back together again, we can begin to see how and why stadiums are such powerful and universal elements of global cultures. I also take some time to set up the ways in which stadiums are especially important in the context of Latin American cities.

Chapter Two takes us to Rio de Janeiro in the late nineteenth century, when there was not a single stadium in Brazil, much less *futevoli* (soccer-volleyball) on Copacabana Beach. We will trace the development of soccer and stadiums through the first half of the twentieth century, exploring the importance of these institutions in the formative years of modern Brazil. By looking at the history, geography, culture, and urban context of four stadiums near the center of Rio de Janeiro, we establish powerful connections between the stadium and issues of race, class, cultural identity, and the development of Brazilian national identity.

Chapter Three grapples with the modern complexities of Rio de Janeiro's twenty-nine stadiums. By following four stadiums from the twentieth to the twenty-first century, we evaluate changes in urban life and public space, local responses to global influences, and gain insight into the social, economic, political, and "footballing" reality in Brazil. As the projected host of the 2014 World Cup, Brazilian and global attention will increasingly turn to the stadiums of its most famous city. As we shall see, there are some serious problems ahead.

Chapter Four takes us thousands of kilometers to the south, where Buenos Aires sits like a coffee-stained tooth in the mouth of the Rio de la Plata. This city of fifteen million is teeming with stadiums. My count puts it at seventy-nine, but you might be able to find one I've missed. In 1880 Buenos Aires had no soccer stadiums and one horse-racing stadium. By 1904 there were more than three hundred soccer teams in the city and stadiums were growing like cattle on the pampas. Today it has more stadiums than any city in the world, and they are among the most intense, violent, and difficult to negotiate (much less understand). By examining the development of urban space and culture in Buenos Aires in the first decades of the twentieth century, when Buenos Aires was assuming its modern character, I identify why stadiums in Buenos Aires are so highly charged with masculine, sexual, and violently aggressive energy.

Chapter Five turns to contemporary Buenos Aires, comparing the stadiums, experiences, and geographies of three sports: rugby, polo, and soccer. Argentina produces world-class athletes and teams in all these sports, but each occupies and constitutes very different social, cultural, and geographic worlds. By entering into these worlds through their stadiums, I piece together a composite picture of *porteño* society that is increasingly fragmented along class lines. By comparing and contrasting the geographies and stadium experiences of rugby, polo, and soccer, we see how stadiums emit and refract the complexities and contradictions of Argentine society.

Chapter Six brings the two cities together and places them in a global context. I demonstrate that by comparing what is happening in the stadiums in Rio de Janeiro and Buenos Aires we are able to discern unique responses to global phenomena that may give us important clues about how we understand and manage these same issues in our own communities. Stadiums in both cities are undergoing changes that are related to larger political, economic, and social processes. I suggest that stadiums are barometers of these changes and that by looking at stadiums as places and spaces of cultural process, sites and symbols of dynamic social interaction, we gain unique insight into who and what we and others are.

Acknowledgments

This book would have been impossible without the guidance and assistance of my friends and colleagues in Buenos Aires, Rio de Janeiro, Durham, North Carolina, and Austin, Texas, among other places. In Buenos Aires I am particularly indebted to Tulio Guterman, whose insight, friendship, and connections opened many doors that I never knew existed. Tulio introduced me to a slew of academics, journalists, and *fútbol* cognoscenti among whom Julio Frydenberg, Roberto di Gano, and Hugo Comesaña stand out. I am also grateful to the Gil and Tomasetti families for opening their homes in some very difficult times. Early versions of the Buenos Aires chapters were read by Elizabeth Jelin and Ines Valdez, and their comments were immensely valuable in shaping the final version. Manuel Balan provided the muscle necessary to push into the *popular* section of at least one stadium. The rest I managed with the help and acerbic humor of thousands of unknown *porteños*. *Es para vos, para vos.*

In Rio de Janeiro, I owe a huge debt of gratitude to Gilmar Mascarenhas de Jesus, whose hospitality and geographic vision helped to shape my perceptions of *a cidade maravilhosa*. Fernando Ferreira also extended untold kindnesses, and his profound knowledge of and passion for Vasco da Gama were inspirational. Thanks are also due to Mauricio, Davidson, Jair, Renato Trindade, the geography students and faculty at the State University of Rio de Janeiro (UERJ) and at the Federal University of Minas Gerais–Carangola. Abbie Bennett earns full marks for sharing the costs of a one-room hovel in Copacabana during the fieldwork. Rodrigo Nunes helped me pick out my first *sunga* and instructed me in some of the finer details of *carioca* culture. Gonzalo Varela and Sofia Alencastro provided critical logistical and moral support in São Paulo, and I am grateful for their friendship.

In the United States, I am indebted to the guidance and support of Paul Adams, who edited and pushed me through the dissertation so this book could be written. Thanks also to those who have participated in conference sessions and contributed to the larger theoretical discussion, particularly Hunter Shobe and George Roberson. Casey and Kristine Kittrell deserve more than I can give in return for their epicurean friendship. Brian Godfrey and Bert Bjarkman read early versions of the Rio chapters and provided valuable feedback. Paul McGinlay and the Trinity University Men's Soccer team deserve some kind of trophy for allowing me to wax philosophic about kicking a ball around a field. I imagine it would look like Rodin's *Thinker* dressed in a Paris St. Germain shirt with a soccer ball underfoot. Thanks also to Jason Reyes and David Salisbury for their design and cartographic aid.

Of course, none of this would have been remotely possible without the faith, confidence, infusions, airline passes, and support of my parents, brothers, and family. And finally, *mil beijos* to Brenda Baletti, whose love and life bring joy to my heart.

Abbreviations

AAFL	Argentine Association Football League
ADEM	Administration of Municipal Stadiums
AFA	Argentine Football Association
AMEA	Metropolitan League of Athletic Sports
APA	Argentine Polo Association
CBD	Brazilian Sports Confederation
CBF	Brazilian Football Federation
CONMEBOL	South American Football Federation
CoProSeDe	Provincial Committee of Sports Security
FERJ	Rio de Janeiro State Football Federation
FIFA	International Federation of Association Football
GEPE	Special Stadium Police Force (Rio)
IMF	International Monetary Fund
ISI	Import Substitution Industrialization
LMDT	Metropolitan League of Terrestrial Sports
SUDERJ	Superintendency of Sports of Rio de Janeiro State
UAR	Argentine Rugby Union
UEFA	European Union of Association Football

Temples of the Earthbound Gods

CHAPTER ONE

The Stadium in Theory and Practice

Have you ever entered an empty stadium? Try it. Stand in the middle of the field and listen. There is nothing less empty than an empty stadium. There is nothing less mute than the stands bereft of people.

EDUARDO GALEANO

Like many others throughout the world, you have probably experienced the drama and passion of sport with tens of thousands of others, screaming, shouting, celebrating as one. Perhaps you have had your memory indelibly scored by a great musical performance, religious ceremony, or political rally. Maybe you have had your heart quickened by a monster truck show or a NASCAR race. Or it could be that you were (or are) skilled enough to play in stadiums and recount your glory days or imagine yourself playing in front of fifty thousand adoring fans. You might work at a stadium, or pay taxes to subsidize stadiums. You might hate stadiums but pass one every day on your way to work or school or get caught up in game day traffic. Regardless of your experience, you have stadium stories to tell. This book connects those stories with places and people across time and space.

Nearly every city in the world has a stadium; it is among the most recognizable features of the cultural landscape. Elliptical tracks circle rectangular fields; fence-bound patches of brown dirt abut acres of genetically manipulated grass surrounded by tiers of silver bleachers. Hectares of black tar envelop giant white domes. Transportation infrastructure leads the anticipated thousands to and from the structure. On the ground, the stadium fills the visual field and road signs point the way. Although not as tall

Photo 1.1 Aerial view of the Maracanã, Rio de Janeiro. Stadiums are frequently dominant elements of the cultural landscape. Their size, location, and importance make them shorthand features for recognizing places.

as skyscrapers, stadiums dominate their local environments and can be products of the cutting edge of architectural techniques and engineering technology.

Stadium lights brighten the night sky, drawing us like moths to the flame. Along with tens of thousands of others, we rush to and from stadiums. Traffic clogs transportation arteries, locals turn lawns into parking lots, enterprising youth commandeer curbsides. Subway cars suddenly fill with scores of people wearing their team jersey. Children drag their parents across the parking lot, groups of friends trot towards the gates, and long lines cause anxiety. Men ply the approaching human tide with upraised fingers, buying and selling scarce tickets.

The rituals of the stadium are familiar: face paint, lucky clothes, consumption of red meat and alcohol, souvenirs, programs, team songs, national anthems, wild gesticulation, yelling at the referee. Stadium events are anticipated well before they happen. Newspapers fill with histories, predictions, statistics, probable lineups, and odds of victory. Dollars, Euros, yen, yuan, and pesos change hands. Media production facilities swing into high gear as millions, even billions, of people gather in bars and homes—even other stadiums—to watch the event. From the "thrill of victory to the agony of defeat," the stadium occupies our attention long after the floodlights have been turned off.

The roar of the crowd may send a tingle up the back of our necks or make us hurry in the opposite direction. As Eduardo Galeano suggests, even when the stadium is empty, it communicates power, history, and meaning. Important for locals and tourists alike, one only has to think of the Roman Colosseum to understand the lasting imprint of stadiums on urban areas.

Stadiums matter to us because they are places where we share common emotions in a common place in a limited time frame. Stadium games, concerts, and spectacles are momentous occasions that live on in our collective memory. The limited space and time of the stadium gives spectators a sense of privileged participation. "I was there when . . . " is a prideful claim made by millions who have attended a stadium event. However, stadiums have also been sites of tragedy, murder, and repression. They represent and reproduce political and economic inequalities. Neighborhood communities organize to stop stadium construction. The effects of the stadium radiate outwards, affecting traffic flows, daily routines, environmental quality, and property values. The stadium has an impact even on those with no interest in what happens there.

Stadiums are the sites of unforgettable human dramas and mundane realities. Jesse Owen's victories in the Berlin Olympic Stadium did not halt Nazi advances across Europe, but they did diminish the glories of the self-styled Aryan race. In 2005 the Louisiana Superdome and the Houston Astrodome housed tens of thousands of refugees from Hurricane Katrina. As you are reading this book, there is an Olympic Stadium under construction somewhere in the world. The ancient Greeks, Romans, Aztecs, and Maya all had stadiums that functioned in ways similar to ours, which suggests that there is something essentially human about them.

More nations compete officially in international sport than in international politics. FIFA (soccer's governing body) and the International Olympic Committee both have more member nations than the United Nations (205, 202, and 192 respectively).[1] This means that nearly every politically organized territory in the world has a stadium where local, national, and international competitions take place.[2] The stadium might be the most global of the globalized.

At the local level, stadiums are monuments, places for community interaction, repositories of collective memory, loci of strong identities, sites for ritualized conflict, political battlefields, and nodes in global systems of sport. On a weekly basis millions of people all over the planet gather at *their* stadiums, *their* home grounds, to participate in sporting events where they renew communal bonds and host teams from other communities. The dying wish for thousands of people is to have their ashes scattered on the field. Others go to the stadium to work as janitors, parking attendants, security, media, or manual laborers. The stadium experience is as particular as the person who has it.[3]

Obviously, stadiums are built so that we can perform and patronize sport, but the ways in which stadiums are constructed, managed, experienced, and understood are as different as the events they host. The meanings and histories they contain, represent, and produce are inseparable from the cultures in which they exist. As fundamental elements of the urban cultural landscape, stadiums impart ideological messages wrapped in discursive frameworks that are in turn informed by multiscalar geographic processes. Which is to say that the more we look at and think about stadiums, the more complex they become. By using stadiums as lenses to observe cultures, we survey historical, economic, political, sociocultural, technological, and globalizing processes as they are expressed on the local level.

This book explores the stadiums of Rio de Janeiro and Buenos Aires in their historical and contemporary contexts. However, before entering into these Latin American mega-cities through their stadiums, it will be instructive to explore how stadiums function on a more general level. What were the historical antecedents for stadiums, and how did they become such important elements of modern cultures? What are the general characteristics of stadiums that make them such apt mechanisms for comparing and contrasting vastly different times and places? And finally, how can we look at stadiums to discover who we are and what we have in common with people past, present, near, middle, and far? After answering these questions, we will be able to make better sense of the stadiums, cities, and cultures of Rio de Janeiro and Buenos Aires.

A Brief History of Stadiums

The word *stadium* comes from the Greek *estadion*, wooden posts that marked the beginning and end points of Hellenic footraces.[4] The

Greeks eventually extended the term to include the entire architectural structure surrounding the race course. As early as 900 BCE stadiums were used as places to celebrate religious festivals through games and athletic competitions. Generally located in rural areas, each religious site possessed a mythical background, and the stadium was intended, along with shrines and temples, to reestablish connections with the divine.[5]

The stone and wood stadiums of the ancient Greeks had dressing rooms, approach tunnels, VIP sections, and tiered seating. Situated within vast religious complexes, a stadium's racetrack ran towards the temple of Zeus. As with modern stadiums, clear boundaries separated judges, participants, and spectators. Greek Games (of which the Olympic Games were but one) were marked by official ceremonies, oaths, and sacrifices similar to modern-day presentation of athletes, singing of national anthems, and pregame consumption of meat. There were wine-fueled Greek hooligans as well. The archaeological record suggests that episodic fan violence sometimes resulted in the destruction of the stadium. Eventually, there were ushers to keep rowdy fans under control. The four-year cycle of pan-Hellenic games that began at Olympia in the sixth century BCE attracted thousands of spectator-pilgrims and hundreds of athletes. As the games became more popular and less religious, the athletes came to be regarded as cult figures in their own right.[6] Athletes underwent rigorous training regimes leading up to the games and were considered paradigms of Greek masculinity. The games also served a larger political role as they began a period of peace throughout the isthmus.[7] The founder of the modern Olympic Games, Pierre de Coubertin, was similarly inspired by the potential of sport to achieve universal, if temporary, and localized peace among nations.[8]

Like the Greeks, de Coubertin also thought it unseemly for women to participate in the Olympic Games. In Greece, other than the priestesses who presided over ceremonies, women were prohibited from entering the stadium, although they were likely part of the large encampments that blossomed around the site of competition. Games brought together a wide spectrum of Greek society: traders and merchants, food and souvenir vendors, wealthy businessmen and landowners, cooks, prostitutes, musicians, religious figures, soldiers, poets, and common people. Wealthy citizens sponsored an early form of athletic professionalism. The conquests of the athletes they funded brought status and honor to the individual, town, or region. In broader terms, Greek stadiums and quadrennial athletic competitions renewed and reflected Greek religious, sexual, and political ideologies. Games were an integral part of Greek life, and the stadiums were important sites and symbols of Greek civilization.

Panem et Circences

To the Greeks, the coronation of a wrestling or running champion with an olive branch symbolized the close association between the human and the divine through bodily perfection. The Romans were not as poetically inclined. They regarded bodily pursuits that did not have a practical end as effete. So while both the Greeks and the Romans sought bodily strength and perfection, the Romans did so with a focus on battlefield performance. It is difficult to say if this bodily pragmatism was the chicken or the egg relative to Rome's militaristic imperialism. However, the gladiatorial competitions and chariot races of the Roman Empire give deep insight into the social and political structures and mores of Roman society.[9]

The bloodiest and most well known of the Roman games were the gladiatorial contests (*munera*) that emerged out of funerary rites in the third century BCE.[10] It was common to erect temporary wooden stadiums that served as a venue for the human and animal slaughter. Later, as the *munera* became instrumental as a political tool, these improvised stadiums took on immense dimensions. "Event producers" hastily constructed wooden bleachers, which the Roman Senate banned after a rash of stadium collapses in the late first century BCE. Legislative control over the development of large amphitheatres effectively placed the production and control of public spectacles in the hands of the imperial elite. Only the state or the very wealthy could afford to build concrete or stone coliseums, amphitheatres, and circuses. The use of these spaces in the service of the state reached its height with the construction of the 250,000-capacity Circus Maximus and the 50,000-capacity Colosseum in Rome in the first century CE.[11]

The circuses of the Roman and Byzantium Empires were scenes of intense chariot competitions with enormous fan groups battling each other in the stands and on the streets. These circus factions counted as many as fifty thousand members and went en masse to the stadium in their team colors: red, blue, green, or white. Partisanship in sport extended to the political realm where factions were able, through sheer force of numbers, to make demands of senators and city councils. In return, politicians courted favor with these groups. Factional loyalties extended across the empire, with one group of "blues" taking revenge for a wrong done to their like-hued brethren in another city. The parallels with modern hooligan groups and stadium cultures are shockingly apparent and merit more detailed analysis than can be given here. There is significant evidence to suggest that the relationships between politics, hooligans, stadiums, urban life, and social control have been part of human culture for millennia.

The archaeological remains of Roman-era stadiums stretch from North

Africa to Scotland, from Portugal to Asia Minor. Roman stadiums were expensive, sophisticated architectural undertakings that held tens of thousands spectators. Then as today, a large stadium served as a badge of urban distinction. Roman stadiums were urban public spaces that allowed for a variety of entertainments, social control mechanisms, and interactions between the state, its citizens, and its slaves. From highly regimented seating arrangements to the control and domination of man and nature, "the social organization of Roman society took on a spatial form in the Coliseums and Circuses of the Roman Empire."[12] Many of these continued to serve a variety of functions long after the sack of Rome: miniature walled cities in the Middle Ages, anti-aircraft batteries in the Spanish Civil War, places to corral livestock.[13] Their continued presence on the landscape is a reminder of the engineering technology, political ideology, and geographic extent of the Roman Empire.

Mesoamerican Ball Courts

A third form of stadiums we have inherited from our ancestors comes from pre-Columbian societies in Mesoamerica. Maya, Aztec, Zapotec, Mixtec, Hohokam, and Olmec societies all had ball courts with tiered seating for spectators. While not as architecturally complex as Roman coliseums, the myths, rituals, and sacrifices associated with the games played in ball courts were an integral part of the social, political, and religious orders of their societies. Spanning a period of twelve hundred years, the architectural evidence of ball courts extends from western Honduras, Guatemala, and southeastern Mexico through central Mexico to southern Arizona. Like Greek stadiums, these stone and wood sporting arenas were located within temple complexes.[14]

The varied mythical, religious, and political significance of ball courts provides clues to social organization, politicoreligious structures, and the use of leisure time in pre-Columbian societies in the region. While only the largest ball courts remain, we can assume that a diffuse sporting culture necessitated the basic shape of the ball court for practice; thus many more informal spaces probably existed. Although they have fallen into disuse as sporting arenas, Mesoamerican ball courts testify to the historically central role of sport in the region.

Ideological, architectural, and cultural similarities between ancient and modern stadiums abound: athletic professionalization among the Greeks; human sacrifice in Mesoamerica; the Romans' politically organized spectacle of gratuitous violence; moralities and ideologies of sport; ritual performance; mythology; record keeping; body culture; eroticism; local,

Photo 1.2 Ruins of Mayan ball court at Copan, Honduras. Mesoamerican ball courts were used primarily for religious ceremonies, but we can assume that the practice of the game was carried out informally, away from temple complexes. The lasting imprint of these ceremonial spaces provides important, yet underinvestigated clues about the importance of sport in Mesoamerican cultures.

regional, national, and ethnic identities; celebrity status for athletes; symbolic warfare; organized fan violence; architectural complexity and achievement (including a retractable canvas roof in Rome); political influence; and discourses of nation, class, and gender. The more we look at stadiums, the more complicated they become.

Industrial Britain and Stadium Diffusion

The stadiums of the Greeks and Romans fell into disuse as empires and states fell apart. Mesoamerican ball courts faced a similar fate in the face of Spanish colonization. Even without stadiums, sport continued to be played, usually around festival days or as part of large social gatherings. Folk games have always been a constituent of human societies, and the undercurrents of centuries-old traditions survived into the modern era.

It was not until the nineteenth century that stadiums coalesced as features of industrialized European and North American cities. These processes by which this happened cannot be separated from larger cultural, economic, and political shifts. Speaking in very general terms, the rise of mercantile capitalism at the end of the long sixteenth century, the enclosure of rural spaces as a result of the agricultural revolution, the migration of rural populations to growing urban centers, the loss of traditional ways of life, the commodification of time and space, the development of a leisure class, the emergence of a global industrial economy, and British domination of the seas all played their part in the formation and diffusion of stadiums.[15] The emergence of stadiums from the morass of early industrial life in Britain and their insinuation into the modern urban fabric was a logical response to these multiscalar geographic patterns and processes. To understand the historical trajectory of stadiums, we need to first explore the development and influence of the games that were played within them.

During the Middle Ages in Britain, games of *foetbol* were played between entire villages and there were few distinctions made between spectators and players. Because the game lasted for several days it was probably common for individuals to alternate between active and passive roles. The biggest games were played on Shrove Tuesday, just before Lent, with thousands of people battling each other in a space of several miles between neighboring towns.[16] As early as the fourteenth century the practice of folk football was banned by British kings because of the destruction that accompanied it.

But folk football continued below the surface of visible culture for some time and was generally practiced in towns along the coal mining belt of northern England. Beginning in the 1750s, the agricultural revolution radically changed the shape and characteristics of the British landscape.[17] As agricultural productivity increased, fences, hedges, embankments, and drainage channels enclosed open space and constrained the "flying game" of folk football. These same processes pushed people from the countryside towards cities, which began to grow as never before.

Industrial urban culture progressively managed and compartmentalized workers' time throughout the nineteenth century. Leisure time was at a premium and was increasingly the focus of evangelical groups or other urban distractions.[18] The limited leisure time of workers and a dearth of recreational spaces in the city stunted the development of an urban sporting culture that could sustain folk traditions. Although we should not assume that folk football had fallen into complete obscurity by the beginning of the nineteenth century, the practice and observation of sport was not yet a generalized characteristic of industrial urban cultures.[19]

In the 1840s Thomas Arnold, headmaster of the Rugby School, wanted to teach his boys discipline, courage, teamwork, and toughness and so had them play sports modeled on folk customs. With the great success of this pedagogical experiment, other headmasters followed his lead. The schools began to play each other but split over the rules they should use for their games of football. Two varieties developed: Rugby Football and Association Football, of which "soccer" is an abbreviation. The graduates brought their schoolboy games (and ideologies) to British cities and factories.

Once modern sports gained a foothold in urban areas, sport associations and teams (particularly soccer and rugby) became central elements in the lives of young men. In a dense urban society segmented by gender and class, pubs and sporting clubs were places where men of similar tastes and predilections gathered. The codification of Association Football rules in 1865 helped to expand organized competitions, and teams grew out of casual associations in the pub, market, or workplace. Groups of young men pooled resources and either found or created spaces to play. The increasing popularity of soccer attracted spectators, and the playing spaces gradually formalized into crude stadiums, where slag heaps and earth mounds functioned as terraces for spectators to stand on. The expansion of rule-based sport required "the leveling of the field," which translated into the creation of relatively homogeneous spaces for the performance and consumption of institutionalized sport. Similar processes happened on the other side of the North Atlantic: Canadian and U.S. cities adopted stadium forms from the British.

As sport and leisure became central components of industrial cultures throughout the world, their associated spaces increasingly defined the cultural landscape. As the global economy expanded, the spaces and cultures

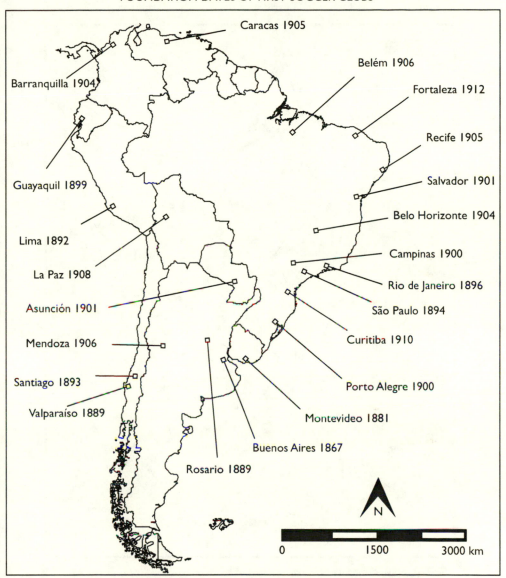

Map 1.1 Foundation dates of soccer clubs in selected South American cities. The map clearly shows that cities along the Atlantic coast of South America were the first to adopt European (British) sporting practices. This was the result of the global expansion of British trade with South American nations in the late nineteenth century.

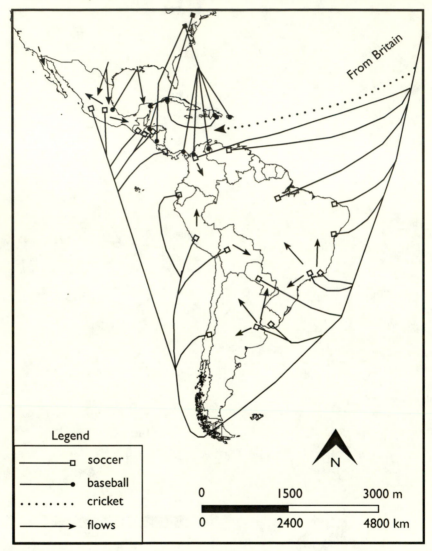

Legend

— □ soccer

— • baseball

· · · · · · · · cricket

——► flows

0	1500	3000 m
0	2400	4800 km

Map 1.2 Diffusion map depicting the spread of modern sports in Latin America, 1870–1930. Baseball was spread by Cuba and the United States to the Caribbean, Yucatán, northern Mexico, parts of Central America, and Venezuela. The British brought soccer (as well as rugby, boat racing, and polo) to much of Latin America in the late nineteenth and early twentieth century. Cricket is a legacy of British imperialism in the eastern Caribbean (West Indies and Jamaica).

of modern sport diffused. The old adage "cricket follows the empire" implies a whole series of interrelated political, economic, and geographic processes related to the development and diffusion of sport and stadiums. The basic premise of this saying is that wherever the British Army went— Canada, South and East Asia, the Caribbean, South and East Africa— cricket became popular with local people. However, it was not just the British Army that carried bats, balls, and wickets in their rucksacks. The emergence of an international industrial economy and the growth of British mercantilism in the nineteenth century gradually brought Argentina, Brazil, Chile, and Uruguay (among others) into the sphere of global capital. By the mid-nineteenth century, Britain was the major trading partner of each of these countries, and the agents of British capital— bankers, industrialists, engineers, managers, dockhands, sailors—were in every major port along the Atlantic coast of South America. As the British economic presence increased so did their cultural influence; British sports and the spaces to play them appeared in South American cities.[20] Similar processes happened with all European and North American colonial powers: the French extended soccer into North and West Africa; the *gringos* brought baseball into Mexico, Central America, the Caribbean, and East Asia.

Patterns of sport diffusion were based in the broad popularity of institutionalized sport at home. As industrial, urban cultures evolved in the metropolis the expansion of the global economy ensured (for example) that British sailors, merchant marines, laborers, and government agents spread it throughout the domain. Not only cricket, but soccer, rugby, golf, horse racing, polo—and their stadiums (spatial forms)—followed the empire. The emergence of local sporting clubs is an excellent indication of when localities were incorporated into global economies or imperial domains. Even within countries such as the United States, the expansion of an internal economy and shifting settlement patterns are reflected in the tremendous boom in professional sport teams and stadiums in the Sun Belt and the West in the last quarter of the twentieth century. We will examine the details of this development in the contexts of Rio de Janeiro and Buenos Aires in the coming chapters.

Stadium Evolution

The geographers John Bale and Martyn Bowden have proposed different and intersecting models that describe the architectural and functional trajectories of stadiums since the late nineteenth century.[21] These models suggest that beginning with crude, open spaces or on the infields of horse-racing grounds, stadiums changed to reflect the increasing organization and sanitization of urban life. While stadiums have always conditioned human movement through architecture, the trend has been from less to more control, from a larger to a more limited public, and from less to more economic and architectural rationality.

Late-nineteenth-century stadiums allowed for a freedom of movement that did not necessarily create clear boundaries between spectators and players. As sport became more organized and competitive, stadium owners imposed architectural divisions that established control over space. The architectural complexities of stadiums evolved fairly quickly, primarily through the efforts of the Scottish architect Archibald Lietch who created the first double and triple tiers as well as cantilevered roofs. By the first decades of the twentieth century, stadiums in Britain, North America, and continental Europe had coalesced into something approximating their modern form. Field dimensions were standardized, spectator capacity was dependent on building materials and architectural know-how, and stadiums were generally dedicated solely to the hosting of sporting events. European stadium models were the templates from which stadiums in many other parts of the world emerged, and architects from Europe were instrumental in the design and construction of stadiums in South America, Africa, and Asia.

Stadium architecture changed in relation to construction technologies: wood and brick gave way to concrete and steel, which yielded to plastic and metal alloys. The internal architecture and location of stadiums also reflected social changes. The United States is a good example of these relationships. Following a period of stadium building in the urban core, the post–World War II era of urban decline and mass movement to the suburbs, cavernous plastic and steel stadiums such as New York's Shea Stadium (1964), Kansas City's Arrowhead Stadium (1972), Pittsburgh's Three River Stadium (1970), Irving's (Dallas) Texas Stadium (1971), Philadelphia's Veteran's Stadium (1971), and Seattle's Kingdome (1976) peppered the landscape.[22] The recent or imminent destruction of many of these plastic stadiums can be understood in the context of a generalized failure of social and urban planning in the United States.

With the reanimation of downtown districts throughout the United States in the 1990s, there has been a commensurate boom in downtown stadiums that attempt to recover the "classic" feel of the early twentieth century: Baltimore, Denver, Pittsburgh, Chicago, San Francisco, Milwaukee, the list of new facilities goes on. These publicly funded stadiums have incorporated architectural influences from shopping malls with the aim of

Stages of Stadium Development

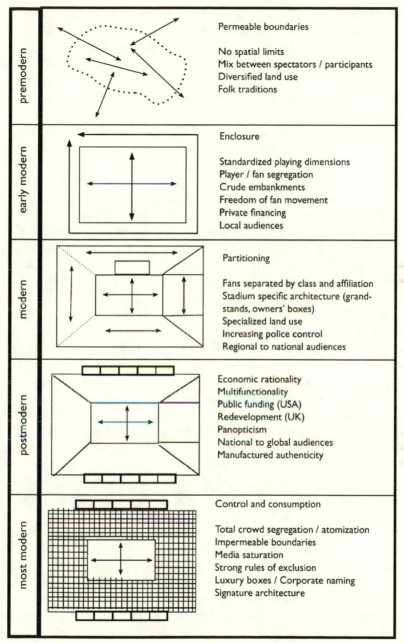

premodern	**Permeable boundaries** No spatial limits Mix between spectators / participants Diversified land use Folk traditions
early modern	**Enclosure** Standardized playing dimensions Player / fan segregation Crude embankments Freedom of fan movement Private financing Local audiences
modern	**Partitioning** Fans separated by class and affiliation Stadium specific architecture (grand-stands, owners' boxes) Specialized land use Increasing police control Regional to national audiences
postmodern	**Economic rationality** Multifunctionality Public funding (USA) Redevelopment (UK) Panopticism National to global audiences Manufactured authenticity
most modern	**Control and consumption** Total crowd segregation / atomization Impermeable boundaries Media saturation Strong rules of exclusion Luxury boxes / Corporate naming Signature architecture

Figure 1.1 Stadium evolution model, modified from Bale 2000. This model shows five stages of stadium development. Moving from disorganization to strict economic and architectural rationality, stadiums have changed to reflect economic, social, and political trends.

maximizing consumption, taking public dollars, and pouring profits into private hands. Instead of responding to population shifts, stadiums are frequently built speculatively in the hope of providing an urban "amenity" that will attract internal migrants and businesses to a city. Unfortunately, the economic realities of stadium building for professional sports franchises in the United States creates significant and well-documented disamenities.[23]

In the 1990s and early 2000s, after decades of stadium-related violence, British stadiums underwent a radical transformation. The biggest change was the elimination of the terraces that were minimalist, standing-only, holding pens traditionally occupied by working-class fans. The government-mandated emergence of the all-seater stadium has had two related effects. First, because the clubs, not municipalities, were forced to pay for stadium renovations, ticket prices increased across the board. This had the effect of pricing out many working- and lower-class fans. Second, those who could afford to go to the stadium were confined to seats, which were monitored by closed-circuit television and increased stewardship. While many bemoan the loss of the traditional atmosphere generated by the fans in the terraces (as the crowds have become older, wealthier, and more sedate), British soccer has blossomed in the post-Taylor era. The all-seater stadium model was adopted by both FIFA and UEFA in 1995, requiring that all international and continental matches be played without standing fans. The trend towards increasing crowd control through seating arrangements is reshaping stadiums all over the world.[24]

In Asia, Australia and New Zealand, North America, and Europe new stadiums have reached a high level of technological sophistication and organizational rigidity designed to extract the maximum profit from fans. It is a rare person who can gain access to all areas of a stadium as the boundaries between differentiated seating sections are patrolled by ushers and security guards. The generalized effect has been an atomization of the crowd, whereby social value is ascribed to an individual's capacity to consume. The traditional public, one that could afford to go to stadiums on a regular basis, has changed to a more limited and affluent crowd. What once were inclusive public spaces are, much like city parks, squares, and other spaces of shared interaction, predicated on the notion that one must consume (and heavily) to be part of the event. Thus, the stadium continues to reflect larger social and architectural trends associated with (post)modern cities. These changes have yet to be chronicled in detail, yet clearly merit more attention.

Terminology

Although *stadium* clearly derives from the Greek, developing a working definition of the word is not as straightforward as it would appear. For instance, some golf courses have "stadium seating" and charge spectators admission to view a tournament, but they are clearly not stadiums. Many stadiums contain hotels, shopping malls, office space, museums, movie theatres, golf ranges, and wedding halls. Is it a mall, a stadium, or both? Bale calls them "tradiums." The ambiguous terminology used to name modern stadiums further confuses: Amsterdam ArenA, Ameriquest Ballpark at Arlington, Wrigley Field, The Den, SkyDome/Rogers Centre, Los Angeles Coliseum, Oriole Park at Camden Yards, Nanjing Sports Park, Cotton Bowl, The Valley, White Hart Lane, Landsdowne Road, Boleyn Ground, and so on. All of these places can hold over thirty thousand people and have the form and function of a "stadium," but apparently none of them are.

The *Oxford English Dictionary* defines *stadium* as "an enclosed area for sporting events equipped with tiers of seats for spectators." Okay, but is a fenced baseball field at a neighborhood park with a single bleacher a stadium? Not really, but it does share similar characteristics. By contrast, an *arena* is "the central part of an amphitheatre, in which the combats or spectacular displays take place, and which was originally strewn with sand to absorb the blood of the wounded and slain." *Ballpark* is simply "a baseball stadium." *Field* has obvious geographic connotations and implies an open stretch of land that has come under cultivation or a generalized, bounded space of interaction. "Fields of play" are essential characteristics of all stadiums and imply the incorporation of natural elements, yet when the word *field* is generalized to an architectural structure we are faced with a paradox.

The words used to describe stadiums are conditioned by local sporting, political, economic, and geographic conditions. In the British vernacular stadiums are referred to as *grounds*. The implication is that without being grounded, a team is rootless and cannot develop lasting place-based relationships. For this reason, soccer stadiums in the British Isles are frequently named for streets or the geographic features in which they are situated.

In the United States, naming rights to professional stadiums are typically purchased by corporations (e.g., QualComm Park, Gillette Stadium, Reliant Stadium, FedEx Field, ProPlayer Field, Coors Field) and links to place are routed through the corporation.[25] In Latin America, most stadiums are named after important political leaders or prominent men associated with the club that owns the stadium. However, most Latin American stadiums have popular nicknames that avoid the need to refer to them by their official names. For instance, the official name of Boca Juniors' stadium in Buenos Aires is Estadio Alberto J. Armando but is generally called La Bombonera, or the Chocolate Box, in reference to its stacked and steeply inclined terraces (itself a term borrowed from agriculture).

Given the wide variety of *sportscapes*, or landscapes of sport, within a cultural landscape, I use the criteria of architectural form, primary use, and micro-physical function as a means of defining the stadium.[26] Although stadiums and indoor arenas have much in common, I focus exclusively on structures that host sports played on natural or artificial grass fields. A stadium is a large, usually permanent, open-air structure that is built, maintained, and primarily used to host field-based sporting spectacles.[27] It has the capacity to accommodate many hundreds or thousands of people in seats or terraces that extend from a focused sphere of action. Entry to the stadium is regulated through ticketing mechanisms that tend to separate spectators by socioeconomic level. Space within the stadium itself is organized to control human movement and action in a patterned and deliberate manner. The multifunctionality of modern stadiums is a recent development that has its origins in Western Europe and North America but has since spread to East Asia, Australia, and New Zealand. In the rest of the world, we know a stadium when we see, hear, taste, smell, and feel it.

The Theory and Practice of Stadiums

From satellite communications to ergonomic seats, stadiums operate at different scales simultaneously. The relations and systems of production that create and support stadiums are nearly impossible to describe in their entirety. There are as many theoretical approaches to the stadium as roads leading to and from it. Each path takes us to different destinations. Stadium architecture and design, financing, law, and structural and social engineering are all pertinent fields of investigation, but as with the city at large, describing the fine details tends to obscure the larger picture. For instance, we can take it as axiomatic that the architectural history of stadiums in the local and global contexts is a rich and complex theme and that stadium- and sports-specific technologies intersect with other arenas of social life.[28] Yet by focusing explicitly on architecture we lose touch with the cultural milieu, historical context, and connections to other stadiums.

In what follows, I examine stadiums from a perspective based in cultural and urban geography highlighting three interrelated themes: the symbolic characteristics of stadiums, how they function as sites of convergence,

Stadium Extensibility Model

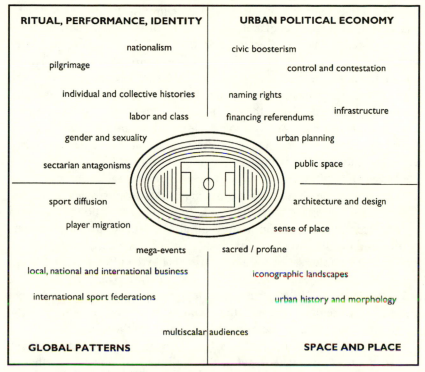

RITUAL, PERFORMANCE, IDENTITY	URBAN POLITICAL ECONOMY

nationalism   civic boosterism

pilgrimage   control and contestation

individual and collective histories   naming rights

labor and class   financing referendums   infrastructure

gender and sexuality   urban planning

sectarian antagonisms   public space

sport diffusion   architecture and design

player migration   sense of place

mega-events   sacred / profane

local, national and international business   iconographic landscapes

international sport federations   urban history and morphology

multiscalar audiences

GLOBAL PATTERNS   **SPACE AND PLACE**

Figure 1.2 Stadium extensibility model. This model shows some of the connections that the stadium has with the larger world. Nearly impossible to describe in their entirety, these networks suggest that stadiums are deeply connected with their physical and cultural environments at multiple scales.

and, taking Latin America as an example, the ways in which they function as urban public spaces. The combination of these elements helps to create powerful yet heterogeneous meanings for individuals and communities. But first, a theoretical sidebar.

You and I cannot step into the batter's box at Yankee Stadium, take a penalty kick at the Maracanã, or hit a crushing forehand at Wimbledon's Centre Court, but we can play baseball, soccer, and tennis in similar spaces. As athletes progress through their sports careers, they move through a series of sporting spaces of which stadiums are the highest expression. Tending towards greater regimentation, organization, and levels of achievement, athletes move from informal practice to high school, college, or apprenticeship leagues before reaching the professional level. Each one of these movements is conditioned by excelling in the previous athletic space. That is, hierarchies of athletic achievement are mirrored by the hierarchies of spaces in which they occur. Zinedine Zidane did not play for his local pub; he played in Real Madrid's Estadio Santiago Bernabeu. Yet the soccer fields of the pub league and Real Madrid's stadium are related, mutually supportive, and together define an interlocking spatial and cultural complex dedicated to the performance, production, and consumption of sport. When sixty thousand people go to a stadium to watch athletes perform, they pay to watch people who have spent their lives practicing, excelling, and moving through a phenomenally diffuse hierarchy of associated spaces and places, each of which shapes the cultural landscape.

The interconnected cultural and spatial worlds of sport suggest that stadiums are some of the most extensible human constructions. The word *extensible* implies that stadiums are "nodal points in communication networks" and that the structures, meanings, and effects of stadiums are predicated on a complex set of social relations that extend forwards and backwards in time and space.[29] Because they are sites of convergence, stadiums bring together a broad spectrum of society in a limited space for a limited period, which tends to increase the social value of stadium time and the economic value of places (seats) within the space of the stadium.

Imagine a map of the paths that fans, players, laborers, team owners, and media personnel take to get to the stadium. The coming together of tens of thousands of people necessitates transportation networks, electricity grids, sewage lines, communication networks, vast human and natural resources, and an implicit set of cultural values that tell us that what is happening in the stadium is worth all the bother. Next, imagine the exponentially larger number of places to which the stadium is broadcast via radio, television, print media, and the Internet. Have you ever read the sports section to see yesterday's results? This effectively transports you through time to the events that took place in the stadium.

As nodal points in interlocking networks, it is difficult to imagine a more extensible place than the stadium. Because of this, as Galeano so eloquently acknowledged, stadiums do not only communicate when they are actively used. They speak to us across generations and help us to imagine our collective futures. The architecture, size, location, and generalized function of stadiums as public spaces shape the memories, texture, and experience of cities around the globe. Continuing with our theoretical exploration of stadiums, we will next examine and compare the general functioning of stadiums as constituent elements of the cultural landscape.

Memorials, Monuments, Spectacles, and the Iconography of Landscape

Montevideo's Estadio Centenario is so called because its inauguration marked the centennial of Uruguayan independence. The Kop at Liverpool's Anfield Stadium is a section of stands named after the 1900 Boer War battle of Simion Kop, in which hundreds of Liverpudlians were killed.[30] The Darrell K Royal–Texas Memorial Stadium on the campus of the University of Texas at Austin memorializes the following "wars": World War I, World War II, the Korean War, the Vietnam War, Desert Storm, Iraqi Freedom, and Enduring Freedom.

Cultural and urban geographers have frequently examined memorials and monuments as elements of cultural landscapes, yet stadiums have generally escaped their attention.[31] Other than the obvious examples above,

Photo 1.3 Postcard of the Estadio Centenario, Montevideo, Uruguay. This stadium was the host of the first FIFA World Cup final in 1930, and its inauguration coincided with the centennial celebration of Uruguayan independence.

retired numbers, statues, busts, names, ceremonies, museums, murals, tourism, rituals, and myths and legends are all mechanisms for preserving social memory in the stadium. We do not consciously think of memorials or monuments in geographic terms but recognize their power and purpose in our interactions with them. Memorials are literally sites of memory, testaments to a time, space, and place that we wish to remember. But because "what is accepted as historical truth is often a narrative shaped and reshaped through time to fit the demands of contemporary society,"[32] we are never quite sure what (or even why) we are remembering.

Even when stadiums are not explicitly designed as monuments, because of their size and public character stadiums function monumentally in a number of ways. First, they serve as nodes of orientation in the city. Bus lines pass them, we can see the floodlights from a distance, they anchor neighborhood or district identities, and we can sometimes smell when we are getting close.[33] Second, stadiums provide communities with a large public space that can be used for a number of mundane and extraordinary purposes. Repeated gathering in a communal space gives it historical significance and public memory. Third, because stadiums are huge and attract a lot of people, local residents tend to identify with them. Throughout the world, stadiums are *the thing* that residents and nonresidents associate with place. For instance, Manchester, England, is globally recognized more for its Old Trafford stadium and Manchester United than its urban history and culture. Fourth, stadium identities are linked with teams and structure subcultural identities within the city: Chicago White Sox or Cubs? Inter or A.C. Milan? Chivas o Tecos de Guadalajara? Boca or River? Glasgow Celtic or Rangers? Fifth, the continuity of the stadium provides us with links to our past in a space that has not changed its basic form and function. Part of the pleasure fans feel in going to Boston's Fenway Park is that they are doing the same thing in the same place as Bostonians in the 1920s. The emotions we put into stadiums are not easily extracted from the structure itself.

Humans produce and interpret the urban landscape on a daily basis. Landscape is an expression of the power—sometimes a will to power—of individuals and collectives to transform the natural world. As landscape is also a way of seeing the world, no two people are likely to experience it in the same way. Geographers read the patterns and transformations of landscape as literal and metaphorical texts that "represent a historically specific way of experiencing the world developed by, and meaningful to, certain groups."[34] The conflicting meanings of landscapes and their constituent elements are representative of ideologies and discourses that structure social relations. The forms and features of the landscape, and the ways in which they change, are the raw materials with which geographers work to understand and interpret culture. Cities and their stadiums provide us with an untapped abundance of resources to work with.

As people we are cautioned "not to make a spectacle of ourselves," but this is not at all what we want from our cities. The bigger, longer, and higher the skyline, the better. We want more wealth, more museums, more entertainment, more movement, more people, more spectacle.[35] From time immemorial, cities were conceived and constructed as spectacles. Within the larger spectacle of the city, stadiums are designed to host the biggest public gatherings, the grandest pageants, and the most dramatic moments of our collective memory. Stadium architecture can be awesome, both reducing our sense of self and aggrandizing our group consciousness. The mere sight of a stadium is enough to stir the imagination.

Sites of extravagance and destitution, consumption and excretion, imagination and desperation, cities are engines of human culture with particular rhythms, characteristics, and life stages. Stadiums are like this too—cities in miniature.[36] And like a city, a stadium is too complex to describe in its entirety. But by connecting the patterns and processes that are expressed by and through its individual components we can begin to understand the whole.

Iconographic Landscapes

Within the larger spectacle of the urban landscape, the stadium is an iconographic feature that provides insight into the political economy, culture, and history of cities. Iconographic features of landscape such as the Eiffel Tower, the White House, the Golden Gate Bridge, or Tiananmen Square provide shorthand mechanisms for characterizing and identifying cities. These structures form part of the conceptual city, a collective image of place that is increasingly homogeneous as we move away from the locale. The proliferation of sport-specific media in the past thirty years has ensured that stadiums are the most frequently viewed buildings in a given urban environment; as such they have become fundamental, iconographic elements of the conceptual city.[37] Further, stadiums are frequently conceived and constructed as symbolic representations of place that project cities to a broad audience, part of a larger competition between cities to attract residents and businesses. Every few years we see cities building extravagant Olympic Stadiums that are intended to convey shorthand messages to global audiences.

At the urban scale, stadiums stand as iconographic representations of political ideologies and social inequalities (e.g., in the public financing of stadiums), reflect patterns of urban development (e.g., in the United States the movement of stadiums to the suburbs), or mark urban boundaries and districts. Stadiums are physical manifestations of labor, and their presence on the urban landscape is a symbolic representation of the actors and processes that created them. The symbolic effects are compounded with the passage of time and the accrual of sedimented layers of history and meaning for individuals as well as local, diasporic, and imaginary communities.

Within the stadium itself iconography abounds. "Popular" sections such as "the bleachers" imply messages about class, behavioral norms, and experience. Many of these are much-loved places, whose destruction or modification are deeply felt. The insinuation of "luxury boxes" into stadiums around the world has created a cultural icon that symbolizes economic privilege and dispassionate spectatorship. The field is also an iconographic landscape that represents exclusivity: only those who produce, maintain, and are skilled enough to perform the spectacle are permitted on it, making "streaking" that much more enjoyable. Merchants and advertisers slather their corporate icons throughout the stadium, linking internal and external patterns of consumption. Stadium postcards, posters, schedules, and team regalia spread the iconography of the stadium throughout the urban realm. Say "Green Monster" to a baseball fan and they will associate it with Boston and Fenway Park, not a furry hobgoblin.

The historical, monumental, spectacular, and iconographic functions of stadiums in the urban realm are profound. Each stadium is a product of geographic processes that are crystallized in its architectural form and social function. These are representative and representational places (and spaces) that structure the lived and conceptual worlds of nearly every urban environment in the world. Stadiums are sites and symbols of power, identity, and meaning that allow us to enter and interpret the cultural landscape through a common medium.

The Sacred and the Profane

Mexico's Estadio Jalisco and Brazil's Estádio São Januário have churches inside them. Pope John Paul II gave dozens of masses in stadiums. His successor, Benedict XVI, canonized the first Brazilian in São Paulo's Pacaembú Stadium. The Promise Keepers is an all-male religious group that introduced 750,000 "men to Jesus Christ as their savior and helped them grow as Christians" in stadiums throughout the United States in 1995.[38] When entering or leaving the field, scoring a goal, saving a shot, or at the final whistle Latin American soccer players frequently make the sign of the cross. After spiking the ball in the end zone, some American Football players kneel in supplication. Stadiums are referred to as temples,

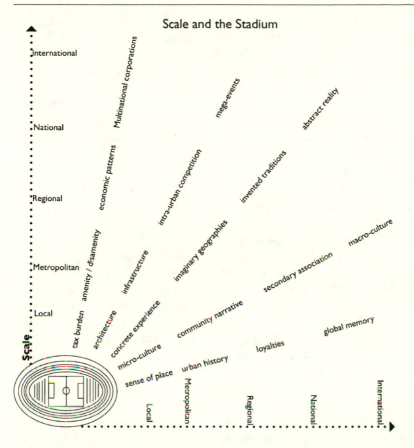

Figure 1.3 The stadium and scale. This model shows the changing nature of stadium space in relation to the scale at which one observes or experiences it.

shrines, cathedrals, and hallowed ground. This is a sacred space for a diasporic community.

Augusto Pinochet used Chile's Estadio Nacional as a prison and torture chamber. During the 1978 World Cup, the Videla dictatorship in Argentina used stadiums to legitimate their government in the face of global criticism of their human rights abuses. Philadelphia's Lincoln Financial Field has a jail, as does New Jersey's Giants' Stadium and New York's Shea Stadium. Stadium violence is common, even at lower levels of sport. Stadium bathrooms are frequently noxious and putrid. Fans become drunk and abusive while celebrating violent and/or beautiful actions on the field. In the stands we are treated to a barrage of swearing, have drinks spilled on us, and throw our trash on the ground. The ever-present media, advertising, and commercialization places our stadium experience squarely in the realm of rapacious capital accumulation. Stadiums take scarce dollars away from much-needed social and educational programs. Surely this is a profane place.

Despite evidence to the contrary, stadiums stand out in the collective imagination as sacred. Much of this lingering sense of specialness has to do with the transcendent characteristics of large gatherings and the emotive capacity of sport. Stadiums have the function of localizing very strong, shared (or contradictory) emotions for hundreds, thousands, or millions of people at exactly the same time. As the ball arcs through the air and bodies move to meet it, the fan moves from I to We, the id connects to the superego, we rise from our seats as one and an enduring connection is etched in space and time. We remember and value what happens in stadiums: good, bad, and mundane.

In addition to the intensity of shared experience, pilgrimage and ritual are two interrelated behaviors that give stadiums a sense of sacredness. People prepare themselves for days or weeks in anticipation of large stadium events. In January 2004 the *Houston Chronicle* advertised more than ninety parties, shows, and concerts in the week leading up to the Super Bowl.[39] Can these be considered pilgrimage stations en route to the larger "shrine" of Reliant Stadium? Consistent with our discussion of sporting hierarchies, "pilgrimage centers can almost be arranged into a ranking order of importance."[40] Going to Mexico City's 110,000-seat Estadio Azteca is simply more memorable than going to Pizza Hut Park in Frisco, Texas. And while this is not to suggest that getting in one's car and driving to the stadium is equivalent to completing the hadj or walking to Santiago de Compostela, they do share many of the same characteristics. It is not infrequently that we encounter stories of individuals who have spent years traveling to every football ground in England or every major league baseball stadium in the United States. When religious ceremonies happen in the stadium, the sense of pilgrimage is obviously heightened. While each culture has its particular stadium rituals, they all serve to connect diverse people through common behaviors in a common place.

The rhythms and rituals of the stadium are similar in many respects to visiting a grave site, parade, memorial, or familiar vacation spot, providing us with a sense of temporal continuity and geographic familiarity. It is also true that they stand out from the linear progression of time that defines modern industrial cultures.[41] Teams play "seasons," a temporal cycle based on natural rhythms that forms the basis of religious worship, holy days, and periods of fasting and feasting. The seasonal, cyclical nature of sport generates hope and comfort for the fan, who knows that his or her team's

Stadium Spaces, Stadium Places

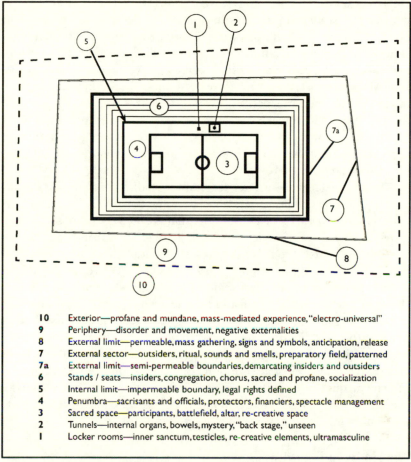

10	Exterior—profane and mundane, mass-mediated experience, "electro-universal"
9	Periphery—disorder and movement, negative externalities
8	External limit—permeable, mass gathering, signs and symbols, anticipation, release
7	External sector—outsiders, ritual, sounds and smells, preparatory field, patterned
7a	External limit—semi-permeable boundaries, demarcating insiders and outsiders
6	Stands / seats—insiders, congregation, chorus, sacred and profane, socialization
5	Internal limit—impermeable boundary, legal rights defined
4	Penumbra—sacrisants and officials, protectors, financiers, spectacle management
3	Sacred space—participants, battlefield, altar, re-creative space
2	Tunnels—internal organs, bowels, mystery, "back stage," unseen
1	Locker rooms—inner sanctum, testicles, re-creative elements, ultramasculine

Figure 1.4 Stadium spaces, stadium places. Adapted from Sabugo 1983. This model shows some of the different attributes associated with distinct areas of a stadium. While some of these boundaries are fluid, some are ossified and heavily defended. This model is applicable in particular to stadiums in Buenos Aires but can be used as a more general paradigm for understanding stadium spaces.

chances of success will be renewed next week or next year. Although it may be coincidental that most professional sporting events are played on Saturday and Sunday, the "religious performance" of ritual behaviors in stadiums on those days puts the stadium in direct competition with church, synagogue, and temple for the attention and money of the masses.

Stadium rituals are syncopated performances of belief systems rooted in fairly new and malleable cultural traditions. They tend to organize and manage the passage of people from one set of rules and normative social positions to another and back again. That is, the nominally transgressive behavior of the stadium is managed and controlled for a brief time in a limited space before returning us to "normalcy." As the Olympic historian John MacAloon notes, this process of "ordering, disordering, and reordering in the same performance process is what makes ritual so apt a vehicle for the making and unmaking of social drama."[42] The stadium is one of the greatest stages for the unfolding of social dramas where tens of thousands of formal and informal actors ritualistically perform identities, beliefs, and scripted and unscripted roles.

The ritualistic, quasi-sacred nature of the stadium provides for liminal experiences whereby people are able to escape their everyday realities by connecting to a larger social group that shares a sense of purpose. Liminal experiences are transformative, allowing us to pass from one state to another or to enter into a different reality. Typically, stadium experiences connect us to a larger community, placing us in the crowd, closing off the outside world for a time. Participants are insiders who establish relationships with the event, the place, and their fellow pilgrims.[43] They are likely wearing the same colors and symbols, or flash each other some kind of hand gesture in solidarity. The intersection of diverse social groups in the rituals of the stadium suggests that the tastes and lifestyles of this place serve to create and celebrate common bonds that allow us to transcend our individual, quotidian reality. It is through the performance of rituals associated with stadium space that potentially disaggregated social actors find a common symbology, language, history, and purpose.

The Limits to Transgression

Stadiums are designed for large-scale entertainment, spectacle, and high-level performance, but the action is not just on the field of play. The crowd is a spectacle unto itself and can be a menacing creature. The anonymity that we feel in large groups of people opens the possibility for behavior that would be considered deviant in nearly any other context. Although they can be escapes from everyday reality that allow us to share common experiences and emotions with tens of thousands of others, the confrontational nature of team sports and the strong identities and emotions associated with teams create the need to control the movement and behavior of the crowd.

As we shall see in greater detail in Rio de Janeiro and Buenos Aires, crowd control can be so difficult that riot police, attack dogs, mounted patrols, and helicopters are needed. The moats and fences found in many stadiums in Latin America and Europe are a response to the unpredictable, kinetic energy of the crowd. For large stadium events in the United States such as the Super Bowl, airline flights are redirected and security costs, paid for by municipal and national government, runs into the millions of dollars. In short, the smooth functioning of stadiums requires a militarized control of space and the uninterrupted functioning of state power. This high level of control is accomplished through what the nineteenth-century philosopher Jeremy Bentham termed the *panopticon*.

As explained by Michel Foucault, the panopticon was a prison design that made the physical exercise of power over inmates unnecessary. A central tower looked down into a backlit cell occupied by a "madman, a patient, a condemned man, a worker or a schoolboy," where individual actions were immediately observable and classifiable. The effect of the panoptic mechanism was to arrange people in space in such a way that the crowd "is abolished and replaced with a collection of separated individualities." Thus atomized, the crowd turns the disciplinary mechanism upon itself, continually modifying behavior because they can never be sure whether there is someone watching. The crowd becomes self-regulating, but in the event that the "unnecessary" exercise of power fails the very structure of the building itself becomes a "machine for creating and sustaining a power relation independent of the person who exercises it."[44]

Modern stadiums are not as much solid entities as they are collections of analytically arranged and segmented territories that distribute, locate, and separate bodies in a system wherein every individual is observable in their ascribed, purchased, or allotted place. This is consistent with the panopticon's "concerted distribution of bodies, surfaces, lights, gazes; in an arrangement whose internal mechanisms produce the relation in which individuals are caught up." Stadium design manuals are explicit in the amount of cubic space allotted to each seat—creating spatially bounded cells in which the fan "becomes the principle of his own subjection."[45] The structural mechanism of the seat creates docile bodies that can be observed and controlled through explicit and implicit panoptic mechanisms. The social mechanism of the crowd multiplies the effect by enforcing acceptable behavioral norms where deviance is quickly extirpated.

The stadium is one of the most highly surveiled spaces of the city and can be considered an archetype of the panoptic mechanism. Dirigibles or police helicopters provide overhead coverage, extending the gaze vertically as television cameras in train stations and intersections extend it horizontally. Stewards, ushers, police, media, and closed circuit televisions monitor the crowd. The crowd surveils itself and the action on the field. The directors evaluate the coaches, the coaches surveil their players, and unacceptable or uncorrected behavior on the field is controlled by match officials, whose behavior is in turn observed, evaluated, and corrected by a sport governing body. Dozens of cameras follow every movement and allow for a retroactive enforcement of discipline on players, team officials, and fans. A great irony of the stadium is that it permits a *sensation* of personal freedom that can only operate within rigidly controlled architectural, spatial, temporal, and behavioral contexts. These contexts are conditioned by the mechanisms of capital accumulation and enforced by the state and private security forces.

The panoptic similarities between stadiums, prisons, hospitals, schools, and other institutions of mass discipline are unmistakable. Their collective role is to discipline individual bodies in a highly regimented architectural space, as well as to "carry out experiments, to alter behaviours, to train or correct individuals. To experiment with medicines and monitor their effects."[46] Steroids anyone? The modern professional athlete is perhaps the most controlled and conditioned human subject—both on and off the field—and is subject to the full force of the panoptic mechanism, which has its highest and most public expression in the stadium. As spectators, we are subject to this mechanism but also enforce it, creating spiraling systems of control that limit its transgressive and transformative potential.

Sexual Space

In most cultures the stadium is male dominated and holds more meaning for men than women. This is particularly true in Latin America and the Middle East. The skewed composition of stadium crowds, intergenerational interactions among fans, and the sexual roles and values promulgated by sport all pile into the stadium in a sweaty male heap creating a lively space of masculine socialization replete with rites of passage, intense bonding, and collective solidarity. Strong, fast, quick, clever, and witty men are valued here. As are those who can mete out and absorb pain, express themselves by and through violence against other men, and "spike" their "ball" in the opponents' "end zone."

Team sport is rife with sexual tension. Athletes are cloistered together in locker rooms and training camps, they stretch, exercise, and bathe together, and they share deep emotional bonds over many years. High-level physical performance and its associated body culture infer sexual performance. The sculpted bodies of athletes are symbolically consumed as sexual and athletic commodities and constitute an ideal vision of human form and movement.

Unsurprisingly, the origins of sexualized sport in the modern context owe much to the Victorians. In the nineteenth century, middle-class men in industrial cultures entered what some social historians have interpreted as a crisis of masculinity.[47] As part of the larger processes of modernist industrialization, men were forced to reinvent traditional gender roles in rapidly changing urban environments.[48] The strict taboos against homosexuality may have allowed men to create meaningful emotional bonds while retaining the characteristics of orthodox masculinity. The social historian Brian Pronger suggests that the world of sports is a "covert world of homoeroticism" and that "lurking *mythically* beneath the ostensible orthodoxy of masculine sport is the ironic subtext of paradox. . . . [T]he paradox of orthodox masculinity is that the hierarchy of gender difference compels men to find satisfaction in one another."[49]

In many cultures participation in sports is taken as a sign of heterosexual normality, and it continues to be unthinkable that a star player could be a homosexual. The pervasive association between sports and orthodox, heterosexual masculinity "remains so strong that psychological tests like the Minnesota Multiphasic Personality Inventory score a male's dislike of sports as an indication of homosexual tendencies, especially when coupled with a preference for the arts."[50] Wow.

The nature of team sports creates an intense emotional bond between spectators, as well as players. The stadium provides a venue for a massive congregation of men who share a common emotional sentiment. The spontaneous hugging that occurs in the stands following a goal is mirrored by kissing, hugging, and piles of sweaty men on the field. The assumed, unchallenged heterosexual masculinity of male athletes allows them to perform homoerotic acts that would be considered overtly homosexual in nearly any other context. Pronger extends notions of homoerotic voyeurism to all sports fans, suggesting that while they cheer the men on the field "who actually get to rub against each other [they wish that] they were doing it themselves."[51]

The transference of gender roles, the public expression of orthodox sexuality, and the idealization of male and female physical forms is yet another way in which stadiums structure social and spatial practices within a larger cultural framework. Even though the meanings, qualities, and modes of transference "are openly textured and imperfectly shared, they are nonetheless connected in an indissoluble, constitutive way to the raw experiences of material history."[52] This material history includes the development of male-dominated spaces within the city that allowed for the expression of masculine solidarity, competition, and rites of socialization. As we shall see in greater detail in Buenos Aires, the gendered space of the stadium is an expression of historical patterns of urban development, paternalistic and clientelistic social relations, and a male-dominated public sphere.

When stadiums first emerged on the modern urban landscape, they were almost exclusively male domains. As women have gained greater cultural, political, and economic agency they have begun to change the hypermasculine nature of stadium space. Billy Jean King's tennis victory over Bobby Riggs in 1973 effectively inverted the masculine space of the Houston Astrodome into a site where women held greater physical and social power.[53] Irrespective of these changes and speaking in global terms, the gender-based moralities, ideologies, behaviors, and expectations of sport performance and spectatorship continue to focus on the production, performance, and transference of masculine heterosexuality.

Stadiums, Public Space, and Culture in the Latin American Mega-City

Part of the problem in using stadiums as a tool to understand cultures is that they do not fit into easily identifiable categories. The general themes and contradictions that I have explored above can be applied to nearly all stadiums in any given culture. What remains is to lay out a framework for understanding stadiums in their specific urban and cultural contexts—in this case, two of Latin America's largest cities, Rio de Janeiro and Buenos Aires. I will treat each city in detail in the chapters that follow, but here I want to present some general principles of how stadiums function in relation to public space in Latin America, with the caveat that each stadium should be understood as an expression of a localized urban and cultural tradition. My goal is to insert stadiums into a larger discussion of urban public spaces in the region, arguing that stadiums are an important, complex, and essential elements of urban public culture in Latin America that merit more critical attention from scholars.

Plazas, parks, historic centers, markets, streets—each of these public spaces in Latin America, emerging from a mixture of indigenous and Iberian urban models, can be said to be fully public in that they allow for unrestricted access, permit free association, and promote a sense of conviviality among diverse sectors of the population. Conceived, constructed, and used by and for the public, networks of public space shape life and culture in Latin American cities to a high degree. Monumental public spaces such as Mexico City's Zocalo are the stages on which national life literally takes place. At the local scale, parks and plazas give Latin American cities and neighborhoods a distinct feeling, anchoring urban identities, serving as sites of community interaction (both contentious and convivial), and providing a pedestrian-scale interface with the city that connects people to urban, architectural, and social histories. Public spaces are also highly visible sites of contestation, where ordinary people confront the state in extraordinary ways. As several prominent urban scholars have argued, it is through analyzing the shifting uses, structures, and qualities of public space in Latin America that we can read larger socioeconomic and political trends.[54]

Although stadiums are important, specialized elements of public culture, they cannot be said to be public spaces in the same way that the above-mentioned are. Stadiums in Latin America tend to be privately owned, to serve a primary function, to be open for short periods, and are as likely to provoke antagonisms as they are to create communal bonds. Even when publicly owned, stadium access is not universally granted but is conditioned by one's ability to pay for or perform a role in the production of an event—even then there are architectural and social impediments to freedom of movement and association. There are some exceptions, such as when stadiums are used for political rallies or religious gatherings, but on the whole stadiums do not belong to a more generalized category of public space.

Yet stadiums do not belong in the private realm either. As some of the most visible architectural elements of public culture and sites for massive, ritualized congregations of urban denizens, stadiums are connective elements in networks of public space and memory. Similar to other kinds of public space, the changes that stadiums have undergone in Latin America and elsewhere reflect larger changes in the planning and organization of urban life. Subject to many of the same globalizing forces as are plazas, parks, city centers, and historic districts, stadiums operate in the public domain and reflect local responses to macro-scale political and economic forces. The complexities that pertain to the social production, physical construction, use, transformation, and contestation of public spaces like parks, beaches, plazas, memorials, transportation systems, markets, and streets also pertain to stadiums. Thus, in order to better understand the public characteristics of stadiums, it is necessary to examine the ways in which stadiums connect to public space in the city at large.

Along with theatres, schools, government buildings, and shopping malls, stadiums belong to a category of spaces and places in the city that I define as *quasi-public*.[55] Quasi-public spaces are those that allow for access to the general public under specific temporal and social conditions determined by their controlling interests. The architecture and social structures of quasi-public spaces are organized according to a specific hierarchy that tends to limit movement and free association with the aid of police forces or other forms of social control. While public spaces tend to be active all the time, quasi-public spaces operate with a certain periodicity. In the case of stadiums, this periodicity heightens the social value of events. This social value extends to the stadium itself, which allows for the communication of meaning and value during phases of inactivity. In the case of stadiums, "inactivity" is a relative term as there is almost always someone at the stadium, be it a groundskeeper, security guard, club official, or tourist.

In order to examine how stadiums function as connective elements in networks of public space, it is first necessary to understand the historical trajectory of public spaces in Latin American cities. While this is by no means an exhaustive treatment of the topic, I hope to provide a foundation on which we will build an understanding of the larger patterns and processes of public culture that shape public life and culture in Rio de Janeiro and Buenos Aires.[56] In the case studies, we will see how stadiums became integrated into the urban and social fabrics of their respective cities.

Public spaces have always played an important role in Latin American cities. The Aztec, Maya, Toltec, and Inca incorporated large open spaces in their temple complexes, and their markets brought a broad spectrum of society together. Frequently laid down on existing public spaces, plazas emerged as one of the defining features of Latin American colonial cities. The grid plan that most towns followed provided for a series of plazas that functioned as commercial and social anchors and diffused the imperial social, economic, and political order.[57] "Originally designed for religious processions, feats of horsemanship, or as a marketplace," the plaza was one of the few shared urban spaces that allowed for a commingling of diverse social groups as well as control over those relations.[58] The central plaza of a town was the site of governmental and ecclesiastical power that provided ample space for daily interaction, community events, official ceremonies, and people watching. It was in plazas throughout the region that nationalist leaders declared independence from Spain in the second and third decades of the nineteenth century, furthering the centrality of the plaza in public life and political consciousness.

In the capital cities of newly formed Latin American republics, the main plaza (*plaza mayor* or *plaza central*) continued to serve as the locus of governmental power and retained its function as the central sphere for social and political interaction. As local and national economies were integrated into the global economy in the late nineteenth century, rural to urban migration and international immigration stimulated tremendous urban growth and generated significant conflict over the use and structuring of public space. From Mexico to Argentina, local and national leaders employed European, "scientific" models of urban design to shape their wildly growing cities, and public space became a stage on which the dramaturgies of social and political life were created, controlled, and contested.

The type of urban reforms undertaken in places like Mexico City, Rio de Janeiro, and Buenos Aires at the turn of the twentieth century responded to the changing dynamics of urban life by creating new kinds of spaces that shifted the form and function of public space. Although the spaces of the street and plaza continued to provide for the casual interaction of diverse social sectors, these same spaces were scenes of violent protests against deplorable living conditions. Control of urban space was of paramount importance for urban elites as they sought to link ideas of social control with civilization. One clear way of doing this was by restructuring urban space in a European image and limiting the expansion of democratic institutions.[59] Historic centers slid into a period of decline, suffering from intentional neglect as urban elites tried to distance themselves from the colonial past.[60]

Coupled with the restructuring of urban space came class-based residential segregation. The out-migration of elites to suburban residential districts and the emergence of rail and streetcar transportation emptied out the urban core and reduced the importance of colonial-era public spaces for providing a mechanism for social interaction. In many cases, Parisian-inspired urban reforms eliminated popular living quarters and restructured urban space with an emphasis on economic functionality, monumentality, the control of social relations in public space, and the creation of a conceptual city that worked very hard to associate itself with cosmopolitan Europe.[61] The spatial dictates of the global economy (dominated by foreign capital) required modern ports, functional transportation systems, and bigger, broader spaces than were needed in the colonial or Republican eras. While the reforms of the early twentieth century did not significantly affect the role of public space at the scale of the neighborhood, structural changes writ large occurred suddenly and shaped the future growth of Latin American cities.[62]

As we shall see in Rio de Janeiro and Buenos Aires, it was during the early decades of the twentieth century that stadiums emerged as a new form of public space that initially served as sites and symbols of cosmopolitan sophistication and social exclusion. Similar to changes that were happening in the larger city, the social model of sporting clubs and the architectural models for their parlors, clubhouses, and stadiums came from Europe. The first modern stadiums in Latin America were self-conscious expressions of European styles, tastes, and habits. These were spaces for a very limited public—not coincidentally the same public that was restructuring urban space through the workings of economic and political capital.

The demographic and spatial expansion of Latin American cities in the first decades of the twentieth century was equaled by an expansion of institutional sports and their attendant infrastructure. As stadiums and sport-

ing cultures expanded to include a larger socioeconomic profile throughout Latin America, stadiums assumed many of the integrative social characteristics traditionally associated with plazas. They allowed for a freedom
of access and association that brought together all sectors in a shared space.
At the same time, they began to lose their foreign profiles and to become
more organic expressions of local urban cultures, using indigenous building techniques, materials, and site designs. Stadiums were gradually woven
into the urban fabric, frequently emerging alongside rows of houses or
industrial buildings, and helped to shape the form, texture, and culture of
Latin American cities.

During the mid-twentieth century, local and national governments
continued to restructure public space to accommodate industrial and
urban modernization. As the geographer Joseph Scarpaci notes, architectural modernism "entailed rational forms that embodied the spirit of this
new image; decoration and ornamentation would become a relic of the
'backward' past."[63] These new forms highlighted the use of the automobile
and incorporated Corbusier-inspired urban designs that further damaged
the functionality of large public spaces. However, at the neighborhood
level, plazas and markets continued to function as integrative public
spaces. Stadiums were also sites of neighborhood identification and helped
to structure the temporal and spatial patterns of urban life.

Commensurate with the innovative technologies that allowed Latin
Americans to build monumental public buildings with reinforced concrete, the 1940s and 1950s were a period of unparalleled stadium building in
Latin America. If not imagined as monuments in their own right, many
state-funded stadiums were of immense dimensions, creating cavernous
public spaces that were more products of political ideologies than functional urban design. Conceived and constructed in a "modernist" moment, these stadiums lacked the intimacy, character, and architectural
nuance of stadiums built in the early decades of the twentieth century. So
frenetic was the pace and scale of stadium building that by 1970 Brazil had
eight of the ten largest stadiums in the world. Many of these drew on traditions of clientelism and political patronage in Latin America—producing
stadiums that had more seating capacity than the towns in which they were
located. Among the long list of Latin American stadiums with the names of
the politicians that sponsored their construction are the Estádio Presidente
Vargas in Ceará, Brazil, and the Estadio Presidente Peron in Buenos Aires'
southern suburb of Avalleneda.[64]

The decline of import substitution industrialization (ISI) economies
and the rise of military dictatorships in the 1960s and 1970s—known as the
"lost decades"—emphasized the political role of public space in Latin
America. In this era the streets, plazas, and public cities of major cities in

the Southern Cone and Brazil became spaces of fear and disassociation as military dictatorships attempted to silence public discourse by controlling public space. The appropriation of Buenos Aires' Plaza de Mayo by mothers who demanded to know the location of their sons and husbands highlighted not only the political but also the gendered nature of public space in that city.

It was also during the lost decades that stadiums became sites of increased violence between rival groups of fans and between fans and the police. By providing governments with malleable groups of young men and allowing for free association, stadiums both abetted and confounded governmental attempts to control public space. Perhaps the most well publicized example is that of the Chilean dictator Augusto Pinochet's use of the Chilean National Stadium as a dungeon and torture chamber for political dissidents. With the return of democracy in the 1980s, public spaces had little chance to normalize before neoliberal economic regimes began to shift the structure of Latin American cities in the 1990s. The historical trend has been towards the reproduction and reshaping of public space in response to the political, economic, and spatial regimes of global capital. Each of these changes can be read in the region's stadiums as well as in the production and control of public spaces.

In the first decade of the twenty-first century, the social and spatial structures of Latin American cities are rapidly changing, with detrimental effects on public life and public space. The emergence of gated communities, the movement of the marketplace to well-guarded shopping malls and large supermarkets, increased automobile traffic, and "over-urbanization" have all contributed to the decline of public space in Latin America.[65] While plazas, parks, and markets continue to give form, rhythm, and texture to older neighborhoods in cities throughout the region, in the rapidly expanding and unplanned urban fringes public spaces are largely absent. Stadiums are also less public as increased violence between fans and the expansion of cable television has had the double effect of expanding audiences while reducing overall attendance. Economies of fear increasingly dictate where, when, and how people move through Latin American cities.

Class-based segmentation of residential space has decreased the effectiveness of public space as a mechanism for creating senses of conviviality and connectedness. Cities are experiencing industrial and residential decentralization as factories and the upper middle classes move to the suburbs. However, the central business district is maintaining its positional advantage due to the inertia of communication and transportation infrastructure. Meanwhile, "empty" space in the *centros históricos* is appropriated by squatter settlements or reshaped to attract global tourists.[66]

These developments have provoked yet more conflict in the production, use, and control of public space in Latin American cities. In Argentina, protesters cut transportation lines; in Bolivia, miners take up arms in the workplace; Rio's beaches and Mexico City's streets are patrolled with machine-gun-wielding police. Overall, the Latin American city (with some notable exceptions such as Bogotá) is a more *randomly* violent place as social and economic polarization increases. This violence is both political and personal, as state economic and social policies create a situation wherein large numbers of people are forced to resort to extralegal means to secure their basic necessities. Social polarization is reflected by increases in kidnapping in Mexico City, highway robbery in Rio de Janeiro, carjacking in Buenos Aires, armed confrontations between federal police and labor organizers in Oaxaca. Stadiums also play a role in these larger urban conflicts, staging ritualized confrontations between groups competing for urban and sporting supremacy. In Brazil, drug trafficking factions battle with police and rival factions both inside and outside the stadium. In Argentina, organized and battle-tested soccer gangs mark city walls with territorial graffiti and engage in hand-to-hand combat with the police both inside and outside the stadium.

Despite the sociospatial fracturing of society along class lines, public space and public culture remain constituent elements of urban life in Latin America. Throughout the region, plazas, parks, stadiums, and churches continue to play vital roles in the expression of collective urbanity (at least at the neighborhood scale) and offer opportunities to investigate the relationships of cultural meaning to designed spaces as well as how these meanings are changing.[67] Even though the decline of public space has not been as linear or as extensive in Latin America as it has been in the United States, the current trajectory is towards greater social segmentation and privatization and the refashioning of public space in the image of global capital.[68] Public space is less public; it is increasingly developed and redeveloped to meet the needs, both real and imagined, of specific and limited communities.[69] As we shall see in greater detail in Rio de Janeiro and Buenos Aires, these trends have also made stadiums more rationalized, territorialized, and militarized spaces that serve an increasingly limited and atomized public.

Conclusion

Stadiums are places where the local intersects with the global in ways so mundane that they have escaped the attention of people trained to think about these sorts of things. Along with a handful of other sites, the stadium is one of the places in the city where a full range of socioeconomic actors comes together at a given time: minimum-wage laborers, middle-class season ticket holders, CEOs, multimillionaire owners, and idolized superstars all have their proscribed places and roles. This congregation gives us a good snapshot of society as a whole, and by comparing pictures over time we can read the changes and patterns of culture.

The stadium is a communicative node in urban and cultural networks that helps to organize human interaction at different scales. A product of the intersecting discourses that shape and inform the cultural landscape, a stadium can no more be understood outside of its cultural context than a key without a lock. Understanding the mechanisms that create, sustain, and shift culture is no simple task, but by focusing on one object of study we can observe, measure, and interpret larger ideas, patterns, and processes.

As we shall see in the coming chapters, stadiums have a physical, cultural, and social geographic presence at the micro-level that profoundly affects surrounding spaces. This presence persists well beyond the playing of games and is a product of historical processes that have exercised progressive and continual influence on the city at large. Stadiums are unique forms that are both connected to and separate from more fully public spaces. This connection implies that a correct reading of them requires an understanding of larger urban and cultural contexts. Yet stadiums are also disconnected spatial and experiential realms, with multiple and overlapping spaces that establish distinctions between inside and outside, sacred and profane, us and them. As constituent elements of cultural and urban landscapes, stadiums communicate simultaneously on multiple levels; understanding their messages and meanings may be critical to making sense of Latin American cities.

As we enter into Rio de Janeiro and Buenos Aires through their stadiums, it will be important to keep in mind the historical and theoretical trajectories I have outlined above. Most of us (literate residents of industrial, urban cultures) have been to a stadium and have strong memories associated with them, or encounter them in such a casual way that we never think much about why and how they came to be—much less their generalized effect on our lives. Universal obviousness may be the essential characteristic of stadiums that makes them such powerful vehicles for opening new ways of exploring and understanding the world.

CHAPTER TWO

Rio de Janeiro

Spiritual Home of World Football

Two blocks from the touristy beaches of Salvador, Brazil, is a bar called Charles Miller. The décor is floor to ceiling soccer: signed jerseys, historical photos of teams and players, flags, scarves, posters—and over the bar hangs a well-dusted photo of Mr. Miller. The Brazilian Gisella Morua begins his account of the early history of Brazilian soccer by musing, "When Charles Miller stepped off the boat in Santos on the 9th of June, 1894, carrying his bag and a ball and other equipment, he couldn't have imagined that this moment would mark the official introduction of soccer to Brazil."[1] The soccer historian Tony Mason writes, "It is well known that association football first came to Brazil in 1894 and that it was Charles Miller who introduced it."[2] And Chris Taylor, a British journalist who traveled throughout Latin America chronicling soccer's multifarious manifestations, calls Charles Miller the "founding father of Brazilian football."[3]

On July 16, 1950, more than two hundred thousand people gathered in the Estádio Municipal do Rio de Janeiro for the final game of the FIFA World Cup between Brazil and Uruguay. It was the largest stadium crowd ever assembled and accounted for 10 percent of the city's population. Outside the stadium, tens of thousands of people filled the plazas, squares, streets, and bars of Brazil's capital city, listening to the radio broadcast of the game. Millions more gathered around radios throughout Brazil, anxiously listening to the game's ebb and flow, anticipating the promised Brazilian victory. The shocking Uruguayan victory was a severe psychological blow to Brazilians that continues to inform national consciousness more than half a century later. People born well after the event suffer from its effects.

This chapter explores the development of stadiums and soccer culture

Map 2.1 Rio de Janeiro and Brazil

in Rio de Janeiro and Brazil from their origins in the late nineteenth century to the dramatic 1950 World Cup Final held in what was then the world's largest stadium. During this brief period, soccer evolved from a game played by British and local elites to a national passion that in many respects defined conceptions of Brazilian citizenship and identity. The astounding pace at which soccer transformed Brazilian cultural and urban landscapes is the central theme of this story, and the burgeoning stadiums of Rio de Janeiro were the collective stage for the transformation.

The development of stadiums in Rio de Janeiro at the turn of the twentieth century occurred simultaneously with a host of urban, political, social, and economic changes. As Brazil began to shed its colonial profile and entered into industrial modernity, its capital city shifted unevenly along class, racial, and geographic lines and was characterized by tension, exclusion, and violence. Consistent with other public spaces in fin-de-siècle Latin America, the geographic space of the Brazilian stadium was initially a venue for the control of race and class relations. But by the mid-1930s, all creeds, colors, and classes were screaming together, and at each other, in the stands. By the 1950 World Cup, the stadiums of Rio de Janeiro were relatively egalitarian public spaces where a wide spectrum of society, from the white-skinned president of the Republic to the dark-skinned manual laborer, understood themselves to be part of a collective national enterprise and shared emotions related to the stadium.

By describing the role of stadiums in the transformation of the cultural landscape in Rio de Janeiro in the early twentieth century, this chapter answers the questions: What were the processes of diffusion and adaptation that made soccer and stadiums central elements of Brazilian culture? How were race and class relations in Rio de Janeiro expressed, contested, and transformed in the stadium? What role did stadiums play in the construction of Brazilian national identity in the first half of the twentieth century?

The Origins and Diffusion of Soccer Stadiums in Brazil

Charles Miller was the Brazilian-born son of British parents who lived in São Paulo. At ten years of age Charles was packed off to Europe for schooling and returned in his early twenties carrying soccer balls and shoes in his luggage. In Britain, organized soccer had been popular for some time, with crowds of more than ten thousand attending matches in many British cities in the 1870s and 1880s. The practice of sport in Britain and continental Europe had a strong footing in institutional settings, and the children of Brazilian expatriate elites had played the game as schoolboys long before Miller strode onto the docks at Santos in 1894. Miller's family was part of a large contingent of British industrialists, engineers, professionals, and capitalists who were the local agents of the British mercantilist empire in Brazil. In addition to the permanent expatriate community, British sailors played soccer on open spaces near the docks, itinerant British managers played soccer on the empty fields near their mills, and British masters released their charges to play soccer on the private grounds of British schools. Thus when Miller began to organize soccer games among his friends and workmates at São Paulo Railway he encountered fertile social ground among the influential agricultural and industrial elite who had the time, money, and cultural habit of vigorous dedication to sport. Miller's enthusiasm helped to establish soccer in the wealthy social clubs of São Paulo, but it is not accurate to credit him with the organization of soccer teams and clubs throughout Brazil, as many historical narratives suggest.

Given the lack of land transportation between cities in nineteenth-century Brazil, there was little popular communication between them and therefore unlikely that Miller traveled throughout his native land spreading the gospel of football. Although they were part of a vast empire, the cities of Salvador, Manaus, Belém, and Recife were essentially islands of urbanism more likely to have trade relations with London and Liverpool than with Rio de Janeiro and Porto Alegre. Thus soccer in Brazil probably began concurrently in many different places by the same generalized processes. Gilmar Mascarenhas de Jesus, one of the few Brazilian geographers to have studied the diffusion of soccer in Brazil, tells us that because of the plurality and isolation of entry points for soccer in Brazil it is "impossible to say the precise time and place of the first soccer experience;" however, "São Paulo was without a doubt the first city to organize soccer and see it disseminated in the streets."[4]

Aided and abetted by figures like Charles Miller, the proliferation of soccer (as well as rowing, cricket, and horse racing) was a direct result of urban, demographic, and industrial expansion. The processes of Brazilian urbanization did not accelerate until the late nineteenth century, after separatist and republican movements throughout the country had been controlled.[5] When Miller was born in the 1870s the population of São Paulo was less than 35,000. By 1890 the population had increased to 65,000, and by 1920 it was 579,000. Following the proclamation of the Brazilian Republic in 1889, the stabilization of national and local government encouraged the highly mobile capital of European and North American firms and governments to invest in Brazil, effectively molding, or "fixing," space in their own image. The emergent industrial modernism of Brazil manifested in a multitude of concrete forms geared towards the export of raw materials:

the space of the factory, the space of the coffee plantation, transportation systems, spaces of production and distribution, and the social spaces in which the expatriate and national elites both literally and figuratively reproduced. The story repeats itself in Belém, Recife, Fortaleza, Salvador, Belo Horizonte, Rio de Janeiro, and Porto Alegre.

Similar to what was happening in São Paulo, as the British became a more established economic, social, and cultural presence in Rio de Janeiro in the last decades of the nineteenth century, they developed private clubs where creole elites mixed with their European counterparts in social and sporting engagements. The peripatetic sons of the British in Rio de Janeiro generally did not have to work, had finished their educations in cosmopolitan Europe, and had a limited social circle to move in. Thus trends spread rapidly and soccer captured the attention and imagination of youth. Soccer not only occupied an increasing amount of their time, but the perceived fashionableness of the sport attracted ever more practitioners. In accordance with European habits, soccer, practiced within the social and physical confines of exclusive social clubs, was becoming a mark of distinction.[6]

Kicking a ball around the club was much more than a way to pass one's leisure time, however. For these elite young men, practicing soccer and moving through its associated spaces was a way of celebrating their British identity. For instance, the Rio Cricket Club organized a soccer game in honor of the coronation of Edward VII in 1902.[7] Soccer games were also a way for expatriates in different cities to socialize and compete as Britons: the first game between British clubs in São Paulo and Rio de Janeiro also occurred in 1902. The *paulistas* (residents of São Paulo) won with Charles Miller on the team. The intercity games gradually became more frequent and more popular and were promoted as spectacles by the clubs. Mirroring the processes outlined by Bale, the increasing numbers of spectators required that clubs invest in grandstands. Playing surfaces and dimensions became standardized and informal "grounds" slowly became "stadiums."[8] While there had been stadiums dedicated to horse racing and grandstands along the beaches in Botafogo to watch the popular regattas, in 1904 the Fluminese Football Club inaugurated Rio's first soccer stadium in the posh Rio neighborhood of Laranjeiras.

For the tightly knit expatriate community, attending soccer matches was initially more of a social than a sporting event. Far from the raucous competitions that were to follow, the stadiums developed on the grounds of social clubs were places to affirm one's Europeanness, places (and spaces) to celebrate cosmopolitanism and refinement, in a process that stamped soccer with the mark of modernity. The stadium of the Fluminese Football Club was a place to see and be seen; the players as much as the spectators were concerned with their appearance and decorum. These were not sweaty, muddy, and bloody battles but a chance to show style and sophistication. The Brazilian social historian Leonardo Pereira says, "With their elegant and well pressed shirts, the belts that held up the Bermuda shorts and their hair curiously arranged, the players demonstrated their class while playing matches."[9] Mario Filho, perhaps the most famous Brazilian sports journalist who chronicled the social history of soccer in Brazil, wrote that it was common to see the players lounging about the clubs in their *smocking* (smoking) jackets, sometimes donning them during half-time while they were chatting up the ladies. This was consistent with early sporting practice in other cities in Latin America.[10]

The expatriate British were not the only ones constructing their geographic and social identities in relation to the burgeoning sport, however. The Brazilian creole elite were also active members of the social clubs of Rio and as early as 1903 played in self-identified Brazilian teams against the British. These early articulations of difference in relation to soccer marked the beginning of a process whereby Brazilian bodies were differentiated from European bodies in the space of the stadium. In 1904, after the Brazilian members of Fluminese beat the British of Fluminese in a friendly match, members of the Brazilian team split to form a club that only permitted native-born Brazilians: the Botafogo Football Club. In the midst of explosive urban development and demographic growth it was inevitable that the British would not be the exclusive practitioners of soccer for long.

While soccer was beginning to show signs of supplanting rowing as the most popular diversion of the young male elite in the first decade of the twentieth century, the processes of diffusion outside this limited social and geographic core of central Rio de Janeiro to other parts of the city were also accelerating. In the same year that the Botafogo Football Club formed, the Companhia Progresso Industrial do Brasil founded the Bangu Athletic Club in a far western suburb of Rio, installing a field in the shadows of the factory. By 1905 it was not uncommon to have more than fifteen hundred people in attendance at a match, and by 1906 more than thirty soccer clubs were active in the city.[11]

The diffusion of soccer to the urban masses in Rio was facilitated by the lack of an identifiable Brazilian sporting culture. The Brazilian working class had some physical social practices and traditions such as *capoeira* and the vigorous sensuality of samba,[12] but there is no evidence to suggest that there was institutionalized sport in Brazil before the arrival of the British in the late nineteenth century. The astoundingly rapid diffusion of soccer in Brazil was also aided, as many commentators have noted, by its flexible and simple rules.[13] In lieu of regulation equipment and spaces, the urban poor

Photo 2.1 Stadium of the Bangu Athletic Club. This stadium, built in the shadow of the factory, was an important element of Rio's early soccer and stadium culture. Far from the city center, it served as a place of recreation for laborers and management of the adjacent factory.

and working classes practiced soccer in the streets with oranges, or wadded newspaper bound with rubber bands, or whatever was available. Played alone or in groups, in empty lots or in the expanding favelas, the soccer practices of the upper classes were observed, imitated, and adapted by all sectors of Brazilian society. The popularity and informality of street soccer stood in direct opposition to the more limited and formal practices of the elites in their well-tended clubs. Charles Miller and his friends were on a collision course with the growing numbers of poor flocking to Brazil's urban centers.

The Explosion, Contestation, and Transformation of Soccer Space

The development of soccer as an integral part of Brazilian culture and national consciousness was effected in a remarkably brief period in the stadiums and informal soccer spaces of Rio de Janeiro. The changes that happened in relation to the sport were part of larger economic, political, social, cultural, and spatial changes in the city, region, and nation. As with baseball in the United States, cricket in India, and gladiatorial games in ancient Rome, soccer in Brazil is imbued with a moralizing discourse.[14] The ways in which the discourses of modernity and social exclusivity in the soccer stadiums of Rio de Janeiro gave way to discourses of nationalism and "racial democracy" were the products of larger social and geographic processes in the first half of the twentieth century. In order to understand the ways in which national, racial, and class narratives were articulated, challenged, and inscribed in the stadiums of the city, we must turn to the historical record.

We can observe at least four concurrent processes in the soccer spaces of early-twentieth-century Rio de Janeiro: modernization, identity formation, social integration, and nationalization. Like many Latin American cities, Rio de Janeiro experienced unprecedented social, demographic, and geographic changes in the late nineteenth and early twentieth century. The decidedly tardy abolition of slavery in 1888 (the prolongation of which had been abetted by North American shipping interests) produced a generation of Afro-Brazilians who had always been free but whose parents and grandparents had been owned by their fellow citizens. The proclamation of the Brazilian Republic in 1889 changed the relationship of the state to the individual and positioned Brazil in a more modern and international context. Millions of Afro-Brazilians were migrating from the northeast sugar plantations of Bahia, Pernambuco, and Alagoas to the cities of southeastern Brazil.[15] This Afro-Brazilian migration, coupled with regional rural migrants into the industrial complexes of southern Brazil, strained the capacity of local governments and urban infrastructures. There were also millions of immigrants arriving from Europe: Italians, Poles, Germans, Spanish, Lebanese, Portuguese, Russians, and others. For many of Rio's recent arrivals, living conditions were difficult, dangerous, and unfamiliar: rampant unemployment, a lack of housing, and pronounced inequality defined urban life. Simultaneously, transportation and communication technologies were bringing places closer together while industrial production and the institution of the factory reshaped conceptions of space and time in the lives of ordinary people.[16] This period also saw the accelerated integration of Brazil's vast hinterlands into the economic and political life of the nation through improved transportation, trade, and communication.

The population of Brazil in 1900 was 17.4 million; by 1920 it had reached 30.6 million.[17] How could all the new arrivals, a hodgepodge of ethnicities, classes, and generations with different traditions, cultures, and conceptions of self and other, be called "Brazilians"? What were the common historical and cultural relationships that could be shaped into a national ideology and identity? Brazilians lacked a cohesive story that they could tell about themselves in the context of modernity. The relative absence of a strong national identity was an opportunity for politicians and elites to present their conceptions of Brazil in a variety of venues. Rio de Janeiro, as the capital of the nation, provided a model for other Brazilian cities, and it was here that the Brazilian government attempted to shape the image of the nation through urban reform projects in which stadiums would play an increasingly important role.

The first major restructuring of Rio de Janeiro in a modernist context was completed under the tenure of Mayor Francisco Pereira Passos (1902–1906).[18] The reforms initiated under his government restructured the physical and architectural forms of the city. Hills were razed and grand Parisian-style boulevards inserted in an attempt to shape the city center on a European model. The physical removal of the working poor from informal settlements in the city center happened alongside the demolition of many colonial-era buildings. Passos also began extensive sanitation works that were critical in halting the spread of disease. The urban reforms of Pereira Passos were effective in developing a visual and functional sense of modernity in the city.[19]

Expansive boulevards and monumental government and public buildings were visually impressive and aided the system of flows, but we can hypothesize that they did not encourage affective relationships with "Brazil" among the lower classes that formed the majority of the population. These reforms were essentially foreign designs imported and imposed on the space of the city by economic, social, and political elites who looked to Europe for their urban and cultural models. Furthermore, the reforms encompassed a limited geographic area as they were concentrated in the city center. However, as the geographer Brian Godfrey has observed, these reforms provided the template from which the city grew in the coming decades. The leveling of major hills in the city center, the modernization of the port, and the development of wide boulevards for commerce and government symbolically and functionally thrust Rio de Janeiro into the twentieth century.[20] However, the social distinctions that pertained in the workplace and the separateness of radically different living conditions and lifestyles demarcated along class and racial lines were not challenged by the newly reformed urban environment. Other spaces of modernity, including the stadium, were much more likely to have the generalized, integrative effects that urban reformers like Pereira Passos desired.

As a means of creating hybridized national identities that would appeal to a broad social spectrum, governments frequently invented nationalist traditions and spaces.[21] The national ceremonies, monuments, and public spaces that were associated with urban reforms all contributed to a sense of belonging and identity—but for a very limited public.[22] The particular trappings of modernity might not have applied to the residents of the favelas or suburban areas, but the idea of modernist progress probably did. So even though there might not have been widespread interaction with modern spaces and places, the idea that these reforms were being made in a modernist context, by a nominally representative government, certainly had an effect on what people thought about Rio de Janeiro and Brazil, which in turn affected their experience of place. As we shall see, stadiums played a central role in the development of this European-influenced and "modern" Rio de Janeiro.

Identity formation is a slippery concept. As it is central to the study of culture, geographers, anthropologists, and others have examined identity formation from a variety of perspectives, but few have compared similar spaces over time as a way of analyzing these spatial and conceptual processes. Identity formation is a dynamic process punctuated by important moments in time and molded through repeated experience of place and space. For example, the "typical" Brazilian identification with samba music and dance results from prolonged exposure and practice in various times and places. Even if a Brazilian does not like the music or cannot perform the dance, there is nonetheless a communicative association between the individual, the nation, and samba. It is difficult to say exactly when or where these identities are solidified as the practice, sounds, and semiotics of the dance are so frequent and diffuse. In relation to soccer we are fortunate to have the more generalized processes of identity formation marked by historical events in identifiable times and places. In this regard, the stadiums of Rio de Janeiro are instrumental in identifying the consolidation of a central element of Brazilian national identity.

As Rio de Janeiro and Brazil became more fully engaged with modernity and industrialization, soccer belonged to the social spaces and cosmopolitan practices of the expatriate British and creole elite. As the city expanded and the population grew, soccer diffused both horizontally and vertically (i.e., among members of the same socioeconomic stratum and between strata) and began to lose its strict association with the tastes and lifestyles of the privileged classes. The burgeoning soccer stadiums of the city were places and spaces to reaffirm elite values, but in the larger society soccer was taking hold (and taking place) and began to reflect the tastes and lifestyles of the middle and working classes. Similar to the spate of urban reforms undertaken by municipal and national governments, the soccer spaces of the elite were not intended for the masses, yet because they were exclusive domains they were visible and symbolic representations of unresolved social, economic, and political differences. In the first years of the twentieth century, the development of an inclusive Brazilian national identity that resonated with most urban Brazilians was still some years away.

Opposites Compel

By the last decades of the nineteenth century, major cities in Britain, Europe, the Mediterranean, and eastern North America had team sports and stadium games that were lucrative and well-established social and cultural practices. Soccer teams that played in the English first division regularly made excursions around the globe to play against local opposition (usually to places where there was a large British expatriate community), and in 1908 several English teams arrived in Rio de Janeiro. Traveling Argentine teams also appeared in Rio's stadiums around the same time. The Brazilian club and Best XI teams (not yet playing as "Brazil") did not fare well, losing all the games they played between 1908 and 1910.[23] Despite the poor showing of the local teams, the stadiums of the Fluminese Football Club and the Paissandu Cricket Club were packed to capacity; the carnival atmosphere that characterizes Brazilian stadiums today was crystallizing. If we can judge the strength of identity formation through the strong negative reaction of fans to the Brazilian losses, then it is evident that soccer had the potential to rally diverse elements of *carioca* society around a common cause, and the stadium was the conduit through which these emotions were communicated and transferred. Following the first defeats, fans were content to protest *after* the game—yelling in bars, causing a ruckus, intimating violence. After losing 7–0 to the Argentines in 1910 there developed a sense of outrage *during* the game and violent disruptions were becoming common in local league games. Police forces were now necessary to control unruly crowds. Within two years what had begun as a collective despondency at Brazilian losses quickly turned into a virulent demand for revenge.[24]

The sense of public outrage associated with the Brazilian defeats had very specific articulations in space. This nascent collective, national identity might have been present in relation to other spaces and places of the city but was not generally appropriated in the way that the national sporting identity was. Soccer was a vehicle that encouraged the development of an "imagined community" and helped to invent traditions that would become invaluable in shaping a sense of national identity.[25] More immediately, the stadium was one of the few spaces in the city to experience such a broad social spectrum in a confined space. Different from plazas or streets, where social distinctions were more clearly articulated and maintained, the space of the stadium conditioned and focused individual relationships and identities in regard to a collective body both on the field and in the stands. Although social distinctions were maintained through regimented seating arrangements, the general effect of the stadium is to create a *corpus generalus* that temporarily elides the distinctions that pertain beyond the stadium walls. The competitive nature of sport, located in spaces built to host ritualized confrontations, ensured that these spaces were imbricated in the construction, manipulation, contestation, and affirmation of "Brazilian-ness" opposed to the English and Argentine "other."

Of course, soccer-related identities were part of a larger matrix of relationships and processes, and the sport was variously appropriated by different groups: the stadium had very different meanings for rich and poor. For the majority, the stadium offered a spectacle that was entertaining, emotional, and affordable as more and more teams began competing and building stadiums. Media coverage expanded, and the leagues were increasingly competitive and organized. The entire cultural complex associated with soccer was booming, the stadiums were filling, and the cultural landscape of Rio de Janeiro rapidly transformed as a result.

From its introduction in the late 1890s through the 1910s, soccer signified elitism, refinement, and exclusivity. With the flowering of nationalist sentiment in relation to the game and the rapid spread of "foot-ball" throughout the city, the rusty doors of the elite were beginning to crack open. These games against the Argentines and English were significant in that they show the presence of several simultaneous processes: the Brazilians were beginning to lose their subaltern position in relation to the English; soccer was shifting from an elite sport to a popular sport; fans from divergent socioeconomic categories were coming together in the stadium under the aegis of Brazilian national identity; and this convergence forced elites to reconcile the inclusion of the lower classes into conceptions of the nation.[26] The meanings of the games played in the stadiums of the Fluminense Football Club and the Paissandu Cricket Club had begun to take on social and political significance well beyond the immediacy of the event. The games against foreign teams between 1908 and 1910 marked the beginning of these processes.

The 1919 South American Championship and the Estádio das Laranjeiras

The localized growth and organization of soccer in Rio de Janeiro, São Paulo, and other South American cities was also happening at the national, continental, and global scales. For instance, the soccer federation of South Africa joined FIFA in 1910, those of Argentina and Chile in 1912, and the United States Soccer Federation in 1913. The first Brazilian soccer federation (Federação Brasiliero do Esporte [FBE]) formed in 1915 not long after the first team to play as "Brasil" lost to England's Exeter City in an exhibition match.

The rebirth of the Olympic Games in 1896 had demonstrated the power of sport to inflame national passions while at the same time providing a venue for the peaceful interaction of geopolitical rivals. International competitions were a natural outgrowth of the formation of national football associations. The first South American Championship was held in Buenos Aires in 1916 as part of Argentina's centennial celebrations. The Brazilian team was composed of players from the major clubs of Rio and São Paulo—the team included a *paulista* mulatto named Arthur Friedenreich. Sadly, because of Friedenreich's inclusion, the Argentine fans labeled the Brazilians "monkeys." The Uruguayans easily won the 1916 tournament with the help of an Afro-Uruguayan striker named Isabelino Gradín. A year later, in a tepid response to the reaction of the Argentines in Buenos Aires, the FBE sent an all-white team to Montevideo, losing 4–2 to Argentina and 4–0 to the hosts and trouncing the hapless Chileans 5–0. Uruguay again won with Afro-Uruguayans on the team. Rio de Janeiro was selected to host the 1919 tournament. Although by this time most South American nations played soccer, the participants were again limited to Uruguay, Argentina, Chile, and Brazil. It is no surprise that Britain was the largest trading partner of each of these nations. All the games were played at the Estádio das Laranjeiras of the Fluminese Football Club.

Since its formation in 1904, the Fluminese Football Club had moved and improved its social and soccer spaces over time.[27] Constructed by and connected to the social club of the Fluminese Football Club in 1917, the Estádio das Laranjeiras was expanded to hold eighteen thousand spectators for the 1919 tournament. The remodeled stadium combined a neocolonial palatial style with the modernist functionality of a large public space. The stadium's architecture embodied messages of the colonial past and the modernist future while at the same time retaining notions of social privilege and exclusion. The general public was welcome, as long as they could pay and could remember their place was in the stands, not in the clubhouse.[28]

Though it was a semiexclusive domain, the stadium became a symbolic home for the nation during the 1919 tournament. The stadium and the club grounds occupied a large area near the center of the city, the beaches of Flamengo, and stylish residential neighborhoods. The proximity to the Palacio de Guanabara, the former residence of Princess Isabel and the Conde d'Eu (purchased by the federal government during the Republic for housing state guests), revealed the symbolic and functional relationships between the general membership of the Fluminese Football Club and the political and economic powers of the city and nation. We can surmise that the stadium and the club helped to consolidate relationships of power and privilege among its members and guests.[29]

The Brazilian team selected for the 1919 tournament was again chosen

Photo 2.2 Estádio das Laranjeiras, 1919. This photo shows the completed stadium and club as well as the grounds of the Palacio de Guanabara. The stadium hosted the 1919 South American Football Championship, which Brazil won for the first time. Fluminese Football Club archives.

by the FBE and included the *paulistas'* controversial mulatto, Arthur Friedenreich. Though the outward representation of Brazil on the field was primarily that of the white elites from the richest clubs of Rio de Janeiro and São Paulo, the crowd was all Brazilian, and twenty thousand of them watched Brazil pummel Chile 6–0 in the tournament's opening game. Thousands more lined the hills surrounding the stadium, and hundreds more stood in the streets, just to be close to the action.

Visiting the Laranjeiras stadium today, it is difficult to imagine the crush of humanity during the 1919 South American Championship. The steeply inclined double-tiered stands rise precipitously from the field of play. The average crowd for Brazil's games in the then-18,000-capacity stadium was 25,000, and the average for the seven games of the tournament was 20,100. These figures reflect the rise of soccer as a mass spectacle, the nascent popularity of the sport, the increasingly strong associations of soccer with the nation, and an apparent disregard for personal space and public safety.

These were by far the largest crowds ever to attend soccer games in Rio de Janeiro and were formative moments in linking the stadium to the nation. The spectacle and experience of an overflowing stadium and the association of that experience with a sense of Brazilian citizenship must have been very powerful for those who managed to get in. Not only were fans privileged participants at a unique event, but they were literally and figuratively incorporated into a singular mass that represented Brazil for the first time in international competition on home soil. The Brazilian team had performed well but needed to beat the favored Uruguayans in a playoff in order to capture their first international trophy.

More than 35,000 fans pressed into the Estádio das Laranjeiras on May 29, 1919. Those who were not able to get tickets to the game filled the hills around the stadium. Others congregated on the principal avenues of Rio to listen to the game being broadcast from loud speakers. The final game against Uruguay was the first moment of a process that has continued unabated today: the almost complete cessation of urban normalcy when the Brazilian national team plays. Banks closed, stores closed at noon, and the president of the Republic gave public employees the day off. When the Brazilian team took the field an enormous cheer of "Viva o Brasil!" erupted from the crowd.[30]

In 1919 blacks and mulattos were still banned from participating in Rio de Janeiro's principal soccer league, the Liga Metropolitana. The presence of many Afro-Brazilians and mulattos in the stands of the Estádio das Laranjeiras during the 1919 Championship undoubtedly caused some cognitive dissonance between the conceptions and realities of the nation. If the team

Teams	Score	Attendance
Brazil × Chile	6–0	20,000
Argentina × Uruguay	2–3	18,000
Uruguay × Chile	2–0	8,000
Brazil × Argentina	3–1	22,000
Argentina × Chile	4–1	15,000
Brazil × Uruguay	2–2	23,000
Brazil × Uruguay	1–0	35,000

Table 2.1 Attendance figures from the 1919 South American Championships. The capacity of the Estádio das Laranjeiras was 18,000.

Photo 2.3 A crowd gathered in the streets of Rio de Janeiro to listen to the final of the 1919 South American Football Championship. There was no radio at this time, so the crowd listened to the game broadcast over loudspeakers connected to the stadium. From Pereira 2000.

on the field could equally represent Brazilians of all classes and colors, then why not extend rights of citizenship and social inclusion to these very same people? Did "Brazil" pertain to the elites or to the undifferentiated, multi-colored mass of Brazilians in the stadium, on the hills, and in the streets?

As the game moved into its fourth overtime period, deadlocked at 0–0, the crowd screamed for the winning goal. When Friedenreich finally tal-lied, he not only won the tournament for Brazil but also signaled the impending inclusion of blacks and mulattos into the nation. Elevated to the status of national hero, the mulatto Friedenreich was valued for his actions on the field and not judged by the color of his skin. His success in a Brazil-ian uniform was an early signal that the rules of the stadium were changing and that these changes would have to be accepted beyond the stadium walls. The Brazilian team were champions of South America, and Brazil-ians of all classes and colors streamed into the streets to celebrate.

King Albert's Visit

A year later King Albert of Belgium made a state visit to Brazil and further consolidated the Estádio das Laranjeiras as a national space. In order to demonstrate the emergent modernity of Brazil, the national government and Rio's principal soccer league (the Liga Metropolitana) organized a parade of Rio's sporting clubs in the Estádio das Laranjeiras. By presenting these clubs as representatives of a highly evolved national sporting culture—the implicit message being that the more one could vigorously pursue leisure activities, the more civilized one was—the image put forth for King Albert was one of a healthy, wealthy society founded on European principles. Despite the obvious exclusion of São Paulo's major clubs (as retribution for the *paulistas'* refusal to send representative players for the fourth South American Championship in 1920), Rio de Janeiro, as the capital of Brazil, was understood to be a microcosm of Brazilian society.[31] The king's parade highlights the emergence of a moralizing discourse associated with sport, the association of stadium space with modernist development, and the flowering of national and regional identities associated with the stadium.

The image projected by the parade organizers was carefully manipulated to show a particular vision of Brazilian society. Only clubs from the Liga Metropolitana's three divisions were permitted, although there were other leagues and clubs in the city, and strict attention was paid to the socioeconomic differences between these clubs. This was accomplished by placing the larger, wealthier clubs at the beginning of the parade queue. Thus the government of Brazil in conjunction with the well-to-do sporting and social clubs of Rio de Janeiro presented the nation in a very deliberate manner, in a particular space, that would highlight their dominance of the sporting and cultural practices of modernity that were intended to present a certain image of the nation to a European monarch. King Albert slept next door to the Fluminese Football Club at the Guanabara Palace. The stadium, as a site and symbol of modernity, became further integrated into an uneasily inclusive idea of the nation.

Zinucati and the "Naturalness" of Brazilian Soccer

Despite discernible movement towards greater inclusiveness, soccer in Brazil retained a European image for many decades. Through the 1920s it continued to be understood as a foreign game suffused with English terminology, equipment, ideologies, models, and styles of play. Though the British were gradually losing their dominance over the Rio soccer scene, the language and codes of the game were still theirs. Mario Filho tells us in his inimitable prose, "Soccer, *made in England,* had to be translated. And when it wasn't translated and Brazilianized, whoever liked to play it had to familiarize themselves with the English names. Of players, of everything. On the field a player who wanted to be respected had to speak in English. Better yet, yell in English."[32]

The exploding popularity of this *esporte bretão* (British sport, still used to describe soccer in Brazil) was inconsistent with the development of Brazilian national identity. There was a growing resistance on the part of the Brazilian intelligentsia to the foreign ideas and ideologies that soccer represented. Brazilians began to look to their own cultural traditions for ways to explain the "naturalness" with which they seemed to play the game. In 1915 a Brazilian army colonel had witnessed Pareci Indians in the north of Brazil playing a game called Zinucati that was similar to soccer in that the participants knocked about an inflated rubber ball with their heads. In an attempt to show that soccer was integral to the Brazilian national tradition and something that the Brazilian "race" was predisposed to excel at, a festival of indigenous games was organized in the stadium of Fluminese in October 1922 as part of the Brazilian Centennial Exhibition.

A group of Pareci Indians were brought to Rio de Janeiro and led out into the stadium to put on a display of their "natural" abilities with the ball. As the "civilized" spectators looked on from the stands, the Indians played their "barbaric" game on the field, dressed in the uniforms of Fluminese. The incorporation of Zinucati into the space and time of the stadium was a way of naturalizing and co-opting the indigenous practice as an expression of national consciousness bridging modern and premodern Brazil. For the Brazilian literary community, Zinucati demonstrated that the national fascination with soccer was an extension of Brazilian traditions and helped to explain the growing fascination with the British game.[33]

By presenting indigenous Brazilians in the space of the stadium, dressed in modern outfits, the organizers of the event also created symbolic and spatial relationships between the modern practices of the city and the traditional cultural practices of pre-Colombian Brazil. A similar nationalization process happened with *capoeira,* the Afro-Brazilian martial art, which was beginning to appear more frequently in Rio due to the continued migration of people from northeastern Brazil where the practice was more widespread. Because these games came from the lower classes and indigenous cultures, they were made into expressions of Brazilian soccer players' "natural" athleticism and ability. As Brazil and Brazilians became increasingly successful on the international soccer stage, the bodily movements, social spaces, and mental characteristics associated with *samba, capoeria,*

Photo 2.4 Zinucati. The caption reads: "Civilized person: Is it true that Zinucati is a barbarous game? Indian: Oh my this is very pretentious! In this respect it is very similar to your game." The Indians' dwellings are depicted within the stadium walls, bringing together the modern and pre-Columbian settlement landscapes of Brazil, even though the houses were not actually brought into the stadium. From Pereira 2000.

and *malandragem* (a way of moving through city space with feints and deception) framed the ideology and moral discourse of Brazilian soccer.

While Zinucati helped to nationalize Brazilian soccer, the hosting of the Fifth South American Foot-ball Championships (the English title is an indication of the sport's profile) in Rio de Janeiro as part of Brazil's Centennial Exhibition in 1922 reignited nationalist passions in the stadium. The capacity of Estádio das Laranjeiras was expanded from 18,000 to 25,000, and Paraguay was added to the competition. After a two-year absence from Brazilian teams due to internal political disputes, the *paulistas* rejoined the national team. Despite the inevitability of integration and the surging talent pool, the FBE was still deliberating the inclusion of blacks and mulattos in the team. The club directors were undoubtedly cognizant of the fact that the team that represented Brazil on the field would be considered a de facto representation of the nation and was thus an opportunity to define the image of the nation in an emotional and dramatically public way. The amplification of patriotic sentiment in the stadium was compounded by the ongoing Centennial celebrations.

That soccer was no longer a game of hobbyists and casual sportsmen was becoming increasingly apparent, if only from the virulently negative reactions of the Brazilian fans. During the 0–0 draw with Uruguay, some of the thirty thousand Brazilian fans invaded the pitch, throwing things at the referee and causing "scenes of real vandalism."[34] The police placed notices in the paper that they were prepared to exercise the full extent of their legal authority in order to control the crowd. This was no longer a place for dandies in their Bermuda shorts and finely coiffed hair—the honor of the nation was at stake and the *cariocas* (residents of Rio de Janeiro) were adamant that it be defended. When Brazil beat Argentina 2–0 in front of 25,000 fanatical Brazilians to claim their second South American title, the Estádio das Laranjeiras trembled under the weight of a nationalist euphoria.

We can hypothesize that once the Laranjeiras stadium had hosted the South American championships of 1919 and 1922, the king of Belgium, and the indigenous games of Atlantic Brazil's vast hinterland there was no way to effectively separate stadium space from the conceptual apparatus of the nation. People walking by the stadium would remember the experience of place and the emotions that were generated there when Brazil took the field against their South American and British rivals. Residents of the favelas surrounding the field could look down on it from above and imagine themselves playing there or having enough money to someday join one of the clubs that had paraded before a European king. In their reserved seats in the stadium, Rio's elite could fantasize that what they were watching was a natural outgrowth of an inherent Brazilian disposition for the sport. The blacks and mulattos of Rio's suburbs and favelas knew of Friedenreich's success and could imagine themselves stepping on the well-tended grass of Laranjeiras to represent Brazil. Soccer was becoming *the* national narrative, and the stadium was the stage on which Brazil projected itself.

Figueira de Melo

Socially distant yet geographically proximate to the dramatic clash of nations and heady brushes with European royalty that were happening in Laranjeiras, a small working-class neighborhood club was building a modest stadium in the northern suburb of São Cristóvão.

The first organized soccer team of the São Cristóvão Athletic Club appeared in 1909, although there had been neighborhood sporting clubs organized around rowing since the mid-1880s. What was initially called Club São Christovam played their games in the Campo de São Cristóvão, which was an open, flat public space in the center of the neighborhood. Informal games had been played there for several years, and we can assume that the field of play was clearly delimited and that there were permanent goal posts. By claiming the Campo de São Cristóvão as a home ground, São Cristóvão A.C. entered into the Liga Suburbana de Foot-ball in 1910 and has been a regular participant in the Rio de Janeiro leagues ever since.

As was common throughout the city, the presence of organized soccer in the social club attracted many young players from the surrounding neighborhood, generally of similar socioeconomic position. The institutional structure of the club and league not only aided the regular practice of the sport but also was instrumental in forming strong bonds among members. Because the members of the São Cristóvão Athletic Club were drawn from the neighborhood, the team embodied a "place" that existed in relation to other places in the city. São Cristóvão already had a strong neighborhood identity, that of Barrio Imperial, and the conflation of team with neighborhood identity was not difficult.[35] Notions of success or failure were not limited to those who were active participants in the club or on the rowing, water polo, and soccer teams. By taking the name of the neighborhood, the São Cristóvão Athletic Club began to represent the people who lived there.

During this period in Rio de Janeiro's history, the social functions of the clubs were as important as the sport functions. These community entities were part of an emergent civil society that produced Rio's famous Carnival parades and samba schools. In addition to providing a mechanism for socialization and sporting practice, the many smaller social clubs of Rio were sites of illegal activity. A public crackdown on gambling and cockfighting led to a readily available underground in the clubs, making it possible to escape police harassment and also solidifying identification with the clubs. Because the clubs were legitimate elements of the public sphere, the repression that affected otherwise marginalized social actors on the streets was neatly avoided. The public manifestations of these club identities in the multiple stadiums of the city gave marginalized individuals social legitimacy and allowed them to participate, at least in theory, in the public sphere. The interaction of these diverse clubs city-wide brought different groups into contact with each other, which had the effect of expanding, integrating, and solidifying urban and social networks.

Barrio clubs like São Cristóvão Athletic had varied social and economic compositions. One club might be composed of commercial employees, another might be related to a factory, another might be composed of people of the same national origin. In many cases, solidarity across labor lines trumped ethnic identities. The clubs hosted dances, dinners, and other social gatherings besides soccer and rowing competitions and helped to give structure and rhythm to urban life. More so in the first half of the twentieth century than today, Rio's laboring classes used the sporting clubs as a principal element of their social organization. The clubs served to integrate migrants and immigrants into Rio's increasingly complex social world. Ironically, these integrative processes were sometimes related to the paternalism of companies and political leaders who had moved against organized labor movements among Rio's working poor.[36]

The growing popularity and success of the São Cristóvão Athletic Club motivated businessmen associated with the team to purchase land for the club on the Rua Figueira de Melo in 1915. This too was a typical process of stadium formation in Rio de Janeiro. The social club of São Cristóvão had moved frequently during its first seventeen years of existence. When the land for the future stadium and *sede social* (social club) was purchased a member of the club who owned a construction company volunteered to clear and level the land. Bit by bit, members of the São Cristóvão community contributed labor and materials, with a large part of the financial resources provided by one of the wealthiest members of the club. By the middle of 1916 the club completed construction and played an inauguration match against Santos F.C. (which traveled 450 miles for the event) with approximately six thousand people in attendance. Inauspiciously, the referee from Botafogo suspended the match fifteen minutes early because of the hostility of the São Cristóvão fans towards him. Despite the ill-tempered home crowd, the local press was taken with the "sober beauty and elegance of the stadium."[38]

Due to the expanding popularity and profitability of soccer, the Estádio Figueira de Melo emerged as a venue where the poor male youth of the neighborhood could hope for upward mobility within the rigid socioeconomic structures of the larger society. By entering the club as a soccer player, young men had a chance to better their life situations, despite lacking the means to become members. As we shall see more clearly in the next chapter, this is consistent with the role the club plays for young men today.[39] As early as the 1910s, players were receiving jobs, housing, and food from the directors of clubs. This was a direct challenge to the discourse of amateur sportsmanship articulated by the larger, elite clubs whose players could aggressively pursue leisure activities without sacrificing significant amounts of income. The wealth and prestige of the larger clubs appeared to isolate them from the social and cultural realities that were driving the rapid growth and popularity of smaller clubs like São Cristóvão. The masses of urban poor were making their way into the social clubs through the practice of soccer. São Cristóvão A.C. was rising through the lower divisions of the Rio leagues; conflict with wealthier, whiter clubs was inevitable.

Although São Cristóvão A.C. was relatively small in comparison to the elite clubs of Rio de Janeiro, its ability to amass the capital to appropriate a large urban space for the practice of soccer is representative of the influence that clubs had over their localities. From the date of its inauguration, April 23, 1916, the Estádio Figueira de Melo functioned as a node in a system of spaces that defined the culture and practice of soccer in Rio de Janeiro, which in turn shaped geographic and social realities in the larger society. The stadiums of Rio de Janeiro, created by the community clubs of the metropolitan soccer leagues, were the literal and metaphorical battlefields between social actors from different geographic regions of the city. These were the places where people from different socioeconomic strata and different ethnic and racial compositions came together to participate in a shared event, identity, and culture.

C.R. Vasco da Gama and the Estádio São Januário

Well-to-do members of Rio's extensive Portuguese community founded Club de Regatas Vasco da Gama in 1898. As the name suggests, the club was a venue for members to participate in the popular rowing competitions of the city (regattas) and was strongly associated with Portuguese ethnic and historical identities. Perhaps the only sport club in the world to be named after a geographer, it took the appellation in honor of the 400th anniversary of the Portuguese explorer Vasco da Gama's discovery of the sea passage to India.[40] In part because of the historical association of the Portuguese community with the neighborhood of São Cristóvão and because land was cheap, C.R. Vasco da Gama chose Barrio Imperial for its home.

At the time of the founding of C.R. Vasco da Gama, there was a growing anti-Lusitano sentiment in Rio de Janeiro. The Portuguese community had dominated the economy and politics of the city and nation for centuries, but by the end of the nineteenth century their influence was in decline. Although they were still influential in the social and economic life of Rio de Janeiro, they were becoming supplanted by new immigrants and the British mercantile elite. The formation of Vasco da Gama helped to structure the Portuguese community along ethnic lines in a way that distinguished them as a particular social entity within the urban polity. Vasco de Gama's membership incorporated blacks, mulattos, and poor whites into its soccer team, which was the most public aspect of the club. Based in the industrial neighborhood of São Cristóvão and playing on an open plot of land at the intersection of Morais and Silva Streets, C.R. Vasco da Gama's soccer team entered the third division of the Liga Metropolitana in 1915, rising to the second division in 1917 and the first division in 1922. By this time identification with the soccer team was so intense that there were Vascainos who would not talk to anyone for three days after Vasco lost.[41]

The social tensions within Brazilian soccer and society were not mitigated by the successes of the national team in 1919 and 1922. To the contrary, the Liga Metropolitana continued to mandate exclusionary practices that discriminated against players according to their occupation, race, and literacy. None of the league champions between 1906 and 1922 fielded a black or mulatto player, much less a lower-class white. The process of integration came to several critical junctures. The first was when the Paissandu Cricket Club, an elite team, finished last in the first division in 1921. The rules of relegation and promotion were changed so that they would not have to compete in the second division with teams that fielded blacks and mulattos. This excluded the second division champion, Vasco da Gama, from assuming its position in the first division. The following year, Vasco da Gama won the second division again and was promoted to the first division.[42] In 1923 Vasco da Gama, with a team composed almost entirely of mulattos, blacks, and poor whites, won the Liga Metropolitana; São Cristóvão Athletic Club finished second. The presence of the marginalized in the stadiums of Rio de Janeiro could no longer be ignored.

Vasco's success in the 1922 and 1923 championships had important implications for the social, cultural, and spatial realities of soccer in Rio de Janeiro. First, because Vasco represented the Portuguese community as well as blacks, mulattos, and poor whites, the rich clubs hid their racist and class ideologies behind a veil of a more generalized anti-Lusitano sentiment.[43] Second, there was wide suspicion within the league that the Vasco da Gama players were de facto employees of the club, receiving payment-in-kind (*bichos*) for their services on the field. This nascent professionalism and the success of a "black" club were a direct threat to the hegemonic discourse of amateurism and "sportsmanship." Smaller, more peripheral clubs were fielding their best players, regardless of class or color, and they were having tremendous success as a result. Third, the increasing presence of uneducated, poor, and dark-skinned players in the same spaces as the educated, wealthy, white players brought more generalized social tensions to the fore. Following Vasco de Gama's 1923 championship season, Flamengo, Fluminese, América, Botafogo, and Bangu left the Liga Metropolitana and formed a separate league.[44]

So they would not appear to have racist statutes in the new league bylaws, the newly formed Metropolitan League of Athletic Sports (AMEA) included a series of "workers" statutes that limited participation. Teams needed to be formed by "students or workers who did not work in subaltern positions, except for factory workers [ostensibly to include Bangu] . . . [and] illiterate players were not allowed."[45] Another statute required that clubs possess a stadium exclusively dedicated to the practice of soccer. League champion Vasco da Gama was prohibited from participating in the AMEA because the majority of the players were illiterate and its stadium was not much more than a leveled, open space at a street corner.

One result of Vasco's 1923 championship season was that from 1924 to 1934 Rio de Janeiro had two independent and simultaneous championships, the AMEA and the Metropolitan League of Terrestrial Sports (LMDT), which included Vasco, São Cristóvão, Bonsuccesso, and other suburban clubs. In effect, this created an apartheid system wherein rich, white teams (again, with the exception of Bangu, which was a factory-based club) played against each other in stadiums while poor, black, and mulatto suburban teams played in "popular" spaces. In an attempt to consolidate their position as league champions and to claim their place among the elites, the Portuguese community associated with C.R. Vasco da Gama began to collect money to build their own stadium.

Estádio São Januário

In addition to being a response to the institutional apartheid of Rio's soccer leagues, the emergence of one of the world's most elegant stadiums in Rio de Janeiro in 1927 was partially the result of Brazil's transformation into a modern, industrializing nation. After Pereira Passos' initial transformations of the city center in the first years of the century, Rio had expanded to the south by tunneling through mountains, exploded to the west and north on electric trams, and connected with São Paulo, Belo Horizonte, and the Brazilian interior by rail. Favelas and entire hills located in the city center were razed with the idea of improving hygiene, morals, and commerce. Wetlands near the city center were filled in with the demolished mountains and the beaches transformed into spaces of leisure. The 1922 Centennial had ushered in a new era of architecture, and a definitive Brazilian style was beginning to emerge.

The 40,000-capacity Estádio São Januário was built between June 1926 and April 1927. The astoundingly rapid completion of the stadium must have come as a shock to the teams that had split off to form the AMEA. The São Januário was a symbolic and functional mixture of Brazilian and European influences with an eye towards the monumental.[46] Designed by the Brazilian architect Ricardo Severo, the horseshoe-shaped São Januário fea-

Photo 2.5 Estádio Vasco da Gama in its urban context. Better known as the São Januário, the stadium was constructed in eleven months, opening its doors in 1927. It was the largest stadium in Brazil until the opening of the Pacaembú in São Paulo.

Photo 2.6 Estádio Vasco da Gama. The elaborate, neo-Baroque facade of the stadium communicates messages about ethnic identity, historical traditions, and community narratives. The building is inlaid with traditional Portuguese blue and white tile work and adorned with the Maltese Cross of Admiral Vasco da Gama. The stadium's Portuguese and Brazilian flags fly at equal height.

tured an extensive, ornate facade that left little room for mistaken identity. This was a powerful expression of the wealth and organization of the Portuguese community. The facade evoked images and memories of the Portuguese colonial past and reminded those who saw it of Brazil's historical and linguistic ties to Europe. Conceived and constructed as a place by and for the Portuguese community of Brazil, the Estádio São Januário was open to all segments of Brazilian society who would honor that tradition. As concerned as it was with history, the architectural style of the stadium as a whole, with its low, sleek lines, innovative features and attention to the flow of human bodies, placed the structure firmly in the domain of the modern.

Though it was the property of C.R. Vasco da Gama, the presence of Washington Luís, president of Brazil, at the stadium's opening ceremonies was the first in a long series of events that would bring the space of the São Januário into the sphere of the nation. Much as the Estádio das Laranjeiras had been used as a vehicle for state ideology in 1919 and 1922, in 1927 the most modern, and therefore most suitably representative space of the nation, was the Estádio São Januário. The symbolic shift from the elite neighborhood of Laranjeiras to the working-class neighborhood of São Cristóvão had a practical side as well: the forty thousand people arriving at the São Januário had better access to public transportation and the neighborhood was located closer to the geographic center of the population. In addition, the São Januário featured an open design that allowed spectators a view of the urban landscape, integrating the life of the city into the events of the stadium.

In Europe and the Americas, the early modern stadium was not just a place of localized sporting activity and recreation. It was also a forum for political figures to disseminate state ideologies or curry political favor with local economic and social elites. The emerging centrality of soccer in Brazilian society and culture ensured that political figures would use the space of the stadium in service of the state. The more the state used the apparatus of the São Januário to further its agenda, the more it had to recognize the validity of the claims made on it by the blacks, mulattos, and poor whites who constituted a large part of Vasco's membership. When the government of the Old Republic (República Velha, 1889–1930) gave way to the New State (Estado Novo, 1930–1945) headed by Getúlio Vargas, the São Januário became a stage on which Brazilian history played out.

Building on his appeal as a populist (and strong-arm) leader, Vargas used the São Januário to announce governmental reforms that helped to define the conditions of labor and citizenship for the majority of Brazilians. Much in the same way that the Estádio das Laranjeiras had been used to promote an elite ideology, Vargas' discourse in the São Januário was one

Photo 2.7 President Getúlio Vargas in the São Januário, 1932. From Pereira 2000. Vargas used the stadium as a platform to launch political initiatives and disseminate state ideology. His use of the São Januário helped to legitimate the claims of Vasco's fans for full inclusion in the national project.

of labor, education reform, and social inclusion. Vargas' government hosted military, athletic, music, and labor ceremonies in Vasco de Gama's elegant stadium. Beginning in 1931, Vargas celebrated Workers Day and Independence Day in the Sao Januário. In 1943 he signed a minimum wage law in the presence of forty thousand laborers. Following trends in Nazi Germany and Fascist Italy, there was a clear attempt to link these official moments with the passions associated with soccer.[47]

One of the reasons for Vargas' successful use of the stadium was that the Brazilian team was excelling in international competitions and soccer was extraordinarily popular in Brazilian cities—especially in Rio de Janeiro where tens of thousands flocked to the stadiums every weekend. After the reunification and professionalization of Rio's soccer leagues through the formation of the Liga Carioca de Futebol Profissional in 1934, Vasco da Gama became one of the most successful teams on the continent. Competition for professional wages was fierce, and the wealthy began to retreat from serious practice as teams from Colombia, Uruguay, Argentina, and Europe began to lure Rio's best players with large salaries. The culture of soccer was firmly rooted in Rio, and participating in mass events at stadiums was commonplace for many. Following Brazil's third-place finish in the 1938 World Cup, the sport assumed a permanent, valorized place in Brazilian national consciousness. Political leaders of all stripes began to use soccer and stadiums as means to their particular ends. The population of Rio de Janeiro probably did not have to make much of a conceptual shift to move from attending soccer games to participating en masse in state-sponsored events in the stadium.

For Vargas, state-centric ideologies were embodied in the stadium and from there disseminated throughout society. For the ethnic Portuguese of Rio de Janeiro, the stadium represented an architectural and historical tradition that functioned as a site of social and cultural memory. For the fans and players of C.R. Vasco da Gama, the stadium was a place where they could freely participate in civil society and celebrate their own identities, histories, victories, and traditions. And lest we forget that the stadium is a site of ritualized conflict, Vasco's rivals had to come to terms with the social power and economic potential of the club that played with the Maltese Cross emblazoned on its jerseys. Beginning in 1927 and continuing today, the Estádio São Januário has hosted the dramaturgy that defines soccer in Rio de Janeiro.

Estádio Municipal do Rio de Janeiro and the 1950 World Cup

Brazil entered World War II on the side of the Allies and emerged ready to assume a more central position in world affairs. Brazilian industry and agriculture had prospered during the war, and the country had assumed economic and political centrality in South America. Governed by the Dutra military dictatorship, Brazil was looking for a way to define itself on the global stage in the early years of the Cold War. The hosting of the 1950 World Cup was an opportunity to diffuse a modern, progressive image to the rest of the world. The most visible elements of this image would be the stadiums that hosted the games.[48]

As early as 1945 Filho had penned an article in his newspaper, *Jornal dos Sports*, titled "O Sonho" (The Dream). He argued for the construction of a national stadium in Rio de Janeiro on the grounds that the stadium would give the Brazilian people a new soul, awakening the slumbering giant within.[49] The relationship between the construction of the stadium and the development of the nation was explicit. However, there was fierce resistance on the part of Rio's intellectuals, who wanted more hospitals and schools instead of another stadium. As the battle raged in the press, the power of Filho's discourse linking sporting to national achievement won

Photo 2.8 Maracanã, June 1950. Very much under construction as the World Cup got under way, the Maracanã nonetheless opened with a crowd of 150,000. At the bottom left of the photo is the temporary settlement where hundreds of laborers lived. Photo from FIFA.com.

out over less visible elements of social progress. In 1946, after the municipal government of Rio de Janeiro voted to fund the stadium, FIFA awarded Brazil the right to host the first post–World War II World Cup.[50]

The construction of the largest stadium in the world in the geographic heart of Rio de Janeiro was a product of local boosterism, nationalist rhetoric, democratic ideologies, and sporting discourses. One motivation was that the construction of the 70,000-seat Estádio Pacaembú in São Paulo had shifted national stadium bragging rights to Rio's biggest rivals. The Pacaembú was almost twice the size of the São Januário. This represented a symbolic shift in sporting centrality from the elegant capital to its more industrialized neighbors to the west. *Cariocas*, foremost among them Mayor Angelo Mendes de Morais, argued for a municipal stadium because Rio needed a public place for recreation and because it needed to one-up the *paulistas*.[51] For all parties involved, it was important that the Estádio Municipal, like the Pacaembú, be constructed with public, not private, money.[52]

The presence of a grandiose stadium in the capital city was also important for its external image. The conventional wisdom of stadium proponents held that the stadium not only attested to the capacity of Brazilian architects, engineers, and laborers to construct on a massive scale but also allowed Rio to be compared with the great capitals of the world. Along with national theatres, opera houses, libraries, and universities, the existence of an immense stadium was thought to constitute an integral part of the public infrastructure of capital cities. Thus a large national stadium would complete the "capital landscape" of Rio de Janeiro and symbolize to a global audience the capacity of the city and county to construct monumental buildings for the rigorous pursuit of national glory through sport.

Of course, the Brazilian Sport Federation (CBD—the successor to the FBE) was supportive of the city of Rio de Janeiro building on a massive scale for the 1950 World Cup. The rhetoric employed by the president of the CBD highlighted the capacity of sports to integrate all sectors of Brazilian society, which, he suggested, would effectively (if temporarily) eliminate social difference. Through the construction of the stadium and the experience of sport the population would share a common feeling of unity and equality. The 1950 World Cup would be "a propitious occasion to forge national sentiments and the stadium would be the ideal stage for national integration." In addition, there was no doubt after World War II of the value of physical education to provide strong bodies for the defense of the nation, and what better place to prepare those bodies than a massive sports complex?[53]

Before the first concrete piling was sunk, the Maracanã was destined to fulfill an important symbolic and functional role in the lives of Brazilians.[54] Located on the defunct grounds of the Derby Club and near the Quinta de Boa Vista, former home of the Portuguese royal family, the Municipal Stadium of Rio de Janeiro was envisioned as a secular palace, where the common man could gather with political and social elites to celebrate the achievements of their sporting idols. With the stadium's proximity to railways and centers of population, supporters could emphasize its urban functionality. The nickname, Maracanã, was the name of a small river that flowed past the stadium that was in turn a reference to a ubiquitous Amazonian bird, further solidifying the linkages between soccer and a "naturalized" Brazilian identity.

Within two hours of the formation of a government agency (Administration of Municipal Stadiums, ADEM) to oversee construction, more than two hundred laborers showed up for work. The monumental scale of the stadium combined with a media onslaught to attract thousands more, and an informal settlement developed next to the construction site. Filho published daily progress reports in the *Jornal dos Sports* chronicling this "engineering marvel" and massive public works project. Conceived and constructed as the largest, most modern building of its kind in the world, the Maracanã was a self-conscious testament to the capacity of Brazil and Rio de Janeiro to lead South America into a postwar world of ordered, progressive, and industrialized democracy. Building the stadium would be a victory in and of itself. Brazilians assumed it would also be the site of their greatest national triumph: the conquest of the Jules Rimet Trophy.[55]

Beset by difficulties and delays in construction and saddled by the inefficient governmental agency created to oversee it, the stadium complex nonetheless opened its gates to the world on June 16, 1950.[56] Filho was effusive: "Brazilian sport is not only great in terms of its tradition. Many years from now, when we write the history of this era, the miracle of the stadium will be noted as one of the most complete dreams ever brought to fruition in our country.[57] The press and government officials celebrated the inauguration of the stadium as a testament to the dedication of Brazilian labor, the ingenuity of Brazilian architecture, engineering, and construction, and the capacity of government to successfully organize monumental projects on behalf of the Brazilian people. The president, mayor, and others gave themselves medals for completing the project, though the details of the stadium (bathrooms, facades, lighting) would not be completed until the 1960s. The following day, 150,000 people came to watch friendly matches between teams from Rio and São Paulo. Now that Brazilian labor and the government had done their part (including the deaths of at least one hundred workers, some of whom are entombed in the stadium's concrete), it was time for the Brazilian national soccer team to do theirs.

In the 1940s Brazil was widely considered to have the best soccer team in the world; its confidence heading into the 1950 World Cup was not unfounded. Brazilian professional leagues blossomed during World War II, whereas European leagues were forced to suspend play. Brazil won the South American Championship in 1949 (70,000 had crammed into the São Januário for the 9–1 demolition of Ecuador) and had recently beaten both Uruguay and Argentina in friendly matches.[58] The core of the Brazilian *seleção* (national team) for the 1950 World Cup was a group of players from Vasco da Gama, whose coach, Flavio Costa, was selected to train the national team for the World Cup. They used the familiar confines of the São Januário as their base camp and training ground for the tournament. The Brazilians were so confident of their ability to win the 1950 World Cup that they offered to paint the drab concrete of the Maracanã in the national colors of the winning team.

By 1950 the World Cup had expanded to sixteen teams, but Scotland, Turkey, France, and India withdrew, the Indians because FIFA would not allow them to play in bare feet. The Brazilians were clearly the class of the twelve-team tournament; their only stumble a 2–2 first round draw with Sweden in the Pacaembú. The disappointment of this result convinced the *cariocas* that the national team should play all its games in Rio de Janeiro, as they had in the 1949 South American Championship. In the Maracanã, the Brazilians played the flowing, innovative brand of soccer that was identifiably theirs. The format of the 1950 World Cup was different from that today. The winner would be the team that had the most points after a second round of three games. In the second stage of the tournament Brazil eviscerated Czechoslovakia 7–1 and trounced Spain 6–1. The third and final round-robin match pitted Brazil against Uruguay, which had performed unevenly in the tournament. Heading into the final game, Brazil held a one-point lead over the Uruguayans and would be champions if they beat or tied their southern neighbors.

More than two hundred thousand people streamed into the Maracanã on the afternoon of July 16, 1950. This was equivalent to 10 percent of the population of Rio de Janeiro. Many tens of thousands more listened to the live radio broadcast in the streets, millions more throughout Brazil. The city and nation were hypnotized. In a pregame speech, the president of Brazil addressed the team over the stadium's public address system: "You who I already consider champions . . . you take the field as authentic representatives of Brazil who will prove the worth of the Brazilian people to the entire world." The mayor of Rio de Janeiro, Ângelo Mendes de Morais, followed up: "The municipal government has done its part by building this stadium. Now, players of Brazil, you must complete your duty!" The ethnic and racial mix of the team had come to represent the best elements of Brazilian society: creativity, playfulness, skill, and determination. The stadium was also considered to represent the present and future of Brazil, helping to realize the development of a democratic society. The elliptical form of the stadium was thought to unite rich and poor, black, mulatto, and white in a common experience, a shared emotion that would be self-reflective and self-sustaining. As a public monument that sought to embody the national spirit, the Maracanã was the embodiment of a dream and represented the possibility of a better future for all Brazilians.[59]

Among the 200,000-plus Brazilians in the stadium were approximately 300 Uruguayan fans, in addition to the seemingly forgotten Uruguayan team. While hailing the Brazilian players as champions before the English referee had blown the first whistle, the Brazilian press, politicians, and people apparently forgot that there were still ninety minutes of soccer to play before they could celebrate their coronation as World Champions.

After a scoreless forty-five minutes Brazil seemed destined for glory when their forward Friaça scored less than two minutes into the second half. The stadium exploded with smoke and music, the fans urging Brazil on to more goals. The noise built incessantly until Uruguay's Schiaffino blasted Ghiggia's cross past Barbosa in the Brazilian goal in the sixtieth minute. A grim panic gripped the Maracanã. For the first time the possibility of losing entered the collective consciousness of the players, the fans, and the nation. As it stood, Brazil would be champions, but could they hold on?

With just over ten minutes to play and the score tied 1–1, the president of FIFA, Jules Rimet, left his seat to prepare for Brazil's victory celebrations. When he emerged onto the sidelines five minutes later, he was met by the absolute silence of the stadium. Gigghia, the Uruguayan right midfielder, had scored on a counterattack in the seventy-ninth minute, beating Barbosa at his near post—an unforgivable error. At the final whistle the only sounds in the stadium were the cheers of the Uruguayan players and their small contingent of fans. The silence was morbid. Rimet unceremoniously handed the trophy to the Uruguayan captain, Varela. There are no photos of the winners with their trophy. The Brazilian dream had been shattered. The Maracanã was born to die a symbolic death.

The loss against the Uruguayans is an event that continues to loom large in Brazilian national consciousness. The game is known as the Maracanaço (the Failure in the Maracanã) and July 16, 1950, is Brazil's infamous day. For many, the loss confirmed Brazil's inferiority complex: the nation was capable of organizing and producing the most modern facilities and grandest spectacles, but its accomplishments were limited due to the intractable complications of their ethnic mixture. While it is difficult to discern the myth from reality at this point, there was a common sentiment that the three blacks on the Brazilian side were singled out as scapegoats for the loss. Barbosa, the unfortunate goalkeeper, was ostracized from Brazilian society and died in shame in the early 1990s.

Alex Bellos says of the 1950 World Cup Final, "To upset the largest amount of Brazilians as possible without loss of life, there is probably no more efficient way than creating the largest stadium in the world, filling it to overflowing, and then losing, in the final minutes, to neighbors you had recently beaten, at a sport that is believed to best represent the nation."[60] Surprisingly, there were no pitch invasions, no violent reactions. The collective sadness that descended on Rio de Janeiro reminded many of Ash Wednesday following Carnival. Attending the games of the 1950 World Cup had become more than a way for Brazilians to entertain themselves. It had become "a patriotic duty. It was an obligation for everyone to partici-

Game	Date	Score	Attendance
Brazil × Mexico	6/24/50	4–0	81,000+
England × Chile	6/25/50	2–0	30,000
Spain × Chile	6/29/50	2–0	20,000
Brazil × Yugoslavia	7/1/50	2–0	142,000+
Spain × England	7/2/50	1–0	74,000+
Brazil × Sweden	7/3/50	7–1	138,000
Brazil × Spain	7/13/50	6–1	152,000
Brazil × Uruguay	7/16/50	1–2	200,000+
Total attendance			837,000

Table 2.2 Attendance figures for games played in the Maracanã during the 1950 FIFA World Cup.

pate in the battle, because it was in the name of every fan that the team was fighting for victory."[61] Uruguay won; Brazil was a defeated nation.

Conclusion

Soccer in Brazil originated as an elite practice that occurred in geographically and socially limited spaces. The social clubs and soccer stadiums of the Brazilian and expatriate British elites were sites and symbols of modernity that communicated notions of privilege, cultural refinement, and exclusivity. As soccer diffused across the socioeconomic spectrum, the spaces of the elite came under increasing pressure from below. The appropriation and adaptation of soccer by the middle and lower classes and the competitive nature of institutional sport ensured that blacks, mulattos, and poor whites would eventually take their places on the field and in the stands. The processes of social contestation and integration that happened in the stadiums of Rio de Janeiro in the first half of the twentieth century ruptured sociospatial barriers that, once broken, could never be re-formed.

In the Estádio das Laranjeiras of the Fluminese Football Club we saw how the diffusion of soccer into and its adaptation by the lower classes made the "natural" skills of mulatto players competitively desirable, though socially unacceptable. For many years the Laranjeiras stadium functioned as a site and symbol of elite privilege that was reinforced through the presentation of Rio's sporting clubs for the Belgian king and the hosting of the 1919 and 1922 South American soccer championships.

However, the social pressures exerted on this elite space required the opening of stadium space to a broader social spectrum.

The development of sporting clubs such as São Cristóvão Athletic Club and C.R. Vasco da Gama began to incorporate marginalized socioeconomic groups into stadium spaces. São Cristóvão A.C. and the Figueira de Melo Stadium were popular social and spatial expressions of the increased popularity of institutional sport. Based in a rapidly expanding industrial zone, these clubs drew their members from their immediate environs and helped to form residential and class-based solidarities in the space of the club and the stadium. Although these clubs were able to endure as social and sporting entities, there is a long list of clubs that formed and folded before the advent of professionalism. Some of these were based in national heritage, such as Club Atletico Syrio e Libanez, while others, like Bangu A.C., were organized around the workplace and had a greater chance of success. The conflation of race and class in Brazilian society was reflected in the composition of sporting and social clubs, positioning soccer stadiums in the center of a polemic debate about the meaning and future of Brazilian society.

The emergence of the Estádio São Januário had a profound impact on the sociospatial dynamics of sporting and social practice in the city. Associated with laboring classes, marginalized ethnic groups, and colonial history, C.R. Vasco da Gama challenged and contested the status quo, which provoked an institutional separation of elite and popular stadiums. However, the populist discourse of President Getúlio Vargas brought the São Januário into the sphere of the nation, which had the effect of legitimizing the claims of the working classes and ethnic Portuguese. This process, along with the increased presence of blacks, mulattos, and poor whites on the fields and in the terraces, helped to transform the stadiums of the city into more fully public spaces that served as sites and symbols of geographic, class, ethnic, and national identities. In addition, the Luso-Brazilian community had repositioned itself in national political and cultural life by constructing the most modern stadium in South America, a distinction confirmed by the installation of the continent's first stadium lights in 1928.

The construction of the Maracanã for the 1950 World Cup consolidated the stadium as a powerful locus of Brazilian national achievement, social integration, and discourses of industrial democracy. More than 830,000 people attended soccer games in Rio de Janeiro in less than a month. The popular conflation of the Maracanã with the space of the city and nation augmented the significance of the 1950 World Cup—losing to the Uruguayans in that space signified a defeat of the nation that continues to figure heavily in Brazilian national consciousness.

The number of stadiums in Rio de Janeiro in the first half of the twentieth century was undoubtedly eclipsed by informal spaces, spread unevenly throughout the metropolitan region. Thus not only did soccer transform the social landscape; it transformed the physical landscape. The location and impact of these informal spaces will never be known, but we can judge their relative extent by the increased presence and cultural centrality of stadiums in the city.

As constituent elements in a network of public space, soccer stadiums in Rio de Janeiro were linked with other spaces such as schools, hospitals, streets, transportation systems, parks, plazas, theatres, beaches, and other spaces of leisure. In the majority of these other spaces, however, there was little or no opportunity to challenge the socioeconomic, political, or geographic status quo. Domestic servants, day laborers, street vendors, and other urban poor used the public spaces of the city as part of their daily routines but not for the expression of their identities as such. The stadiums of the city were unique venues for the expression of horizontal class, racial, and ethnic solidarities that extended vertically to connect with the idea of the nation. True, the idea of the nation was initially formed in relation to elite conceptions. However, it was in the stadiums of the capital city that these conceptions and relationships were visibly and ritually challenged, making claims for a wider spectrum of Brazilian society to be included in the national project. These complicated and contentious processes happened unevenly and simultaneously in a variety of geographic locales. The stadiums of the city formed an important, dynamic network of spaces that allowed for the emergence of a potentially new social order while at the same time permitting social, economic, and political control. This paradox lies at the heart of the Brazilian stadium and is what makes it such an elusive and tantalizing object for geographic investigation.

CHAPTER THREE

Stadiums and Society in Twenty-first Century Rio de Janeiro

On the way to the beaches of Rio de Janeiro from the Tom Jobim International Airport one gets a sense of the city that exists beyond the realm of the popular imagination. The elevated Red Line (Linha Vermelha) whisks eight lanes of traffic past the industrial neighborhoods of Penha, Ramos, and Vila do João: favelas extend to the western horizon, kites bob in the sky, political propaganda is smeared on unsteady brick. The Carlos Castilho Olympic Village appears on the right; locals plod around the dusty track, boys kick about on the hard-packed dirt. On the left snippets of Guanabara Bay float in and out of view, obscured by warehouses, oil storage tanks, and the enormous Saint Francisco Xavier cemetery.

Looking to the right, the roof of the Estádio São Januário is suddenly at eye level, the closed end of the horseshoe hiding the emerald grass, the working-class neighborhood of São Cristóvão close by the stadium walls. To the left, Rio's port is framed by the graceful bridge that spans the bay and the dilapidated warehouses along the waterfront. The old public space of the Campo do São Cristóvão comes into view as the saddle-shaped Centro Luiz Gonzaga de Tradições Nordestinas, a permanent exhibition of cultural traditions from northeastern Brazil. Continuing south, the mountains begin to define this sprawling metropolis of 12 million. Christ the Redeemer can be descried on his hazy perch, and the Brazilian fascination with Formula One racing becomes evident—it's a participatory sport! As the underphotographed downtown comes into view, the dilapidating concrete walls of the Estádio Figueira de Melo flash below, uncomfortably close to the four-lane, two-tiered auto-duct. The sky blue Maracanã hovers like a spacecraft, improbably low on the western horizon—the immense, elliptical bowl seems to create its own gravitational field. Passing over the modernist width of Avenue President Vargas, the car speeds on, skirts through the Redeemer's mountain, and after zipping by the rowing installations on Lagoa Rodrigo de Freitas, emerges into the dog-eared postcard of Ipanema (Map 3.1).

Rio de Janeiro is a mosaic of contradictions. Stunning and repulsive, accessible and forbidding, rich and poor, mountains and sea, refined and vulgar, obvious and hidden, exotic and common, tranquil and violent, lively and deadly—the list goes on. It is a place where the flowering of imagination collides with a frequently harsh reality. Rio confuses and frustrates those who are most familiar with it. Given the difficulties of making sense of the self-proclaimed "Marvelous City," it is logical to pick a singular point of reference and work outwards. Because of the centrality of sport in Brazilian culture and because there are so many of them, stadiums may be the easiest place to begin.

The North American sociologist Janet Lever was one of the first foreign academics to recognize the potential of using soccer to decipher Rio de Janeiro's complex social worlds. Long before Brazil had won its fourth (1994) and fifth (2002) World Cups she found that investigating soccer teams in Rio de Janeiro was a mechanism for "understanding the role they play in symbolizing the real divisions within the city. Rio's soccer clubs help

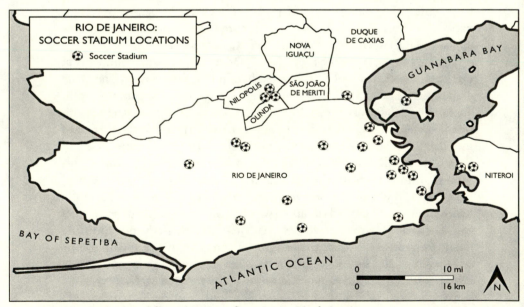

Map 3.1 Soccer stadiums in twenty-first-century Rio de Janeiro

House, Street, and Other World

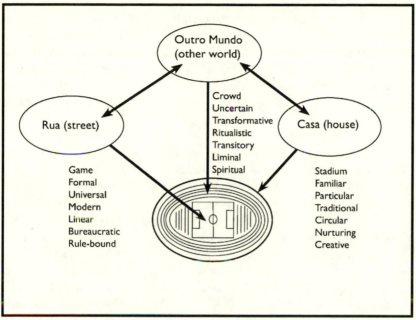

Figure 3.1 House, street, and other world. Author's diagram relating Roberto DaMatta's view of Brazilian space to the stadium. The arrows indicate to which part of the stadium each element pertains. *Rua* is the rule-bound field of play. *Outro mundo* is the transformative stands. *Casa* is the stadium itself.

break down the urban mass and integrate people into subgroups."[1] Lever's sociological perspective provides a useful paradigm for understanding the complexities of Brazilian society through soccer, although we must also appreciate the space of the stadium as a mechanism for informing cultural process and meaning. Brazilian social scientists have long understood soccer as an instrument for critical self-reflection and understanding.[2] One of the most insightful is the anthropologist Roberto DaMatta, whose contributions to an understanding of the organization of space and society in Brazil are an excellent place to start making geographic sense of Rio de Janeiro's stadiums.[3]

In his book *House and Street: Space, Urban Life, Woman and Death in Brazil*, DaMatta partitions Brazilian society into three distinct spatial realms: house (*casa*), street (*rua*) and other world (*outro mundo*).[4] His tripartite division identifies "house space" as having the qualities associated with family, friendship, isolation, tradition, reproduction, and privacy. He characterizes "street space" as bureaucratic, formal, universal, modern, and linear. The "other world" is uncertain, neither here nor there: it is shifting, liminal, and transformative, ever-moving. DaMatta correlates these three spaces to the Holy Trinity of the Catholic tradition. If *casa* is the Christ figure with its intimacy and individualism, *rua* is God, represented by universal laws and a sense of inevitability, and *outro mundo* is the Holy Ghost, which facilitates communication and movement between these two worlds.

If, as DaMatta suggests, "the secret of a correct interpretation of Brazil is to study that which is between things,"[5] then the Brazilian stadium is an ideal place to start. Stadiums are the *casas* of the teams that play in them where we find a sense of family and belonging, personal stories and experiences, strong loyalties, revenge killings, and tradition. But the stadium is also a *rua*—a public, universalizing, law-ridden place where we enter into a world of political power, economic necessities, social hierarchies, externalized and objectified ethnicities, local, national, and international dramas. In the stadium as *outro mundo* we find superstition, belief in magic, rites of passage, transgression, personal and collective transformation. The stadium is a truly *catholic* place (and space) in that it is inclusive and universalizing, where the conditions and practices associated with the everyday melt away, at least temporarily. The Brazilian stadium, then, is *rua*, *casa*, and *outro mundo* and presents deep insight into the geography, history, and culture of Brazil.

The Stadiums of Rio de Janeiro

The first stadium in Rio de Janeiro was the Derby Club, a suburban horse racing track, built in 1868. It was demolished eighty years later to make way for the Maracanã; its replacement, the 80,000-capacity Joquei (Jockey) Club, sits on some of the most expensive land in the Americas. In the southern suburb of Barra de Tijuca, the Nelson Piquet Auto-park can accommodate 60,000 people and is the largest stadium in the city by area. The 100,000-capacity Sambodromo is where Carnival judging of samba school competitions takes place. There are also stadiums for tennis, baseball, softball, and other sports associated with the 2007 Pan American Games, including the 45,000-capacity João Havelange Olympic Stadium, named after the longtime Brazilian president of FIFA. From time to time temporary stadiums with capacities of 10,000 arise on Copacabana Beach to host the professional beach volleyball circuit, international beach soccer tournaments, or mega-concerts like the Rolling Stones. While it is

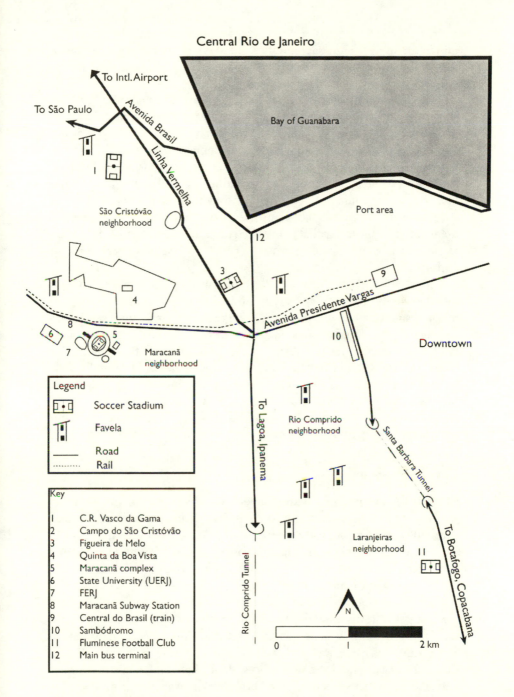

Central Rio de Janeiro

To Intl. Airport

To São Paulo

Avenida Brasil

Linha Vermelha

Bay of Guanabara

Port area

São Cristóvão
neighborhood

12

3

9

4

Avenida Presidente Vargas

8

6

5

10

Downtown

7

Maracanã
neighborhood

Legend

Soccer Stadium

Favela

Road

Rail

Key

1 C.R. Vasco da Gama
2 Campo do São Cristóvão
3 Figueira de Melo
4 Quinta da Boa Vista
5 Maracanã complex
6 State University (UERJ)
7 FERJ
8 Maracanã Subway Station
9 Central do Brasil (train)
10 Sambódromo
11 Fluminese Football Club
12 Main bus terminal

To Lagoa, Ipanema

Rio Comprido
neighborhood

Santa Barbara Tunnel

To Botafogo, Copacabana

Rio Comprido Tunnel

Laranjeiras
neighborhood

11

N

0 1 2 km

Map 3.2 Map of central Rio de Janeiro

difficult to arrive at an exact number, there are at least thirty stadiums in Rio de Janeiro, the vast majority of which are unfamiliar to *cariocas* (Appendix A).[6]

Soccer stadiums and informal soccer spaces dominate the sporting landscape of Rio de Janeiro. Soccer is everywhere: parks, favelas, clubs, streets, beaches. Every bar and restaurant shows soccer on television, almost every day. Soccer is an unavoidable element of Brazilian life: soccer jerseys, soccer hats, soccer tour buses, soccer street performers, Maracanã key chains, Flamengo postcards, conversation, football, "fu-chi-bol," *futebol*. Soccer is a fundamental element of Brazilian culture; its players and styles are some of Brazil's best-known exports; the canary yellow jersey of the national team is a global icon. The stadium is the apex of the soccer world and is where Brazilians ritually gather to celebrate, bemoan, and perform.

This chapter traces the four stadiums discussed in the previous chapter into the twenty-first century. By examining the spaces, urban contexts, and meanings associated with the Estádio Figuiera de Melo, the Estádio das Laranjeiras, the Estádio São Januário, and the Estádio Jornalista Mario Filho in a contemporary context, it provides insight into the dynamics of Brazilian society. Located within a four-kilometer radius in central Rio de Janeiro these stadiums represent divergent and intersecting geographic worlds, social trajectories, and cultural trends. Taken together, they provide a historically (and spatially) continuous vision of *carioca* society and also reveal stark contrasts of fortune.

Estádio Figueira de Melo

Constructed in 1916, the Estádio Figueira de Melo is the oldest surviving stadium in Rio de Janeiro and looks it. The field is concrete-hard and nearly devoid of grass. The downtrodden pitch is surrounded by white-washed concrete walls with a shallow row of bleachers running along one side. There is no facade, only a chain-link fence separates the entrance from the stadium's eponymous street. The club that owns the stadium, São Cristóvão de Futebol e Regatas, sold most of the bleachers in 2002 to create space to generate revenue from monthly parking fees. Soon after, they sold the lights—the empty stanchions frame Cristo Redentor in the distance. The stadium shares a wall with an abandoned textile factory that reads: Campeão 1926. Behind the club offices, dance hall, and concrete training field, the elevated, two-tiered Linha Vermelha highway rises ominously; the smell of exhaust and dust permeates the air.

On a hot September afternoon, thirty teenage boys have gathered in the

São Cristóvão Futebol e Regatas Environs, Rio de Janeiro

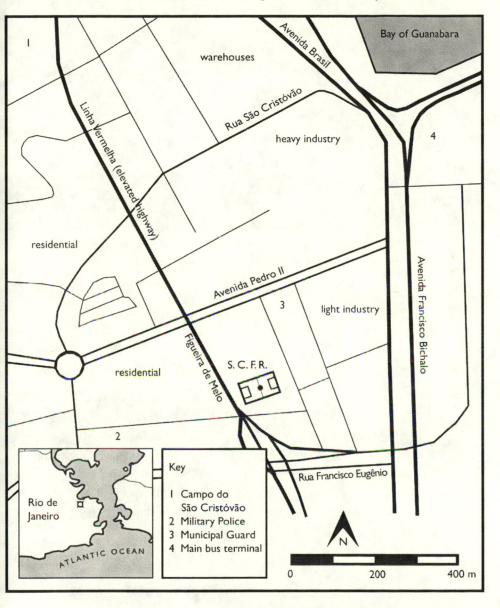

Map 3.3 Estádio Figueira de Melo and environs, Rio de Janeiro

Photo 3.1 Figueira de Melo looking east. The wall behind the goal is shared with an abandoned textile factory. A favela rises up the hill in the distance.

Photo 3.2 Figueira de Melo looking south. Corcovado mountain is to the right of the empty light stanchion. The space on the far side of the stadium is leased for monthly parking.

Photo 3.3 Figueira de Melo, north stand. This stand has been in the same location since the stadium was constructed in 1916. The training facilities and locker rooms of S.C.F.R. are just behind it.

shade of the team dugout to listen to the rambling discourse of the coach.[7] A glass-encased figurine of St. Christopher, buried in a wall, mirrors the players' disinterested stares. Many have traveled here from the northern suburbs of Duque de Caxias and Nova Iguaçu, a three-hour round trip, looking for a chance to break into the team: they are here to work, not play. They come here three or four times a week, hoping to follow in the footsteps of Ronaldo Luis Nazario de Lima, aka Ronaldo Phenomeno, the leading goal scorer in World Cup history, by playing for and leaving São Cristóvão F.R. in search of greater footballing and financial glory.[8] A handful of middle-aged men gather in the bleachers to watch the future unfold.

Clube São Cristóvão de Futebol e Regatas is one of the few small, working-class social and sporting clubs formed in the early twentieth century that has survived into the twenty-first. The space of the stadium is of importance to our story in that it was an archetype for the generalized processes of social contestation and integration described in the previous chapter. It is also a good example of what has happened to smaller clubs and their stadiums throughout Latin America in the face of accelerated economic globalization. The club and the stadium were central elements of soccer culture in Rio de Janeiro from the 1920s until the 1980s but in recent years have become marginalized, increasingly peripheral spaces. By examining the relative social and geographic positioning of the stadium over time, we can discern larger processes that are articulated in a multitude of similar stadiums throughout the city.

Just as time in Brazil can be measured in the four-year intervals that coincide with the World Cup (at least since 1950), so can Brazilian space be measured through soccer. The relative isolation of the major population centers of Brazil, which continued into the last half of the twentieth century, led each state to develop soccer tournaments that teams from the largest cities dominated. The teams of each city (and state) rarely competed against nonlocal opposition; when they did, it was likely to be against teams from the nearest big city. Thus teams from São Paulo and Rio, Fortaleza and Recife, Goiás and Belo Horizonte developed significant rivalries, but they were nothing compared to the intensity of the state tournaments, which were essentially city tournaments that included a few teams from smaller towns. It was because of the geographic conditions of Brazil and the structure of the state tournaments that smaller, neighborhood-based clubs like São Cristóvão F.R. were able to survive if not thrive in the local context.

With the advent of the Brazilian national championship in 1970 (Campeonato Brasileiro or Brasileirão), itself a result of improved transportation and communication technologies as well as the political ideologies of a military dictatorship, the spatial structure of Brazilian soccer began to shift. Incorporated into a national framework, smaller teams found it difficult to finance trips to games that could be as far as 3,000 kilometers away, and the confusing, ever-changing rules of the competition discouraged impartiality and transparency, which in turn benefited bigger clubs with more political clout. Even as the Campeonato Brasileiro became more profitable for the Brazilian Soccer Federation (CBF), the state tournaments continued to hold more significance for fans: a historical and local rivalry between (for example) the Rio giants of Vasco da Gama and Flamengo or smaller clubs like São Cristóvão and América was much more compelling than a midseason Brazilian league game between Coritiba and Flamengo, or Goiás and Vasco. The persistence of state championships is essentially a remnant of a different geographic context, one that emphasized the regional over the national. The notoriously confusing Brazilian schedule, which has the state championships between February and April and the national league between April and December, is a symptom of the dilemma of Brazilian history and geography.

When Brasilia became the capital city in 1960 as part of the "national project," Rio de Janeiro suddenly lost political, economic, and cultural influence. These losses, combined with an acceleration of rural to urban migration, overurbanization, and political instability, created a crisis of urban governance that is far from being resolved. By the late 1960s one-third of *cariocas* lived in 250 favelas; by 2006 there were at least 700 favelas with several million inhabitants. The well-publicized escalation of violence between drug lords and police has produced one of the most violent cities in the world: between July 2004 and June 2005 there were more than 3,200 murders.[9] These larger socioeconomic problems have had a negative impact on smaller clubs, which have seen membership numbers decline as people curtail leisure and recreation activities. The clubs have responded by eliminating services, reducing investment in stadium infrastructure, and cutting payroll. Because clubs have long been an important cohesive element at the neighborhood level, providing community space and a vehicle for communal identification, the decline in membership and services has contributed to an overall decline in lived or shared neighborhood space. In the case of São Cristóvão F.R., the vicious cycle of impoverishment and social atomization has been exacerbated by structural changes in the production and consumption of soccer on the national and global scales.

As the explosion of cable television and global media accelerated the global reach of soccer in the 1990s (with the 1994 World Cup in the United States as an important moment), television revenues increased and wealth further concentrated in the hands of bigger clubs in wealthy European leagues. Teams like Manchester United, Arsenal, Barcelona, Real Madrid, A.C. Milan, Bayern Munich, Benfica, and Paris St. Germain scoured Latin America, Africa, and Eastern Europe for soccer talent. This was nothing new as professional soccer players had been making their way to Europe from developing nations as regularly as shipments of timber, coffee, cacao, and precious metals. However, the amount of money changing hands increased along with the pace at which "raw talent" was brought to Europe to be "refined."

At the same time, the Brazilian championships were gaining in importance at the expense of the state championships, but only for the larger clubs that could afford to compete. The state championships have continued because they are an entrenched part of the political structure of Brazilian soccer, are an important part of local soccer traditions, and provide an institutional structure that allows for the development of athletic talent that is sold for ever higher values as it progresses through stages of refinement on its way to European markets.

The impact of these globalizing processes on smaller clubs like São Cristóvão has been particularly severe. With more televised games (state, national, and international), uninteresting, low-quality matches (because the best players were in Europe) and unkempt, dangerous stadiums, attendance decreased and clubs suffered a loss of membership and ticket revenues. In addition, Brazilian soccer is beset by corruption at all levels, further concentrating money in fewer hands. Added to this, the increased socioeconomic and spatial polarization of Brazilian society positioned stadiums and teams as vehicles for public expressions of discontent. Stadiums and associated urban spaces became battle grounds between the Brazilian "hooligans," the *torcidas organizadas*, and the police.[10] In order to contain and control these battles, stadium architecture militarized, which made them even less comfortable, and more people than ever stayed at home. In the absence of strong membership, in the face of increasing operational costs, and occupying one of the lowest rungs on the unevenly spaced ladder of global soccer, São Cristóvão F.R. has become dependent on its ability to recruit, identify, develop, and sell human talent. This is a dramatic change from the days when the club could rely on its neighborhood-based membership and gate receipts for financial stability.

As the midday sun beats on Figueira de Melo, the coach ends his talk and the boys take the field. The pace and skill are nearly unbelievable given the field conditions. The ball hits the ground and bounces twenty feet in the air, cleats skid across the hard-packed dirt. The sprinkling of men in the stands cross their arms impatiently or shield their eyes from the sun. Bone-crunching tackles fly in, the coach blows his whistle, the boys help each other off the ground as dust rises with the heat. They are walking a fine line between playing within the team and showing individual ability, determination, and force of personality. It is unlikely that any of them will earn a living wage playing soccer. Even if they do, the average wage for a Brazilian professional playing in Brazil is US$400 a month. In Rio, it is common for even the bigger clubs to be several months late with salaries, offering prompt payment as incentive for greater effort.

São Cristóvão F.R. competed in the first division of the Rio de Janeiro state tournament (Campeonato Carioca) in 1991, 1993, and 1995; after falling to the third division for several years, they now compete in the second division.[11] It is a long way from there to the Brazilian national leagues.[12] Between 2000 and 2005 club membership declined from 1,500 to 600, with most of the club revenues coming from dues paid by members of the club's nautical center located on Governor's Island. Attendance at the traditional Saturday night *forró* dances hosted in the club's ballroom has declined due to competition from the massive weekly festivals held at the nearby Exposition Center for Northeastern Culture. There is not a sense of optimism at the club. They cannot afford to pay their players much more than a *bicho*, and developing and selling players to larger clubs is made more difficult by the sheer numbers of others doing the same thing. The team continually extends invitations to Ronaldo Phenomeno to visit when he is in Rio de Janeiro, but he has yet to return to the stadium and club where he began his professional career.[13]

In 1916 the Estádio Figueira de Melo emerged in the midst of a growing industrial suburb of Rio. By the mid-1920s the stadium was a central component of Rio's soccer world and the team was consistently in the top flight of the Rio state championship through the 1980s.[14] Over the past fifteen years, the club has experienced a contraction of its geographic network as a direct result of changing urban, economic, and sporting dynamics. Although it is centrally located, close to major transportations lines and the port, the neighborhood of São Cristóvão has not fared well, losing industry and jobs while gaining favelas. It has come full circle, moving from a residential suburb that was the center of the Portuguese empire to a productive industrial center to a zone of socioeconomic marginality.

Similarly, a stadium that once occupied a central position in a network of soccer spaces in the city has become marginalized as the scale of soccer in Brazil has shifted away from the local to the national and international. Yet there is always the hope that one of the players will reestablish these geographic connections by changing the pink, white, and black of S.C.F.R. for the red and black of Flamengo, the blue and maroon of F.C. Barcelona, or the canary yellow of Brazil.

Estádio das Laranjeiras (Manoel Schwartz)

The Estádio das Laranjeiras sits on the elegant, neoclassical grounds of the Fluminese Football Club. From the top of the double-tiered bleachers there is an excellent view of the next-door Palacio de Guanabara, the official visitors' residence for guests of the state of Rio de Janeiro. Large apartment buildings tower over the east end of the field, palm trees shade the sidewalks. Hovering over the west end of the stadium is Cristo Redentor, who appears to be celebrating a goal. Located near the city center and the beaches of Flamengo and Botafogo, the stadium is ensconced in the well-to-do Laranjeiras neighborhood. The main entrance is off a quiet, tree-lined street—a bucolic scene in the midst of a mega-city.

Behind gold-trimmed, wrought-iron gates, the manicured grounds contain four clay tennis courts, an Olympic swimming pool, a diving pool, and a large, ornately decorated clubhousee with a restaurant, bar, club offices, and two ballrooms that can seat 800 comfortably. The clubhouse, built in the 1920s by French architects, incorporates high ceilings, chande-

Fluminese Football Club and Environs, Rio de Janeiro

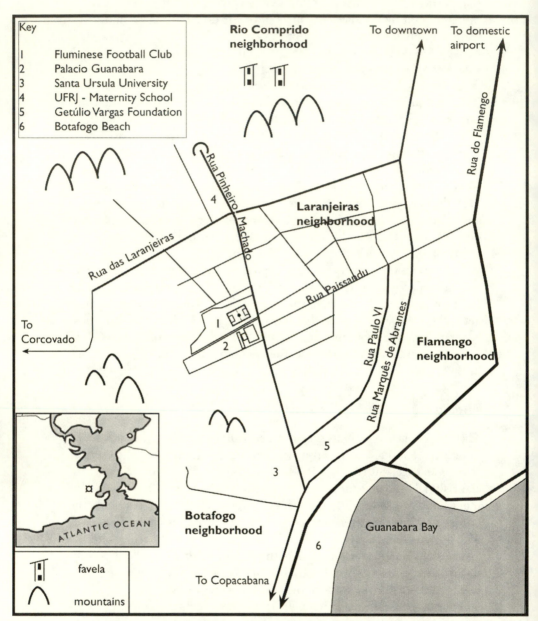

Map 3.4 Fluminese Football Club and environs, Rio de Janeiro

Photo 3.4 Estádio Manoel Schwartz. The steeply inclined and shallow bleachers of the stadium are the same as when they were constructed in 1917. After the removal of one section of stands and the enforcement of more rigorous public safety measures, the capacity of the stadium is 8,000.

Estádio das Laranjeiras

Photo 3.5 Fluminese mascot and club (from team Web site). The club's mascot is indicative of the persistent association with the Fluminese Football Club and elite social status, even though the majority of fans come from the middle and lower classes. Courtesy of Fluminese Football Club.

liers, cascading stairways, and extensive ornamentation—reflecting the history, wealth, and tradition of Rio's oldest soccer club.

Moving through the foyer, past the restaurant, and around the trophy room, one comes to a salon that overlooks the stadium through twenty-foot double French doors. The bar that offered halftime drinks to British dandies stands at the ready to serve the Brazilians that have taken their place. Stepping through the doors, one finds the VIP section and its rows of comfortable seats for taking in the stadium scene.

Renamed after a former president of Fluminese in 2004, the Estádio Manoel Schwartz will never again see Brazil lift a South American Championship. Nor will it host games in the state or national championships. After expanding to a maximum capacity of 25,000 for the 1922 South American Championship, the stadium gradually contracted to 8,000, losing stands to the city of Rio de Janeiro in 1961 as the Rua Pinheiro Machado widened. Stricter occupancy regulations also affected the stadium, which as late as the early 1990s occasionally opened its gates for competitive senior team matches. Since the 1950s the Fluminese Football Club has played the majority of its home games at the Maracanã, which is also considered the home ground of its main rival, Flamengo.

Whether by design or association, the name Manoel Schwartz has yet to enter the vernacular. Most *cariocas* refer to this legislatively decreed element of Brazil's cultural patrimony as Estádio das Laranjeiras. The stadium functions as the principal training ground for the Fluminese Football Club, and sitting in the bleachers to watch practice stirs the historical imagination. The space bounded by the main grandstand, double-tiered bleachers, and field is essentially the same as it was in the 1920s. One gets a good sense of the intensity that 35,000 people crammed into this space would generate. The stands rise precipitously from the field and the words "Sou Tricolor de Coração" run along the top of the white concrete. Heavy fencing indicates that the competitive youth and women's team games that are played here are taken very seriously.

The Fluminese Football Club was formed as a province of the British expatriate and Brazilian elite. The club's (2006) mascot is evidence of this continuing association. One of the curious elements of fandom in Rio de Janeiro is that the assumed socioeconomic profile of a club frequently has little to do with that of its fans. Thus while the club self-consciously identifies with elevated socioeconomic sectors, the majority of Fluminese fans come from the middle and lower classes, if only because they are the dominant sectors of the population. As Fluminese has more than 2.2 million fans in Brazil, it is unlikely that the vast majority have any associations with the geographic space of the club itself.[15] Even for fans who live in Rio de

Janeiro, club membership is only within reach of those who can afford the thousand-dollar inscription fee or practical for those who live close enough to use the club's facilities regularly.

Because of the ways in which fandom acts as a means of personal identification for Brazilians there are several distinct groups associated with the Fluminese Football Club and the space of the stadium. One set of identities cuts across class and ethnic lines and is completely dependent on soccer as a vehicle for identification. Another, more limited set of identities is strongly associated with the geographic space of the social club and stadium. The former can be understood as a product of the larger social changes that transpired in the Estádio das Laranjeiras in the first decades of the twentieth century when soccer expanded its reach well beyond the limited geographic space in which it occurred. The latter identities reflect the continuing geographic, cultural, and socioeconomic associations of the Fluminese Football Club with dominant segments of Brazilian society.

This segment of the population plays or participates in sports such as water polo, diving, swimming, synchronized swimming, shooting, volleyball, basketball, table tennis, tennis, fencing, athletics, and martial arts. In addition to providing facilities and training for the above, F.F.C. offers its members a host of other services, including medical evaluations, discounted shopping at sponsoring stores, continuing education courses, and, of course, tickets to Fluminese games. Fluminese is one of Brazil's leaders in on-line registries, and its Web site is detailed and sophisticated. After falling on some difficult times in the 1990s when the team was languishing in the Brazilian third division, the Fluminese Football Club has ridden the rising tide of the Brazilian economy and its soccer fortunes have also improved.

In addition to being steeped in aristocratic iconography and elite social practices, Fluminese fans have one of the more curious traditions in Brazilian stadium culture. When the team takes the field, Fluminese fans toss massive quantities of rice or talcum powder into the stadium air. While there are several versions of the origins of this tradition, known as *po-de-arroz*, the most prevalent (and the one put forth by the club) is that in 1914 a mulatto player by the name of Carlos Alberto tried to disguise his skin color by applying rice powder (*po-de-arroz*) to his face. As he ran and sweated, the powder streaked his face. The opposing fans noticed and began a derisive chant of "po-de-arroz." The Fluminese faithful adopted the nickname and nearly a century later continue to cover themselves in the stuff.

Another version of the story proposes that Carlos Alberto was being mocked by fans of the América team who cried out that a mulatto would only become aristocratic (like the other Fluminese players) by putting rice powder on his face. At halftime, the entire team went into the stands, borrowed face powder from their female friends, and emerged for the second half with whitened faces, saying, "Hip, hip, hooray! Now we're aristocrats!"[16] In either case, the association of whiteness with social and political power continues to have profound associations in all realms of Brazilian society. These connections are ritually performed and confirmed every time the Fluminese Football Club takes the field.

While the most important events in the Estádio das Laranjeiras occurred in the first half of the twentieth century, the stadium and social club continue to function as sites of social memory as well as serve a limited public in the immediate geographic context but an ever-expanding public in the realm of associative geography. The Fluminese Football Club is a highly recognizable institution throughout Rio de Janeiro and Brazil. When club elections take place, candidates for president take out advertising space on city buses, on billboards, and in newspapers. The club and stadium are strongly associated with the neighborhood of Laranjeiras, a zone of prosperity close to the city center.

"Being Fluminese" no longer explicitly suggests belonging to a certain class or having a particular set of tastes and values. Yet the persistence of *po-de-arroz* and the use of elite iconography among Fluminese fans of all classes and ethnicities implies that the elite historical associations of the club are understood and accepted among all fan groups. This reinforces the idea that the social geography of fandom in Brazil does not follow predictable patterns. The relative wealth of F.F.C. does not mean that it has escaped the structural conditions imposed by the shifting political economies of sport and society. It may be that the club is simply farther up the food chain than clubs like São Cristóvão F.R. Yet the space of the club has maintained its function as a repository of elite practices and ideologies. And while the world around the stadium has changed significantly, its meanings have remained remarkably constant. It is through examining the trajectories of spaces and ideologies through time that the contemporary meanings and textures of culture in Rio de Janeiro can be brought to light.

Estádio Vasco da Gama (São Januário)

> *Casaca, Casaca*
> *Casaca-zaca-zaca*
> *A turma é boa*
> *É mesmo da fuzarca*
> *Vasco, Vasco, VASCO!*
>
> Untranslatable C.R. Vasco da Gama fight song

Clube Regatas Vasco da Gama and Environs, Rio de Janeiro

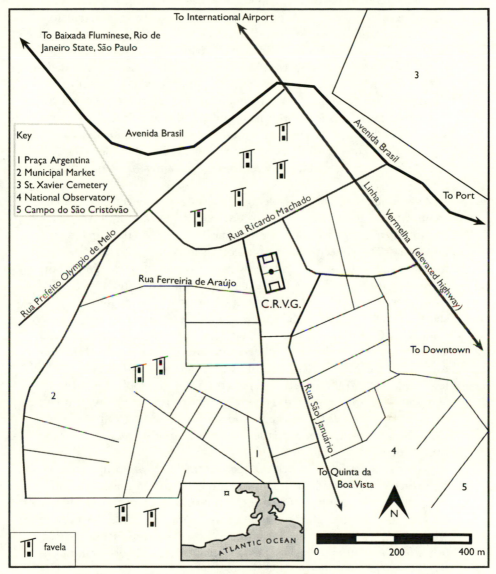

Key

1 Praça Argentina
2 Municipal Market
3 St. Xavier Cemetery
4 National Observatory
5 Campo do São Cristóvão

To International Airport

To Baixada Fluminese, Rio de Janeiro State, São Paulo

Avenida Brasil

Avenida Brasil

To Port

Rua Ricardo Machado

Linha Vermelha (elevated highway)

Rua Prefeito Olympio de Melo

Rua Ferreiria de Araújo

C.R.V.G.

To Downtown

Rua São Januário

To Quinta da Boa Vista

ATLANTIC OCEAN

N

favela

0   200   400 m

Map 3.5 Estádio Vasco da Gama and environs, Rio de Janeiro

When attending a game at the Estádio Vasco da Gama (better known and hereafter referred to as the São Januário), especially on a weekend, it is advisable to arrive early and hungry. The buffet line forms hours before kickoff, and families, friends and Vascainos of all descriptions get their fill of *feijoada* (soupy black beans and meat), *bacalão* (salted cod, potatoes, and onions) and the ever-present *frango e insalada* (chicken and salad). Sitting down, tables are pushed together and conversation inevitably focuses on the impending game as acquaintances are renewed, the odd visitor introduced. This is a very friendly place (if one is inclined towards Vasco), and the walls are saturated with the past. At ten million and counting, Vasco da Gama has the fifth-largest fan base in Brazil. Pride in the club and stadium runs generations deep among Vascainos, they are quick to inform.

After lunch it is also advisable to take a quick turn around the trophy room, where the blinding glitter of Carioca, Brazilian, South American, and Intercontinental triumphs remind one of C.R. Vasco da Gama's sporting legacy. The sixteenth-century accomplishments of Vasco da Gama himself are also on display: an oversized bronze bust of the Portuguese admiral guards the ornate entrance to the stadium, a traditional blue-and-white mosaic recalls his arrival at Calcutta in 1598. Walking into the main stand, the full extent of the São Januário complex comes into view. To the right is an Olympic pool and ten-meter diving facility, a 2,500-capacity gymnasium, a row of houses, a three-story hotel, and Our Lady of the Victories Catholic church. Across the grass, formerly surrounded by an athletic track, the two-level press box spells out what the trophy room shows: *campeão, campeão, campeão*. The Maltese Cross is painted twelve times, thirty feet high across the bleachers and seats, intersecting with the letters C.R.V.G. An angled, three-meter fence with sharp prongs discourages the overzealous from entering the field.

As the stadium fills and the teams go through their warm-ups, children chase each other around the field and members of the press jostle for interviews. Adrenaline pumps as unexpected fireworks go off overhead. Shot by the club, not the fans, they continue for five minutes, filling the stadium with smoke. It seems very unlikely that a game will emerge out of the chaos, but it happens; the singing crowd lights even more fireworks, enormous flags sweep through the redoubled haze.

The São Januário is located in the mini-neighborhood of Vasco da Gama, a politically motivated entity that is wholly contained within the neighborhood of São Cristóvão.[17] As it is surrounded by favelas in a zone of industrial decline, leisurely walks in the area are not advised. At night getting to and away from the stadium is much more complicated and the

Photo 3.6 Pregame at the São Januário

Photo 3.7 Vasco fans regain their equilibrium just after a goal. The white blur is a huge flag being waved.

Photo 3.8 *Vascaínas e um gringo*, ready for the game.

hard-sell tactics of Vasco's multiple *torcidas organizadas* can make for high-intensity ticket negotiations. As with most clubs in South America, Vasco da Gama is an ostensibly democratic institution, its governing board elected by dues-paying members. As democratic elections are highly suspect throughout the Americas, the dominance of an oligarchic elite is perpetuated through manipulation, propaganda, favoritism, vote buying, fraud, and electoral malfeasance. The stadium functions as a place from where political power is projected into other social arenas, complicating Vascainos' strong emotional and geographic associations with place.

Constructed as the site of power and memory for the Portuguese community between June 6, 1926, and April 21, 1927, the Sao Januário has fulfilled that role for more than eighty years. This is a space and place that is deeply connected to narratives of Portuguese colonization, Afro-Brazilian migration, social welfare, labor unions, the discourse of "racial democracy," and the formation of modern Brazil. Because of this legacy the stadium has always been more than a simple sporting arena; political and social ideologies are ever-present. As we saw in the previous chapter, the São Januário was a product of a multitude of cultural and economic forces that helped to reposition the Portuguese community in Rio de Janeiro and Brazil. The importance of the stadium in redefining the relationships of poor whites, blacks, mulattos, and the working class to the larger society is an active part of memorialization among Vascainos throughout Brazil. Indeed, the club attracts fans because of this.

The strength and proliferation of Vascaino identities has generated considerable wealth and power for the club.[18] This power is expressed in part through the local, national, and international successes of the soccer team, the elegant stadium and social center, and a large fan base. The strong emotions associated with the team, its icons and history, have also opened avenues for manipulation and propagandizing. The abuse of power in Brazilian soccer has a long, inglorious history extending back to the formation of its first institutions. In recent years Vasco da Gama has been in the midst of repeated corruption scandals as the dictatorial, strong-arm tactics of Vasco president and three-time federal deputy Eurico Miranda have drained club coffers, violated local and national laws, overturned the club's constitution, and brought the club into disrepute.[19] Miranda is the iconic prototype of the *cartola* (literally, "top hat"): haughty egoists who dominate Brazilian (and global) soccer. Answering to no one but themselves, *cartolas* run their clubs as personal fiefdoms, forging paths to political and economic power in a realm where the ends justify the means. As one example in a long list, in May 2007 Miranda was convicted of tax evasion and sentenced to ten years in prison and fined 53 million reales, about US$27 million. He appealed the decision and will likely never serve time or pay for his documented and undocumented crimes.[20]

It is the persistence of figures like Miranda that have mired Brazilian soccer, its teams, clubs, and stadiums, in self-perpetuating cycles of scandal, corruption, and graft. Recognizing that the *cartolas* use stadiums as instruments to secure local and national political power, the Brazilian government outlawed the posting of political propaganda in and on privately owned public-use buildings. Miranda ignored this law as well, illegally slathering the São Januário with posters for his 2002 federal deputy reelection bid (he lost—Vasco was not having a good season). During his campaigns, the São Januário became a place of conflicting associations for many Vasco faithful, many of whom detest Miranda.

While Miranda and his cronies drain the Vasco coffers and use the stadium to augment personal power, it is not just the top hat that uses the São Januário for political and economic gain. In a textbook example of political clientelism in Latin America, Vasco's multiple *torcidas organizadas*

VEREADOR **ROBERTO** MONTEIRO

65789

Torcidas Vascaínas apóiam Roberto Monteiro:

Roberto Monteiro disputa sua segunda eleição para Vereador. Em 2000, sua campanha contou apenas com o apoio da Força Jovem, tivemos pouco tempo de campanha e, mesmo assim, ele teve uma votação que demonstrou a força da torcida vascaína. Nessas eleições, além de contar com o apoio da FJV, a maioria das torcidas organizadas do Vasco estão com Roberto, com isso, estamos muito próximos de ter um verdadeiro vascaíno na Câmara de Vereadores do Rio de Janeiro. Um torcedor de arquibancada que tem a cara do Vasco - Roberto Monteiro.

Propostas

Roberto vem debatendo com vários setores cariocas projetos e idéias para a nossa cidade, muitas delas, certamente, vão ao encontro das necessidades da sua comunidade.

Esporte:

Utilizar escolas, igrejas, clubes populares e associações para a prática desportiva da população. Aplicação de (no mínimo) 1% do orçamento nessa área. Prioridade para o esporte amador.

Moradia:

Envolver Universidades, a sociedade e moradores na busca de projetos que melhorem as condições de vida nas diversas comunidades cariocas, levando em conta questões como urbanismo, transporte e saneamento.

Educação:

Mais vagas no ensino fundamental, supletivo noturno e creches públicas. Programa de nutrição escolar e valorização do magistério.

Saúde

Fortalecimento da rede pública de saúde, com melhores salários para os profissionais da área e melhor atendimento à população. Criação de um centro público de diagnóstico de imagens (Raio X , Tomografia, Ultra-sonografia etc).

Photo 3.9 Vasco political propaganda. The symbols below the text are the icons of the various *torcidas organizadas* that are supporting Monteiro in his election bid for city council. The number 65789 is Monteiro's election number. Note the background picture of the stadium in the bottom section of the flyer.

compete with each other for political favor from the directors, doled out in the form of tickets for resale, phantom jobs, or other gifts. These groups would be fascinating case studies for anthropologists, sociologists, and cultural geographers as their use of urban space and negotiation of institutional structures is closely allied with residential patterns, socioeconomic status, culturally specific notions of masculinity, and ritualized identity performance. As a lived phenomenon, the *torcidas* give the Brazilian stadium much of its color, sound, movement, and emotion.

In addition to intraclub political intrigue, candidates for local governmental use Vasco iconography and the space of the stadium to align themselves with the ideologies of labor and traditions of the club. Aspiring politicians also employ sympathetic *torcidas organizadas* to promote their candidacy by passing out leaflets, wearing and selling T-shirts, waving flags, or shouting down the opposition. The Brazilian Communist Party's (PCB) candidates draw on Vasco's historic association with leftist and labor politics to promote themselves within the ranks of the Vasco faithful. Plumbing the depths of political patronage and club association is beyond the scope of this book—it is a wide open field of investigation and yet another example of the cultural centrality of stadiums and soccer culture in Rio de Janeiro.

In its neighborhood context, the C.R. Vasco da Gama complex is an island of relative stability and security in a sea of industrial decline. The city government has for many years neglected its northern neighborhoods in favor of developing the tourist-friendly southern zones. This neglect has resulted in decaying social infrastructure and public safety, the growth of favelas, and a commensurate rise in violence in São Cristóvão. As it did in the early twentieth century, São Cristóvão continues to attract migrants because it is the terminus of rail and bus lines. One of the reasons for Vasco's national profile is that when migrants from the north and northeast of Brazil arrived in Rio de Janeiro, they were incorporated into the local Vasco community. Vasco fandom was then transferred through space and time to diverse regions of Brazil.

This transference is also happening within the city itself. In part as a response to the shifting residential patterns of the city, Vasco opened a social center in the southern suburb of Barra de Tijuca that combined with their nautical center on the shores of the upscale Lago Rodrigo de Freitas has extended the traditional membership demographic of the club. Similar to Fluminese but in the opposite sense, Vasco identities are not limited by "popular" categories of class, labor, or race.

While the most public face of Vasco da Gama is the soccer team, it has one of the best basketball teams in Brazil and a long history of success in sports such as cycling, tennis, swimming, and diving. Similar to programs at Rio's other major clubs, the sporting organization at Vasco da Gama is intended as a civilizing mechanism that will generate successful athletes and citizens. The emphasis on soccer is unmistakable, as this is where the club stands to recoup its investment in youth training programs. However, the wide range of social, sporting, and educational activities at the club create a continual flow of people who use the São Januário complex for multiple purposes.[21] This is a community anchor.

Because of its longevity, architectural elegance, and hosting of significant national events and the role of C.R. Vasco da Gama in the social, urban, and sporting histories of Rio de Janeiro, the Estádio São Januário is a readily identifiable feature in the conceptual geography of most *cariocas*, even though the vast majority have not been there. For Vascaínos, the stadium is *the* repository for the twin narratives of social inclusiveness and antiracist practices that define the club's history. An eightieth-year retrospective article calls the stadium "a mark in the fight against segregation, a flag confronting preconceived notions . . . that today should be recognized as a monument against social and racial differences."[22] In this light, the use of the stadium for political ends is not altogether distasteful. However, the realities of Brazilian society are such that darker skin generally indicates lower socioeconomic status. Sadly, a continuing legacy in Rio de Janeiro is that democratically elected club officials shamelessly hijack the team, stadium, and heritage of social inclusiveness to serve their own needs at the expense of the Vasco and São Cristóvão communities.

While the stadium has undergone significant changes in recent years as part of routine updates and modernization (i.e., replacing wood seats with metal, installing cameras, luxury boxes, increasing points of sale, renovating the press box, trophy room, etc.) the lived experience of the club and stadium has remained constant for several generations. This is one of the few stadiums in Latin America with a dedicated family section where people can be thrown out of the stands for audibly cursing. The strong emotions associated with soccer are fueled by a real sense of belonging to a community of people with a core set of values that is anchored in the space of the stadium.

As with the city at large, the São Januário is a maze of contradictions, comforts, the mundane and the spectacular. Controlled by corrupt officials, beloved by millions, and home to one of Brazil's most famous soccer teams, the São Januário embodies a distinct narrative of *carioca* society. This narrative is confirmed and renewed every time Vasco da Gama takes the field—the voices of the São Januário sail down the centuries, stirring the old geographer's bones.

Estádio Jornalista Mario Filho (Maracanã)

On Wednesday June 30, 2004, more than eighty thousand people descended on the Maracanã to see Flamengo of Rio de Janeiro play Santo André, a second division team from the interior of São Paulo State, in the final game of the Brazilian Cup. Many thousands of fans never made it inside. A pulsating mass of human bodies gathered outside the gates, pushing and shoving to maintain balance, looking for a way into the stadium. Surrounded by mounted police and cordoned off by riot police linking batons, the crowd pushed to enter the stadium, agitating as kickoff approached; no one seemed to know what was causing the delay. The turnstiles were functioning properly, but the police forces responsible for frisking people as they entered the stadium decided to make every person pass underneath a single baton held between two officers. This created a highly effective bottleneck, and the crowd swelled in an unorganized mass several thousand strong. As more people arrived, mounted police arrogantly forced their way through the crowd giving blows where necessary to clear a path. Those who tried to bypass the bottleneck were beaten or shoved away. Police cars nudged and forced their way across the crowd, ignoring the open streets available to them. The danger of being knocked down, run over, or trampled increased by the minute. At a lateral entrance to the stadium, Military Police shot tear gas into the crowd, beating some of those who had fallen to the ground.[23] Near the main entrance, nervous groups of foreign tourists lined up like schoolchildren waiting for an opening to dart through. No one had extra tickets. When a caravan of buses carrying Santo André supporters passed a large group of Flamenguistas they were greeted with a shower of rocks and bottles that shattered windows. The Military Police charged and scattered the crowd with raised batons.

Beyond the immediacy of the stadium, thousands of cars were deadlocked; no police had been dispatched to control traffic. The newspaper *O Globo* estimated that two thousand people listened to the game in their cars, tickets in hand.[24] After the game, won by Santo André, "revolted fans began to break windows of cars parked around the stadium, robbed people in cars as well as pedestrians. It was a large-scale assault with the Military Police nowhere to be found."[25] One fan broke through the bodyguards surrounding the president of Flamengo and punched him in the face. One member of the Military Police lost an eye; another was hospitalized when homemade bombs were thrown into their midst. On the slow walk out of the stadium, tearful Flamengo fans vowed that they would never return to the Maracanã.

In the days after the game, the media initiated a debate as to who should

Estádio Jornalista Mario Filho and Environs, Rio De Janeiro

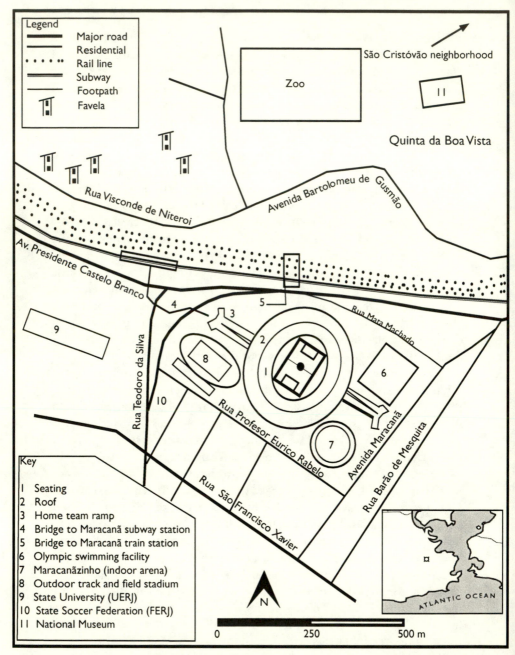

Legend

———	Major road
———	Residential
• • • • •	Rail line
———	Subway
———	Footpath
🏠	Favela

São Cristóvão neighborhood

Zoo

Quinta da Boa Vista

11

Rua Visconde de Niteroi

Avenida Bartolomeu de Gusmão

Av. Presidente Castelo Branco

Rua Mata Machado

9

4

3

5

2

1

Rua Teodoro da Silva

8

6

10

Rua Profesor Eurico Rabelo

Avenida Maracanã

7

Rua São Francisco Xavier

Rua Barão de Mesquita

Key

1 Seating
2 Roof
3 Home team ramp
4 Bridge to Maracanã subway station
5 Bridge to Maracanã train station
6 Olympic swimming facility
7 Maracanãzinho (indoor arena)
8 Outdoor track and field stadium
9 State University (UERJ)
10 State Soccer Federation (FERJ)
11 National Museum

N

ATLANTIC OCEAN

0   250   500 m

Map 3.6 Maracanã and environs, Rio de Janeiro

DISCUTINDO FUTEBOL

— Ô Ricardo Teixeira, essa história de demolir o
Maracanã... 'cê tá chutando!
— Não, tô falando sério!
— Tá chutando!

Photo 3.10 Lula and Teixeira. The text reads: "Hey, Ricardo Teixeira, this story about you wanting to demolish the Maracanã, you're joking. No—I'm serious. You're joking!" *Chutando* is a double entendre, referring to shooting a soccer ball. Cartoon from *O Globo.* Courtesy of Chico Carouso.

take responsibility for the chaos. Television stations showed clips of the violent confusion; newspaper columnists expressed their dismay over the reprehensible state of organization. The Maracanã appeared to be in a crisis situation. Ricardo Teixeira, president of the CBF, suggested that the stadium be demolished. His comments gained him an immediate audience with the president of the Republic, Luiz Ignacio "Lula" da Silva, who asked him if he was joking.

Francisco Carvalho, president of the Superintendency of Sports of Rio de Janeiro State (SUDERJ, the state agency responsible for the operation of the Maracanã), suggested that the violence and disorganization was a "social problem" and a "generalized fault of education amongst the populace."[26] He considered the unruly behavior of the fans the responsibility of the soccer clubs. Only willing to take responsibility for the unexpected overcrowding of the special seating section, he attributed the generalized confusion to free admissions given to 1,200 underprivileged children to sit in a "reserved family space." He would not be held accountable for the thousand-odd counterfeit tickets that had been rejected at the turnstiles.

The head of the Special Stadium Police Force (GEPE) assured the public that the Maracanã was safer than it had ever been. Pointing to a recent decline in criminal incidents in the stadium, the police recorded only three incidents on the night in question. This despite the fact that rival drug trafficking factions had forced their way into the stadium and invaded the press area during the game. For their part, the Military Police justified their aggressive tactics on the grounds that they were afraid of a large-scale invasion of the stadium by these same rival drug trafficking factions. No one knew why the transit police had been given the night off.

Neither SUDERJ, the Rio de Janeiro State Football Federation (FERJ), the CBF, the GEPE, the Military Police, the Guarda Municipal, the transit police, nor the two clubs involved further investigated the events of June 30, 2004.[27] The world's most famous stadium was at sea without a captain, and more bad news was on the way.

On October 6, 2004, the police unit responsible for organized crime suppression in Rio de Janeiro (DRACO) indicted Eduardo Viana, president of FERJ, on charges of forming a thievery ring, abuse of power, fraud, and identity falsification. Viana and five other FERJ functionaries were accused of diverting more than 886,000 reales (about US$280,000) of gate receipts from the Maracanã into private bank accounts during the 2003 Rio de Janeiro State Championship (Campeonato Carioca). It was the fourth time criminal charges had been leveled against Viana during his strong-arm, eighteen-year tenure as president of FERJ. Each time he escaped unscathed and undaunted. This time Viana's lawyers claimed that the actuarial differences noticed by DRACO "owed to the fact that the value for the tickets of the white-seated tribune [which has a higher value than other sections of the stadium] are not made public, and for this, they are not directly accountable."[28] The problem for the *cartola* nicknamed "Caixa de Agua" (Water Tank) was that the total number of white seats multiplied by ticket values fell staggeringly short of the missing cash. Viana took an immediate leave of absence for reasons of health. In August 2006, while the case was still making its way through the Brazilian courts, he died of heart failure.

For millions of soccer fans around the world, the Maracanã is the world's most important shrine, considered by many the spiritual home of world soccer. It is known as much for the passion and size of the crowds as for its history and sense of place. This is the presumed "birthplace" of

Photo 3.11 Estádio Jornalista Mario Filho. The entrance ramps to the stadium give an indication of its monumental size. The Maracanã has hosted the biggest stadium crowds for field events in modern history.

Brazilian soccer idols such as Garrincha, Falcão, Zico, and Romário. Here, Pelé scored his officially recognized thousandth goal. The largest recorded stadium crowds (for a nonmotorized contest) in modern history happened here. The repeated presence of 100,000, 120,000, 175,000 screaming fans echoes down the years. This is the biggest soccer stage in the most successful soccer nation. Not surprisingly, the stadium figures heavily in the conceptual geography of Rio de Janeiro; it is seen on tour buses, T-shirts, postcards, travel brochures, tourist maps, and Web sites. It is the subject of books, the backdrop for movies, and the site of innumerable and powerful memories.

The elliptical, monumental enormity of the Maracanã reduces one's sense of individual agency and highlights the connection between the earth and sky. Pope John Paul II must have felt this when he performed Mass here in 1980. There is something magical about the Maracanã that defies the written word. Perhaps a hundred million Brazilians have gathered here over half a century, each one confronted with the sky blue of the Uruguayan flag, a concretized reminder of Brazil's greatest national tragedy. It is more than a metonym for the city and nation: in the 1950s the partially completed stadium became Brazil's principal stage for national and international soccer and an important public space. By the time of the famous journalist Mario Filho's death in 1966, the facades, bathrooms, dressing rooms, and electronic scoreboards of the Maracanã were finally completed and the stadium was renamed in his honor.

Owned by the Rio de Janeiro state government, the Maracanã is a heavily subsidized public works project, public space, private fiefdom, global icon, and cultural patrimony. In 2000, as the Maracanã was preparing to host the FIFA World Club Championships, the municipal government of Rio de Janeiro passed a law to preserve the structure in perpetuity, forbidding its demolition without the consent of the president of the Republic. The stadium is part of a larger athletic complex that includes a 30,000-seat indoor arena, an Olympic swimming pool, and a 5,000-capacity outdoor track and field facility. In addition to a yearly average of seventy-six soccer games and swimming and athletics competitions, the Maracanã complex is used for a multitude of civic events: military training, public university entrance examinations, school outings, and thousands of tourist visits per year.

Given the functional, cultural, and historical importance of the Maracanã in the city and the nation, it is surprising that more careful attention has not been given to its management and maintenance. The 2004 Copa do Brasil and the indictment of Eduardo Viana were merely two more incidents in a long history of mismanagement, corruption, and neglect. Unraveling the multiple reforms, histories, and complexities of the Maracanã warrants longer treatment than can be given here. An examination of the managerial structure and recent changes to the Maracanã reveals some of the larger cultural and geographic influences on this globally recognized Brazilian icon.

The managerial structure of the Maracanã can be considered representative of the mind-boggling complexity of Brazilian bureaucracy. The reasons for such complexity are both historical and cultural. When the Maracanã was constructed between 1948 and 1950, Rio de Janeiro was still the capital of Brazil and housed the national congress and president's residence. Rio's municipal government was organized under the independent state of the Federal District (much like in Mexico), which itself was contained within the state of Guanabara. Thus three levels of government wielded simultaneous authority over and housed their various agencies in the same city. The tradition of bureaucracy redundancy has its roots in the nineteenth century when the Portuguese constructed parallel governments to rule the empire and the nation from the Quinta de Boa Vista, a solid goal kick away from the Maracanã. Because of the symbolic power and cultural import of what was then the Municipal Stadium of Rio de Janeiro, all three levels of government were involved in the construction process or had a vested political interest in it. In 1948 the municipal government formed an independent agency,

Management and Organization of the Maracanã

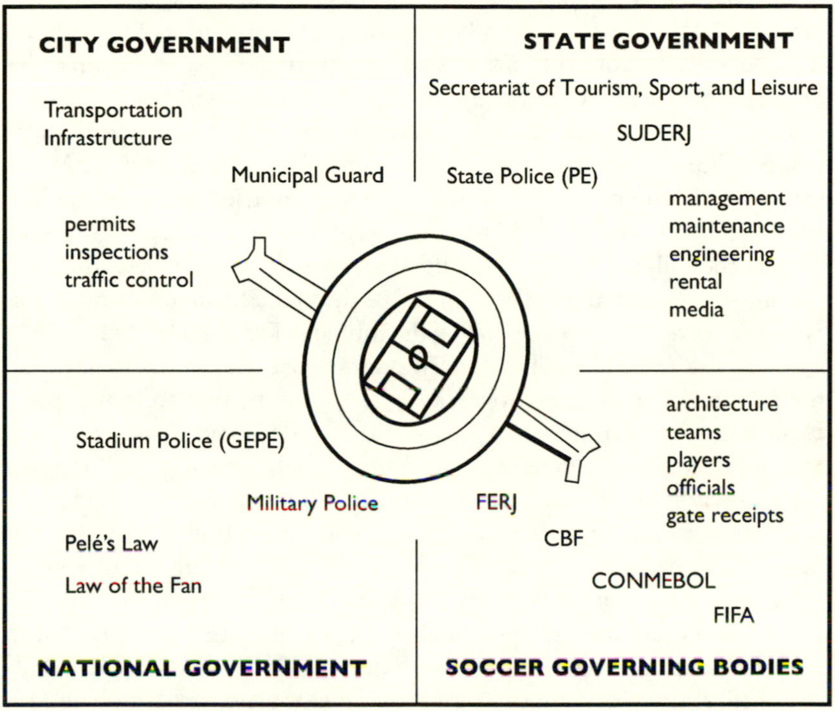

CITY GOVERNMENT	STATE GOVERNMENT
Transportation Infrastructure	Secretariat of Tourism, Sport, and Leisure
Municipal Guard	SUDERJ
permits inspections traffic control	State Police (PE)
	management maintenance engineering rental media
Stadium Police (GEPE)	architecture teams players officials gate receipts
Military Police	FERJ
Pelé's Law	CBF
Law of the Fan	CONMEBOL FIFA
NATIONAL GOVERNMENT	SOCCER GOVERNING BODIES

Figure 3.2 Maracanã management. This figure depicts the multitude of governing agencies that share in the management of the stadium.

ADEM, to oversee the monumental project. This agency answered to the mayor, the state governor, the congress, and the president of Brazil. It is perhaps not surprising that soon after construction began it was halted for several months due to administrative and judicial delay.[29]

The shifting of the Federal District to Brasilia in 1960 simplified and lessened the bureaucratic burden of the city, but complexities still abounded. In 1970 ADEM was transferred from the municipality of Rio de Janeiro to the state of Guanabara. When the state of Rio de Janeiro (the old Federal District that had been transformed into a state but was really just the city of Rio de Janeiro) fused with the state of Guanabara in 1975, ADEM was eliminated in favor of the Superintendency of Sports of Rio de Janeiro. This agency operates all publicly owned stadiums in the state of Rio de

Janeiro: the Maracanã complex, Caio Martins in Niteroi, and the multiple stadiums constructed for the 2007 Pan American Games.

The head of SUDERJ is appointed by the governor of the state of Rio de Janeiro. SUDERJ employs 380 full-time administrators and staff, in addition to 1,000 *operarios*. SUDERJ has its own engineering corps, police force, fire brigade, civil defense corps, press secretary, archivists, restaurant workers, museum employees, lifeguards (for the swimming complex), and tourist guides. Thus the day-to-day administration and maintenance of the Maracanã stadium complex is carried out by more than 1,300 full-time employees.[30] SUDERJ leases the Maracanã to commercial interests, religious groups, the Military Police (for training and orientation), private individuals, and concert promoters. The lands that the SUDERJ stadium complexes occupy are exempt from taxation by the municipality of Rio de Janeiro.

Since the 1950s Flamengo and Fluminese have played the majority of their "home" games in the Maracanã.[31] For reasons that are not entirely clear, when the two other major teams from Rio de Janeiro, Vasco da Gama and Botafogo, are scheduled to play against either Flamengo or Fluminese the games are always held in the Maracanã, despite the fact that the former two teams have their own stadiums.[32] For these and other games, FERJ leases the stadium from SUDERJ, provides tickets and turnstiles (a semi-permanent feature of the stadium), staffs the ticket booths, hires game officials, and assesses the "risk potential" (i.e., potential for violence between fans) of each game in coordination with the Guarda Municipal, federal Military Police, and GEPE. Once SUDERJ has met the infrastructural requirements for the event, they are only responsible for maintaining that infrastructure (fire brigade, structural soundness, lights, electricity, plumbing, etc.). The profits that SUDERJ receives from its lease agreements go into the state treasury, which in turn pays SUDERJ employees' salaries. FERJ functionaries collect the ticket money and count it in a secret, ostensibly secure room within the stadium. The Estatuto do Torcedor (Statute of the Fan) of 2003, essentially a bill of rights for soccer fans passed by the Brazilian national congress, requires that gate receipts, match events, and attendance be made public information. One of the charges made against Eduardo Viana and his FERJ colleagues was a violation of this law.

In addition to local and state laws regarding parking, public behavior, minimum wages, vendors' licenses, and zoning, Brazilian national law has special provisions for criminal acts carried out in stadium space. For instance, if a fan is arrested for throwing a bottle at a police officer *outside* the confines of the stadium, he or she will be tried by a different set of laws than if the bottle had been thrown *inside* the stadium. In order to facilitate the detention and prosecution of unruly fans in the Maracanã, SUDERJ built a judge's chambers and jail within its walls. Thus fans can be arrested, arraigned, tried, and imprisoned under local, state, and national laws without leaving the stadium. The multilayered complexity of Brazilian government is overlaid with the bureaucratic structures and strictures of international sport that dictate the minimum requirements for officially sanctioned competitions.

Moving from the global to the local, FIFA is the governing body of world soccer and is subdivided into six regional governing bodies. CONMEBOL (the South American Football Confederation) controls soccer competitions among its member nations (i.e., Copa América) and organizes continental club competitions (i.e., Copa Libertadores de América). The CBF organizes and regulates soccer in Brazil, parceling out the organization of local competitions to twenty-six state federations. FERJ is the governing body for all amateur and professional soccer in the state of Rio de Janeiro. It organizes state championships for its three divisions and is subject to the rules and regulations of the CBF, CONMEBOL, and FIFA when its member teams participate in the three national divisions or international competitions. When Rio's teams cannot provide their own stadiums to host games, FERJ leases the Maracanã from SUDERJ. When the Brazilian national team plays, the CBF must rent stadiums. Thus the Maracanã must adhere to local, state, national, continental, and international regulations, laws, and statutes. The managerial complexity allows for vacuums of responsibility, and the shifting dictates of these different organizations have forced SUDERJ to radically change the form and function of the Maracanã in recent years.

The design of the Maracanã as a democratic space is reflected in its architecture. The public spaces outside the stadium encourage clustering and guide people towards the entrances to the low-lying bowl. The elliptical design and large approach ramps allow for the fluid commingling of tens of thousands of people who could, until the 1990s, flow freely around the enormous bowl. As with most stadiums, seating was differentiated but to a relatively minor degree given the total capacity. The original seating structure of the stadium was comprised of the *palco de honor* (dignitaries' box), *arquibancadas* (large stands), *cadeiras cobertas* (covered seating) and *geral* (general section). The vast majority of the concrete ellipse was occupied by the *arquibancadas*, simple gradations covered by an inclined, cantilevered roof. Because there were no assigned places, as many as 160,000 people could cram into the bare concrete bleachers. The *geral* was an uncovered, open space located below the *arquibancada*, in front of the covered seating and separated from the field by a three-meter-wide moat.

The *geral* was the populist heart of the Maracanã. It was closest to the action and had a ground-level view of the field, making it possible to relate to the size and pace of the players. If seated, there was no view, so fans stood on eight-inch tiered steps that led down to the moat. More than 25,000 people could fit in the *geral*. This was where fans could run back and forth with the action, yelling encouragement and abuse at teams, players, and coaches, who would sometimes yell back. The *geral* was affordable, if not designed, for those who could not afford to pay for a ticket in a seated area. In 2004 an entrance to this section was only three reales (US$0.95). In the *geral* fans could hear the pregame prayers of their team emanating from the locker room or listen in on the halftime exhortations of irate coaches. It was also a dangerous zone because of the *torcidas organizadas* that sometimes intimated and occasionally acted out their aggressions against the police and rival *torcidas*. The spaces between rival fans were invariably occupied by Military Police and their attack dogs.

Photo 3.12 Maracanã sections. This photo demonstrates all the sections that existed in the Maracanã before the 2006 renovations. At the bottom right of the photo is the *geral*, separated from the lower, covered seating section by a gap of two meters. At the left side of the photo is the *arquibancada* where the *torcidas organizadas* of the Botafogo Football Club have placed their banners on the railing.

Photo 3.13 Entrance to the *geral*

Photo 3.14 In the *geral*. This open, fluid space gave fans a field-level view of the action. Used primarily by men, the *geral*, now replaced by seats, was the democratic heart of the Maracanã.

In response to a FIFA statute that international matches be played in all-seater stadiums, in 1998 SUDERJ reduced the official capacity of the stadium from around 175,000 to 103,022 through the introduction of plastic seats in the *arquibancadas*. The Maracanã could no longer claim to be the largest stadium in the world, falling behind a handful of U.S. college football stadiums. When the Brazilian national team played in the Maracanã, SUDERJ was forced to close the *geral* because of the FIFA regulations. With the reforms, tickets were no longer issued for a section of the stadium but for a particular seat and row in that section, making individuals more read-ily identifiable and therefore controllable. In addition, more than thirty luxury boxes were installed. Besides raising revenues for SUDERJ, the lux-ury boxes had the effect of reducing air circulation, exacerbating the prodi-gious heat generated in the concrete bowl. The deteriorating conditions of the stadium and the open hostility of *carioca* fans when the Brazilian team did not score goals quickly or often enough dissuaded the CBF from rent-ing the Maracanã.

The year 2004 was a watershed for the Maracanã. In addition to corrup-tion scandals and highly publicized incidences of inept management, SUDERJ unveiled a plan to bring the stadium's architecture into complete accordance with FIFA statutes and to prepare it to host events for the 2007 Pan American Games. This plan called for the lowering of the playing field by 1.2 meters and the elimination of the *geral*, to be replaced by 18,000 seats. In addition, two new entrances to the covered seating sections would be added and sixty closed-circuit security cameras installed. The number of bathrooms would increase, and 2,800 parking spaces would be added (also a FIFA requirement). In 1999 there was a similar scheme to modernize the Maracanã, the majority of which did not leave paper.[33] In anticipation of a public uproar over the loss of cheap seats, the state governor promised that she would work to maintain prices at their current level. In interviews with SUDERJ functionaries, the story was somewhat different: only a small sec-tion (behind the goals) of the redesigned *geral* would be made available at current prices. Despite promises, the redesigned seats cost ten to twenty times more than a ticket to the *geral*.

A vice president of SUDERJ defended the architectural modifications as being consistent with a change in the social logics of the stadium. Between 1995 and 2005 attendance in the *geral* was around 750 per game. The sight lines were poor, there were no permanent rest room facilities and no con-cessions, and it was notoriously difficult to police. He suggested that Brazil-ian soccer fans now expect a higher level of comfort than could be found in the *geral*. With the proliferation of cable and pay-per-view services, more people are inclined to watch games from home or at bars than risk the uncertainty of the stadium, much less the *geral*. He noted that very few women, children, or elderly use the geral and that the consistent violence between fans and police was a deterrent for others. The reforms were justi-fied, he said, because the "Brazilian population has evolved to expect more from their public spaces. This ecumenical temple needs to reflect the needs and desires of the people, and the proposed architectural renovations will reposition the Maracanã among the great stadiums in the world."[34]

There is empirical evidence to suggest that the behavior and expecta-

tions of Brazilian fans have changed over the past fifteen years. Many people prefer to watch games among friends and neighbors rather than run the
risk of violence and discomfort at the stadium. Forty-nine percent of stadium-goers say that they do not bring their children to the stadium because
of violence; 43 percent say that their attendance at matches has diminished
in recent years due to violence in and around stadiums.[35] Cleared of the
relatively sedate middle-class and family elements, the *torcidas organizadas*
have been able to exert more of an influence in stadium space, making it an
even less attractive entertainment option. *O Globo* defined the relationship
of the fans to the Maracanã as a mixture of pride and fear.[36] Yet 90 percent
of local fans who frequent the stadium recommend it as a must-see desti-
nation for visitors.[37] Ironically, because of the increased police presence
stadiums may be some of the safest places in Rio de Janeiro. Getting there
and away is a different story.

The desire for increased order in the stadiums of Rio de Janeiro is con-
tradicted by the opacity and corruption of soccer's controlling interests.
The architectural modernization of the Maracanã has not been matched by
a commensurate modernization of the institutional structures that govern
it. The Maracanã embodies many of the contradictions of Brazilian society.
On the one hand, it is one of the most recognized and cherished symbols of
Brazil and has functioned for more than half a century as a public space in
the geographic heart of its most well known city. On the other hand, it is a
private fiefdom used by corrupt bureaucrats such as Viana to augment their
political and economic power. The recent architectural reforms intended
to modernize the Maracanã have struck at the core of the stadium's democratic ideology, the *geral*. However, without the reforms the Maracanã
would risk demolition because its open spaces were remnants of a bygone
era and did not meet the social, economic, or spatial dictates of an increasingly globalized political economy of sport. For some, the sacrifice of the
geral was a fair price to pay for the preservation of the stadium. For others,
the disappearance of the *geral* is emblematic of the loss of traditional public spaces associated with more generalized social changes predicated on
neoliberal economic regimes.

The Maracanã is perhaps the most well known stadium in the world. Its
formerly huge crowds have become the stuff of legend. Born in a moment
of national optimism, it remains stained with one of Brazil's greatest
national failures. Yet the Maracanã remains a symbol of the Brazilian
nation, the city of Rio de Janeiro, and the intensity of soccer culture in
South America. It is not only a shorthand mechanism for identifying Rio
de Janeiro and Brazil, however. The governance, function, and shifting
architectural form of the Maracanã tell us much about the larger patterns

and processes that are acting on the city and country as a whole. In 2007 the Maracanã hosted the opening and closing ceremonies of the Pan American Games, welcoming all Americans (and booing a few) to the nation in its most representative space. As Brazil prepares for the 2014 World Cup, the Maracanã will again be the focus of the world's attention as it was sixty-four years earlier. Next time they just might paint it green and gold and blue.

Conclusion

Communal organization and social hierarchy take spatial forms in the Brazilian stadium. For more than a century, stadiums in Rio de Janeiro have reflected and changed the structure, ideologies, and identities of Brazilian society. The stadium forces us to reconcile and recognize the underlying organization, trajectories, and discontinuities of society. These conflicts exist in other arenas of social life, but rarely are they so compactly, structurally, and ritually presented as they are in the stadium.

That urban landscapes are imbued with ideologies and discourses is demonstrated dramatically in Rio de Janeiro where the beauty of the natural landscape collides with the deplorable living conditions in the favelas or is mirrored in the elegant buildings and neighborhoods of the middle and upper classes. As we saw in soccer's formative years in Rio de Janeiro, sport and spatial practices were always ideologically and therefore discursively laden. Put differently, playing soccer in a space designed for it was an acting out of economic, political, social, and geographic realities.

Since the late nineteenth century, Brazilians have considered sport a civilizing mechanism; spaces of sport are also spaces of socialization.[38] The Brazilian use of sport to solve social ills is more powerful and prevalent than ever, especially in Rio de Janeiro, which has hitched its near-term development plans to the 2007 Pan American Games. Yet how can this civilizing sentiment be reconciled with the violence, decay, chaos, and corruption that plague the stadiums of Rio de Janeiro? As clubs are forced to professionalize their organizations in order to compete in a global marketplace, city, state, and national governments are beginning to link issues of stadium governance with social reform agendas. As city managers, government agencies, and nongovernmental agencies look for ways to deal with the crises generated by the increasing socioeconomic polarization of Rio de Janeiro, sporting venues are increasingly seen as a way to build and repair communities.

The idea that sport clubs provide a positive space for community interaction and identity is deeply implicated in the generalized processes that I have outlined. Part of the reason for this is the strong association in Brazil between soccer and the nation. The international success of Brazilian soccer teams and athletes has centralized the notion that sport is one of the few legal mechanisms available to the poor to escape the structural conditions of poverty. The cultural centrality of sport, actuated in the space of the stadium, does nothing to change the existing socioeconomic structures. To the contrary, the success of Brazilian soccer on the international stage is largely a product of economic polarization. Brazil will continue to produce world-class soccer players because the poor will continue to strive to escape poverty through it. Thus the very form of the stadium is a reflection of dominant ideologies, discourses, and socioeconomic structures. Stadium development projects such as those completed for the 2007 Pan American Games are a continuation of the processes through which sport reifies the stratified and hegemonic social, cultural, and geographic landscapes of Rio de Janeiro.

In Rio de Janeiro, local geographic identity is complexly linked to social stratification. Industrial neighborhoods such as São Cristóvão have very few urban amenities, and the soccer teams and stadiums serve as collective representations of neighborhood identity. In the wealthier southern neighborhoods, there is a marked absence of stadiums, and the spaces of the beach, commercial zone, restaurant district, shopping mall, or park serve as mechanisms of social integration and identity.

In addition to reflecting, refracting, and reproducing social spaces, ideologies, and discourses, the stadiums of Rio de Janeiro continue to function as stages for the social, cultural, and political dramas of the city. The ritualized confrontations between teams (and their fans) that occur in the stadiums are anchored in geographic, labor, ethnic, and class identities with century-long roots. Brazilians describe their allegiance to a team or club through the use of personal adjectives. When asking someone about which team they support, a likely response would be "Sou [I am] Botafoguense" or "Sou Vascaino." Much in the way that one might say "I am a Brazilian" or "I am a geographer," these phrases position the person as a subject of the team, something immutable and unchanging. There is an axiom regarding identity in Rio de Janeiro: "You can change your job, your wife, your house, even your gender—but you can never change your team."

Most residents of Rio de Janeiro (even those who never go to the stadium or have no interest in soccer) are familiar with the histories of the major clubs and teams in the city. The rise and fall of team fortunes is the starting point for conversations and can lead to gross generalizations about the social, ethnic, or class composition of the clubs. Some relationships between clubs are more harmonious than others. For example, Botafogo and Vasco da Gama refer to each other as cousins or brothers, whereas the relationship between Vasco and Flamengo can be described as one of virulent distaste. The historical knowledge of clubs, stadiums, and the accomplishments of teams in the local, national, and international competitions forms an integral and continuous part of the social history of the city and nation.

The four stadiums highlighted in this chapter describe four very different trajectories through geographic and social space. Figueira de Melo tells the story of a small community association that once featured prominently in the soccer world of the city and nation. Its past sporting successes have been preserved in the larger social memory, yet the stadium and club have been shunted into a peripheral position through the unequally applied dynamics of global capital and urban morphology. The club is in crisis, which can be understood as a reflection of neighborhood-based community organizations throughout Rio de Janeiro.

The Estádio das Laranjeiras was one of the most influential stadium spaces in all of Latin America. Constructed as a site of modernist accomplishment in close geographic proximity to economic and political centers of power, the stadium remains the province of an elite socioeconomic class, yet has broader significance for many segments of Brazilian society. The continued association of the club and stadium with elitism speaks to the enduring power of stadiums in a collective social memory and the decoupling of that space from its original signification.

The Estádio São Januário reveals intersecting discourses of social marginalization and the problems of constructing a multiethnic democracy. Co-opted as a site of power by Brazilian president Getúlio Vargas, the stadium has been an instrument for the exercise of political and economic power for generations. The stadium is a powerful locus of historically situated ethnic, religious, labor, and geographic identities that help to frame larger discussions of class and marginality in Rio de Janeiro; it functions as a site of memory for millions of Brazilians. As a result, it has accrued a great deal of symbolic, political, and economic power. This power is subject to abuse and is implicated in larger patterns of corruption in the city and nation.

The Maracanã, conceived and constructed as a monument to Brazilian ingenuity, skill, and potential, bears the stain of Brazil's greatest national tragedy. Despite its inauspicious beginnings, it became a site and symbol of cultural processes and an integral part of the collective imagination of the city and nation. Its close proximity to the former seat of Portuguese imperial power integrates the colonial and modern landscapes of Brazil into a cohesive pattern (Photo 3.16). The sky blue stain has not been erased

Photo 3.15 Maracanã and the Quinta da Boa Vista. In the foreground is the defunct water tank for the palace, now the national museum.

because of the powerful and lasting impact the loss to the Uruguayans has had on national consciousness. The Maracanã is a place for the ritualized renewal of social bonds and represents the democratic ideals of the Brazilian Republic even as those ideals are shifting. And while it is neither orderly nor progressive, its public nature and powerful symbolism establish and renew connections between the local, the national, and the global.

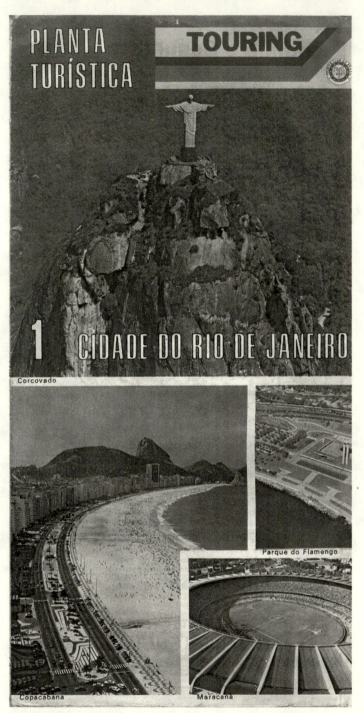

Photo 3.16 Rio de Janeiro tourist map from the 1980s. Perhaps more than any other stadium in the world, the Maracanã both shapes and represents its urban and cultural contexts. This map is but one of a multitude of examples that positions the stadium on par with Rio de Janeiro's other globally recognized iconographic landscapes.

The use of the stadium as a political tool has a long history in Rio de Janeiro and is part of the ongoing social and cultural history of the city. However, the proliferation of smaller stadiums such as Figueira de Melo demonstrates that stadiums also serve to anchor local identities, function as nodes in a wider network of sport and economic production, and accentuate neighborhood solidarities. Although most, if not all, of the clubs of Rio de Janeiro are under intense financial pressure, these smaller stadiums and clubs continue to play an important role in binding an increasingly fragmented society.

It should be emphasized that there are other stadiums in Rio de Janeiro that also function as sites and symbols of sociocultural processes. In addition to the four clubs and stadiums I have focused on, there are twenty-eight more soccer clubs in the city and a total of eighty-nine in the state of Rio de Janeiro. Each of these clubs and its associated spaces form part of the larger social and spatial matrices of sport. Each stadium and club is deeply imbricated in localized identity formations, neighborhood histories, community organizational structures, and relationships to the city and nation. The geographic proximity of the four stadiums in this chapter highlights the complexity and variety of Rio de Janeiro's geography and culture.

The matrix of stadiums in the city informs us about historical and geographic processes that contributed to the production of urban space; the narratives and identities associated with neighborhoods, ethnic, class, and labor groups; and the ways in which these different groups come together as Brazilians. Their collective identity is deeply rooted in the space of the stadium. To understand those places is to make sense of the culture and geography of both city and nation. Rio de Janeiro is one of very few cities in the world where the proliferation of stadiums has influenced the urban cultural landscape to such a large degree. It is to another of these cities that we turn next: Buenos Aires, Argentina.

CHAPTER FOUR

Buenos Aires

Estadiolandia

As the bus rolls alongside the Rio de la Plata towards the working-class neighborhood of La Boca, it steadily fills with fans wearing the blue and yellow shirts of Club Atlético Boca Juniors. Legend has it that these colors were chosen when team founders standing on the docks adopted the flag of the next ship they saw pull into port. It was a Swedish ship, and more than a century later blue and yellow flags adorn the houses of this impoverished barrio at the southern extremity of the Ciudad de Buenos Aires. By the time the bus arrives at the Casa Amarilla (Yellow House), Boca's training ground next to the stadium, it is standing room only and very loud.

As we descend from the bus, we see smoke billowing from an enormous *parrilla* (barbecue grill) decorated with Boca flags. Music blasts from a portable stereo, and a dozen blue and yellow-clad fans are scattered around the grill drinking beer from liter bottles. On offer are *choripan* (pork sausage sandwich) and *morcipan* (blood sausage sandwich), and for two pesos each my friend and I relish in the taste. Hundreds of people file past, making their way to the gates. The Bombonera rises up in the distance; the singing can be heard from half a kilometer. "What will the score be?" I ask one of the men standing around the grill. "Tres a cero [3 to 0], goles de Schavi, Delgado y Tevez."

Walking towards the stadium's hundred-foot walls, we are incorporated into a sea of fans. Groups of young men loiter dispassionately along the broken sidewalk, sizing up the crowd. The game is sold out and late arrivals are turned away from the heavily barred ticket windows. Parents carry young children, jersey-clad couples trot, and heavily tattooed groups of young men swagger towards the gates as vendors of flags, scarves, and hats clamor for their attention. Residents stare down on the passing throng from balconies, blue and gold shirts confirm their allegiance.

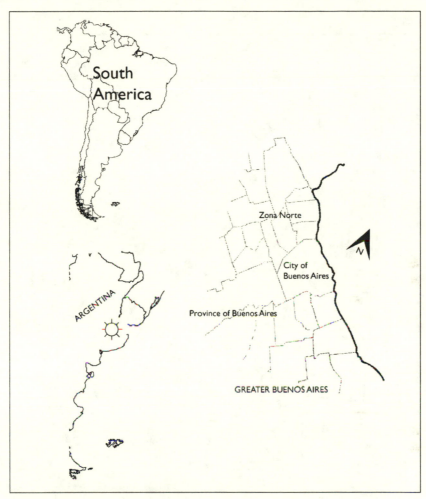

Map 4.1 Greater Buenos Aires, Argentina

A long line has formed in front of police barricades; there is a swarm of activity ahead. When our turn comes we step in front of a police officer, raise our arms, and are perfunctorily searched. Even a modest attempt at concealment would allow one to bring a flask, fireworks, or weapons into the stadium. After passing through the checkpoint we take care to avoid the mounted police lording over the crowd. The helmeted officers are not there to comfort, and I am cautioned not to take a picture. The walls of the stadium are decorated with enormous murals depicting life in La Boca: labor, tango, and the glories of Boca Juniors. The pounding of drums and

La Boca, Buenos Aires

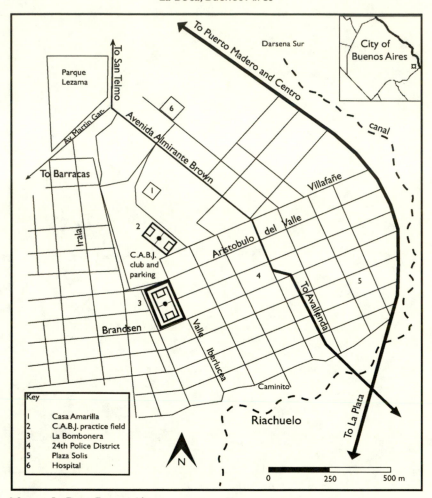

Map 4.2 La Boca, Buenos Aires

combined voices of tens of thousands quicken the pulse. Skipping by a formidable line of riot police, we are ushered through the turnstiles and into a concrete cave smelling of urine and smoke. The flood of people coming through the gates hastens the climb up the concrete steps.

An hour before kickoff we emerge into the light of day. Tens of thousands of fans have arrived long before and have decorated the stadium for the game—large banners emblazoned with the names of their neighborhoods: BUDGE, MORON, TIGRE, SAN JUSTO, SAN MARTIN. Large flags

Photo 4.1 The Bombonera. Ensconced in its neighborhood context, the stadium has undergone significant renovations since its construction in 1938. One can see ships on the Rio de La Plata from the upper tier of stands.

Photo 4.2 Bombonera walls, southwest corner. The stadium's compact, three-tiered form necessitates a very tall structure. The nickname "Bombonera" is derived from the architectural similarities to a chocolate box.

decorated with stars, marijuana leaves, Rolling Stones iconography, and airbrushed paintings of famous players wave in the assembling crowd. A deep bass drum pounds out a rhythm, building energy. As the *popular* fills, the teams are completing their pregame exercises on the immaculate grass. As they disappear into the bowels of the stadium to prepare for battle, fans climb up and shake the fences to jeer the visitors.

A throaty human tide rises to fill the stadium. A large, empty space emerges in the center of the *popular*. From here the *barrabrava* will orchestrate the spectacle.[1] There is no need to reserve this space; it is theirs. Hundreds of police take up their positions and stand guard in the empty spaces between rival fans and along the interior of the field. Police in riot gear enter the field, firemen ready their hoses. If it is hot they will cool the crowd with gently falling spray, if it is violent they will beat them back with water. In the more sedate *platea*, modest banners are scattered on the railings. Fathers sit down with sons, old friends get out their radios, tourists take pictures of one another. A forlorn blue and white flag with a smiling sun hangs limply.

The noise builds as the stands fill. Already the fans are singing well-rehearsed insults, lighting flares, jumping in unison, moving the stadium. They say that the Bombonera does not shake, it beats. Whatever it does, it feels like an earthquake. Finally, slowly, erotically, two long plastic sheets connected to the edge of the playing area inflate into long tubes that have the appearance of giant condoms. The referees emerge onto the field and are greeted by a chorus of whistles and the chanting of "¡Hijos de puta! ¡Hijos de puta! [Sons of a whore!]" Moments later, the visiting team streams out of a tube. The visiting fans release confetti into the air but their cheers are drowned out by ear-splitting whistles, catcalls, and vitriol. Still the *barrabravas* have not entered the bleachers. Older men press radios to their ears like young boys with seashells.

Scantily clad, shimmering women flank the eleven Boca players as they exit their tunnel and run to the center of the field. There, they turn to the crowd with their arms upraised, applauding their fans. Television and radio crews swarm them, scrambling for pregame interviews. An enormous roar erupts as a blizzard of confetti fills the air. It is difficult to see anything but swirling paper. Long rolls of accounting tape and toilet paper rain onto the field, covering the manicured grass. Fires light in the *popular*, smoke fills the air. Little attempt is made to clear the field; only the goal-keepers diligently remove toilet paper from their goal mouths.

Soon after, the home team, Boca's *barrabrava*, La Doce, makes a dramatic entry into the stadium.[2] Scores of young men carry rolled banners to the tops of the stands. Others fasten long vertical spools of colored cloth to

Photo 4.3 Tunnels and clean field. Before the game, the grass is immaculate. The tunnels slowly inflate as the field of play is prepared.

Photo 4.4 Empty space and banners. The names on banners are taken from neighborhoods in Greater Buenos Aires. The *barrabrava* will take up their positions on either side of the long banner in the middle of the second tier.

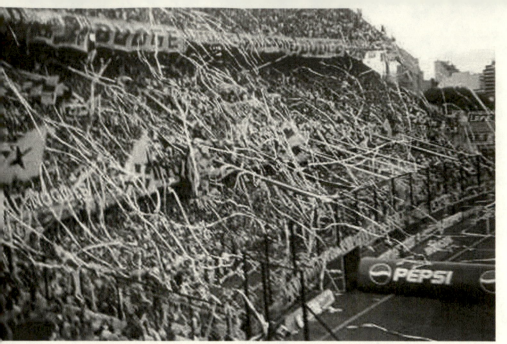

Photo 4.5 *Barrabrava* and ejaculation. The *barrabrava,* having completed the home crowd, orchestrate the release of *serpentinas,* or little snakes. They fall over and around the tunnel extending from the perimeter.

Photo 4.6 Postcoital flag waving. Having claimed the field as their own, the *barrabrava* more formally announce their presence with an enormous flag. The tunnel is now deflated and the crowd steadies itself for the game.

the top and bottom of the bleachers. They will hold onto these banners as they stand on the *para-avalanchas* (human avalanche stoppers) directing their orchestra, backs to the field. The appearance of the *barrabrava* is coordinated to produce the maximum dramatic effect. They transform the *popular* into an undulating sea of waving flags, twirling umbrellas, and smoke. They never enter before their team; visiting *barrabravas* frequently delay their entry until the second half.

As the game begins, the crowd in the *popular* remains standing while those in the *platea* assume their more expensive seats. La Doce begins chanting:

> We are the glorious Doce
> Those that follow Boca don't ask anything
> Even if you lose we will always support you
> Because through everything we will love you.

> I give everything to the *xeneixe*[3]
> Win or lose I will follow
> It is an inexplicable sentiment
> That I carry within me
> And I cannot stop.

From the opposite stands, the fans of River Plate chant:

> You are the "half plus one"
> From Bolivia and Paraguay
> I always ask myself
> You dirty nigger, do you bathe?
> Boca, you disgust me
> Go wash your ass with acid.
> This is the famous River Plate
> The famous River Plate
> Drop your pants
> Because we're going to fuck you.[4]

The referees manage to clear the field of media personnel, players make a modest attempt to clean up toilet paper, and the game is on. Tension rises and falls as the game ebbs and flows. The stadium trembles (or beats) from the force of thousands of fans jumping up and down in unison chanting, "If you don't jump you're a fag!"[5] Fans on both sides make gestures that resemble the throwing of knives. An enormous banner descends from the top of the Boca *popular*. It covers the entire stand, hundreds of feet wide, and moves back and forth to the rhythm of the singing. After several minutes it rises to the top of the terrace and disappears. Then, one green ball of fire is launched from a hand-held firework. Yellow and red quickly flare up and over the field. Then dozens, then hundreds, and then thousands of fireworks are shooting out of the stands and exploding over the field. An acrid taste rises in the throat and the stadium takes on the appearance of a battlefield, mortars falling from the sky. There is a profound sense of normalcy about all of this.

There are few moments in sport as delicate and explosive as the culmination of a flowing goal in soccer. With every possession there is the possibility of success, but failure is most common. When the home team comes close to scoring, there is an audible and physical release of pressure as the fans let out a collective OOOOOOHHHHHH!!!! An anticipatory cascade of bodies falls down a few steps before recovering equilibrium. When the visiting team comes close, there is a sharp intake of breath followed by nervous glances. Neutrality is nowhere to be found. Invariably, the *barrabrava* begins a new chant and the crowd follows:

> Olé, Olé, Olé
> Olé, Olé, Olá
> Da . . . Dale Boca . . . [Give . . . Give it Boca]
> Es un sentimiento [It's a feeling]
> No puedo parar. [That I cannot stop.]

If and when it happens, the stadium erupts in an orgasmic, echoing "GOALLLLLLLLLLLLLL!" Radio and television commentators spread the word to all of Argentina. Fireworks explode over the field and flares burn in the upraised arms of young men. A wave of sweaty, half-naked male bodies tumbles down the bleachers. The ripple effect continues for several minutes as people work their way back up the stands. Strangers are hugging each other in the *platea* and couples give each other a celebratory kiss. Children are held high by their fathers and a handful of loonies scale the four-meter fences, yanking on the barbed wire for effect.

Throughout the game there is a continual threat of violence. When visiting players take corner kicks, riot police stand with upraised shields to protect them from coins, batteries, spit, and cups of urine. The referees warrant a special police escort to their dressing room. Frequently, members of the *barrabrava* will invade the stands of the visiting fans in an attempt to steal banners or engage in hand-to-hand combat. Visiting fans attempt to break through the retaining fences to invade the field. They are beaten back with water cannon, truncheons, and pepper spray. Through-out the stadium a streak of invective is hurled at the players, the referees, and opposing fans. "La concha de tu madre" (Your mother's cunt) and "Hijo de puta" are crowd favorites. Some fans climb barb-wire topped fences, begging the opposition to come closer. The police casually watch them tire before shunting them into the crowd. For these fans, there is no question that what is happening in the stadium is worth bodily sacrifice.

At the end of the game, the Voz del Estadio (public address system) announces that visiting fans will be given a fifteen-minute head start to clear the vicinity. During this time, the singing continues apace. If the home team has lost, the *barrabrava* may remain in the stands long after the game, singing and chanting. If they have won, it is less likely that there will be a prolonged chorus.

When a team has won a local, national, or international championship, the field is invaded by youths who have climbed over the *alambrado olímpico* (perimeter fencing). They literally assault their own players, tear-ing off their shirts, shorts, socks, shin guards, and shoes to take home as souvenirs. The nearly naked players jump around each other in a circle amidst the chaos of reporters, television crews, police, and fans. Later, tens of thousands of people will gather to celebrate their victory at the *obelisco*, a huge phallic structure on Avenida Nueve de Julio that is an iconic symbol of the nation. Here, they sing the songs of the stadium, jump up and down while circling the obelisk/phallus, and party long into the night.

Stadiums and Urban Space in Buenos Aires: 1870–1930

Twenty-first-century Buenos Aires has seventy-nine professional soccer stadiums, more than any other city (see Appendix B). The outra-geously commonplace scenario described above has the potential to boil over into direct, immutable, physical violence in most of them. In trying to decipher the contemporary relationships between stadiums, violence, and sexuality, this chapter examines the formation of urban space and public culture in Buenos Aires at the turn of the twentieth century. I argue that the contemporary presence of sexualized, violent stadium cultures is inex-orably linked to the social and geographic conditions of the city and nation a century ago. The concurrent phenomena of unprecedented demographic increase, rapid urban growth, and British-influenced industrialization combined with the gendered production of urban space to create stadiums as domains for territorial competitions between men.

Though my discussion touches on only a few of the complexities asso-ciated with stadiums and urban space in the period 1870–1930, in what follows I begin to answer the questions: What were some of the geographic processes that produced a superabundance of stadiums in Buenos Aires? How did stadiums combine with other public spaces to create masculine identities in the city? How can contemporary stadium cultures be interpreted through the lens of urban historical geography?

El que no salta es inglés[6]

As with soccer, cricket, horse racing, and rowing in Brazil, the British introduced modern sports to Argentina.[7] In the last decades of the nineteenth century the approximately forty thousand expatriate British in Argentina founded private schools and social clubs where they continued the institutionalized sports that had so recently become a part of their culture.[8] As early as 1876 the Sociedad Sportiva installed a 10,000-capacity horse-racing stadium in the neighborhood of Palermo on the site of today's Hipódromo Argentino, and club members played soccer, polo, and cricket on the infield.[9] The first soccer team in Buenos Aires was organized at the English High School in the 1880s, and modern sporting practices were generally limited to the private clubs and schools of the local elite and British expatriates.[10] It was out of these institutional settings that the first soccer league in Buenos Aires emerged in 1893; by 1899 there were two divisions—a first division of four British high school teams and a second division of nine teams from Buenos Aires' public secondary schools.[11]

As was the case in Rio de Janeiro, soccer's diffusion occurred both formally and informally, between and across socioeconomic groups. The likeliest spaces for informal diffusion were in the dock areas where British mariners played with local laborers or in industrial settings where British managers played with and against their Argentine employees.[12] Globally, Argentina was just behind England and Scotland in developing organized soccer leagues, and we can be fairly certain that the sport's diffusion was not strictly a top-down phenomenon.[13] The spread of soccer (and stadiums) was aided and abetted by its plasticity, a lack of autochthonous urban sporting culture, and recent European immigrants' familiarity with it. Informal practice could happen on nearly any level ground. In the rapidly expanding city there was an abundance of open space. By 1901 there were four divisions in the Argentine Association Football League (AAFL); by 1907 there were about 350 soccer clubs in Buenos Aires.[14] The local press referred to the growing popularity of soccer as a "fever," "wave," and "social mania," which suggests that soccer spread contagion-like among young *porteños* of all classes.[15]

A demographic boom and localized settlement patterns abetted the

rapid spread of soccer in Buenos Aires. Between 1870 and 1930 the population of Buenos Aires exploded from 180,000 to 2,250,000, primarily as a
result of European immigration.[16] Argentina did not develop an export-
oriented industrial system until the last third of the nineteenth century.
Along with the population, the economy grew in response to British capital investment, the development of refrigeration (which allowed for the
transport of Argentine beef to Europe), and the development of rail and
streetcar transport. These technological and globalizing forces also caused
the city to expand away from the coast into the pampas. Many new immigrants settled into ethnic enclaves, retaining their languages and cultures as
they tried to make sense of their new and rapidly changing urban environment. The space of the neighborhood frequently helped to organize these
identities, marking boundaries in a complex urban world.[17]

The association of ethnic, class, and labor identities with the space of the
neighborhood was fortified by the development of locally based sport and
social clubs. These clubs, organized by friends and neighbors, provided a
way for people to develop social bonds in a new home. In addition to
strengthening geographic bonds in the locale, clubs brought together individuals and families from diverse ethnic and socioeconomic backgrounds.
Among the young men, soccer helped to overcome linguistic and cultural
barriers. The solidification of neighborhood identities was therefore inter-
twined with the space of the club, the soccer team, and the burgeoning stadiums of the city.[18]

As Buenos Aires and Argentina grew, national and local officials were
looking for ways to organize the capital city. Swept up in the wave of Eurocentric, modernist thinking that was prevalent throughout Latin America,
Argentine elites took Paris to be the universal functional and visual model
for the capital of a modern nation. They began to shape Buenos Aires in the
Parisian mode by demolishing old thoroughfares, widening streets, eliminating slums, creating public works projects, and building monuments.[19]
The public spaces of the colonial era were reorganized in a modern context. Because Buenos Aires is almost completely flat, it was relatively easy to
organize urban space on a grid system. This system included an extensive
series of public parks and plazas that served as anchors for residential districts and helped to establish a vibrant public culture.

The myriad urban reforms undertaken in fin-de-siècle Buenos Aires
helped to create a more livable city and an increased civic consciousness.
These reforms were predicated on notions of elite privilege, urban order,
and visual consumption of modernist architectural spectacles. Not only
were the wide, paved streets, lighting, sanitation, and leisure spaces
intended to discipline urban space, but they were meant to communicate

ideas and impressions of the sophistication of Buenos Aires to foreign visitors. While the popular classes benefited from the development of public
works in the form of parks, plazas, sanitation, and transportation lines, we
can surmise that the spaces were not intended for them, except as corrective, disciplinary measures.[20]

Since the successful rebirth of the Olympic Games in 1896 stadiums had
figured heavily in European conceptions of urban modernity. To this end,
the municipal government of Buenos Aires was quite aggressive in regulat-
ing the city's burgeoning stadiums. The increasing popularity of soccer
required that the government employ inspectors to control the capacity of
the stadiums on game day. Similar to processes in Rio de Janeiro, many
teams were prevented from participating in formal leagues until they could
construct a stadium that met the architectural standards of the soccer
league as well as government building codes. In many instances, the empty
lots that teams used as a home ground had not been sufficiently maintained
for "fair play," with the result that "landless" teams were barred from league
competitions. The ability to claim space and create and maintain a stadium
was a principal criterion for the permanence of sporting clubs.

In addition to the grid and park system, Buenos Aires formed along
transportation lines that terminated in or near the city center. The historical record regarding the impact of urban morphology, development of
public space, neighborhood growth, and settlement patterns is fairly complete.[21] However, foreign scholars have completely ignored the importance
of soccer stadiums for developing a sense of urban cohesion. The Argentine historian Julio Frydenberg suggests that the development of soccer
leagues in the late nineteenth and early twentieth century helped to integrate disparate zones of the city as teams traveled back and forth to games.
Initially, it was neither easy nor convenient to cover large distances: travel
between stadiums, or in many instances empty spaces that a team had
claimed and improved, frequently took several hours using different
modes of transportation. The constant movement of teams between stadiums or *canchas* (fields) consolidated patterns of transportation and created
a network of associated spaces that served to stitch together the urban environment. One result of this process was that groups of young men identified with the city as a whole and took the word *porteños* (port dwellers) as
a name.[22]

As soccer expanded among nearly all segments of *porteño* society it
began to occupy a tremendous amount of urban space. It also increased as
an element of public culture, gaining increased attention in the press and
providing employment in sporting goods manufacturing and sales. The
proliferation of stadiums, most of which were very small, served to bring

residents of different zones together and facilitated the development and identification of neighborhood-specific identities. These evolving identities and geographies helped to position individuals and groups within the larger urban matrix, not only in relation to each other, but in opposition to other people and spaces. In addition to Porteños, many teams took the name Argentinos in order to distinguish themselves from recent immigrants. Defensores and Unidos were also prevalent names and implied defense of the locale and a united front, respectively. Many teams also took the name of their neighborhood. As teams were formed with the explicit intention of confronting others, it is not surprising that the space of the stadium hosted contests between subcultural groups that that were in direct competition with others for sporting and territorial supremacy in the rapidly evolving metropolis.

Urban Space and Sexuality

Stadiums developed simultaneously with other spaces linked with modernity: factories, parks, plazas, transportation systems, bordellos, and tango bars. All of these public spaces existed in relation to the space of the home, where traditional patriarchal structures tended to limit the public role of women, although in Buenos Aires women played a more prominent role in business and government than in most Latin American cities. As in Rio de Janeiro, the domestic and public spheres are not independent realms but constituent elements of a larger social world controlled and regulated by the state.

One of the problems associated with rapid industrial growth and massive European immigration was that young men between twenty and forty constituted a majority of the population in Buenos Aires at the turn of the twentieth century.[23] The shortage of available women was a problem for both church and state. While prostitution was clearly a violation of traditional Catholic values, its legalization was useful to counter a more generalized fear of male homosexuality. If men were going to be "weak," the logic went, better that they visit a bordello than have sexual relations with other men. If prostitution was to be legal, the state needed to control it through legislation because by the end of the nineteenth century Buenos Aires had a "terrible international reputation as the port of missing women, where kidnapped European virgins unwillingly sold their bodies and danced the tango."[24]

Legalized prostitution reinforced the function of the state in defining the role of women in the public sphere. The state regulated prostitutes through mandatory medical examinations and bordello licensing and made them carry identity cards. Although so-called decent women worked as seamstresses, teachers, domestics, and laborers, the state discouraged middle-class women from working outside of the home, and their ability to move through the city was limited.[25] For men, the roles and spaces of the prostitute and homemaker broadly defined the gendered parameters of their public and private lives.

The gendered segmentation of social life created spaces and places in the city that were defined according to particularly narrow conceptions of masculinity and femininity based in a Catholic and patriarchal heterosexual normality. Because traditional feminine roles were strongly associated with the domestic sphere the public presence of women confused the boundaries between the two. This was consistent with themes of domestic contamination found in Rio de Janeiro around the same time.[26] The Argentine anthropologist Eduardo Archetti suggested that the gendered production of urban space

> created new conditions for public participation and enjoyment, where cultural life, sports and sexual concerns dominated. Three institutions in particular provided the public with new excitement and opportunities for the deployment of sexual fantasies: the modern legal brothel, the "dancing academies" or "cafés with waitresses" and the cabaret. These arenas provided a space of freedom for men and women, albeit of a special kind.[27]

The relationships between men and women in the three arenas that Archetti mentions defined the accepted sociospatial parameters of gendered interaction in the city. Men and women were free to gather in government-sanctioned spaces, where they performed their gender roles and identities in relationship to each other in front of a public audience that enforced the dominant sexual ideology. Which is to say that people acted out their desires in a public space designed for it. These interactions formed a sexual-spatial public consciousness that extended throughout the city. But men do not only define themselves in opposition to women or in relation to the family. They are especially conscious of their relationships with other men. Men were together in the workplace, in labor movements, in government agencies, in the bordellos, and in sporting clubs. The imbalanced gender ratios in the city, coupled with the gendered regulation of public space, meant that men probably spent more time among themselves than with women. Because the places where the most men gathered the most frequently were the stadiums, it is likely that they too functioned as sites of sexual sublimation.

If the legalized bordellos of Buenos Aires functioned to address the "problem" of homosexuality generated by imbalanced gender ratios and defined a dual binary between domestic/public and feminine/masculine, then the emergence of tango as a popular cultural form in the second decade of the twentieth century provided another public stage for the performance of gender identities. Developing in parallel with the soccer clubs and stadiums of Buenos Aires, the performance of tango music and dance in bars, cafés, streets, and neighborhoods created spaces of masculine performance, social integration, and cultural identity.

Similar to the formation and solidification of masculine and geographic identities that happened in other public arenas, particular notions of sexuality, morality, and geographic identity developed in the tango bars and cafés of Buenos Aires. Archetti's seminal work *Masculinidades* is an unmistakable signpost on the road to understanding the development of *porteño* masculinity in these spaces. Archetti suggests that the lines that divided public and private space were bridged in the tango bar through highly localized behavioral codes, expectations, signals, and styles. Tango orginated as a dance between men in the popular zones of the city, notably La Boca and San Telmo, and tango bars were fraught with sexual insecurity. The sanctioned, secure heterosexual love of the domestic sphere and the more illicit lustfulness of the bordello were challenged by a melodramatic, risk-laden pursuit of romantic love in the public space of the tango bar. This more fluid sexuality placed men, both married and single, in direct competition for female attention. The dominant theme of tango lyrics is a strongly felt love gone awry, through betrayal, bad luck, or the loss of a woman to a more masculine competitor. Thus not only is the pursuit of romantic love a risk to one's sense of masculine self-worth, but by entering into the social and physical spaces of the tango, men put their masculinities on display for others to evaluate. Their success or failure in the tango bar confirmed or denied their masculine selves.

The café was also an important element of masculine urban culture in fin-de-siècle Buenos Aires. These were neighborhood- and street-based public spaces where men gathered to drink and socialize. Cafés were distinct from tango bars in that women were (generally) not present. An adolescent male's first entrance into the world of the café signified a transition to adulthood where his ability to act as a man would be evaluated and shaped by other men.[28]

Cafés were spaces where men entered into locally based social networks, and we can assume that social clubs and soccer teams occasionally sprang from these associations. Because the spaces of the cafés, tango bars, bordellos, workplaces, and soccer stadiums of the city were linked both spatially and socially, we can also assume that the quest for masculine legitimacy occurred in all of them. The inner workings of these sexualized spaces has yet to be brought to light. Given the importance of the relationships between masculine public space, public consciousness, and the development of nationalist modernity in Buenos Aires, it is curious that there is an "almost complete silence on how men use public space and in what ways that has changed over time."[29] Looking at stadiums in their historical and contemporary contexts gives fresh insight into male cultural worlds.

Given the predominance of male-dominated spaces in Buenos Aires, it is surprising that issues of homosexuality did not comprise a central element of either tango lyrics or general public discourse.[30] It is likely that homosexuals in Buenos Aires were able to create their own places, fashions, sexual tastes, and customs that existed in opposition to both male and female heterosexual gender constructions.[31] By referring to other cities during the same time period, we can surmise that the strict taboos against homosexual relationships created a complex network of spaces, codes, and behaviors that allowed for an underground homosexuality to express itself.[32]

The involvement of the state and the church in the construction of gendered urban space in Buenos Aires continued in conjunction with the modernization of the city in the first decades of the twentieth century. Although women played an important role in the public sphere, they did not participate as political or social equals, and their ability to move freely through urban space was greatly circumscribed.[33] Clearly, women's activities and spaces were much different from men's. The gender roles and relationships that developed in relation to bordellos, tango bars, cafés, and sport in the period 1870–1930 has become part of the national consciousness. These processes of identity formation and transference were complicated by the relationships that men had with each other. The most visible, public, and sexualized expression of these relationships occurred in the bordellos, tango bars, cafés, and stadiums of the city.[34]

Sos un cagón [35]

It appears that men in fin-de-siècle Buenos Aires were constantly embroiled in masculine competitions of various kinds. In the tango bars they competed to attract the attention of women, in the cafés they performed and evaluated one another's masculine qualities, in the workplace they competed for wages, and in the larger urban matrix they competed for land, political influence, and social status. It is only by linking these spaces that we can arrive at a more complete understanding of the cultural landscape. The proliferation of stadiums in Buenos Aires was a product of this generalized competition.

Within the burgeoning metropolis, it was through soccer that many of

Networks of space in Buenos Aires 1900–1930

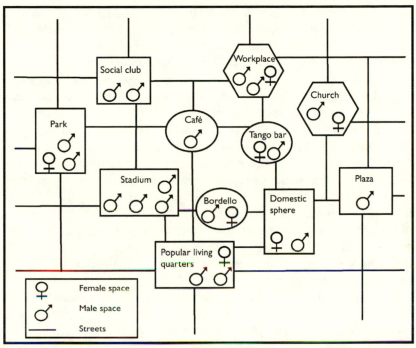

Figure 4.1 Gendered networks of space in Buenos Aires, 1900–1930. This diagram is an imaginary grid of particular kinds of space in Buenos Aires. Connected by streets, each place functioned as a node in a gendered network. Putting the stadium into this network has long been a forgotten element of urban scholarship in Latin America.

the basic values amassed by a large segment of society were actuated in space. After several decades of foreign dominance, soccer shifted from an elite to a popular sport in Buenos Aires, from foot-ball to *fútbol.* In the mid-1910s Spanish replaced English as the official language of the Argentine Football Association (AFA).[36] The British also lost control over the ideological banner under which soccer grew. The British sporting idiom was (and is) one of "fair play" and gentlemanly, rigorous pursuit of the game. However, the majority of Argentine soccer players were adolescents from the "popular" and middle classes—students, laborers, and small business employees who brought a somewhat rougher ethos to the pitch. The games played in *potreros* (open spaces for the informal practice of soccer) were defined by skilled dribbling, rough play, invention, and subversion of the rules. The iconic figure of these spaces, *el pibe*, is a male adolescent who never fully matures into adulthood.[37] As local practice expanded and formalized, the values, skills, and spaces of the *potrero* and the *pibe*, not the old school tie, characterized soccer in Buenos Aires.[38]

It is likely that the majority of the young men in the city participated in some kind of formal or informal recreation. As soccer teams and social clubs developed histories, their stories were etched in the space and place of the teams' playing spaces, or *canchas*. Over time, the relationships between teams and their fans became associated with the spaces that hosted their encounters. As soccer took on more rigid spatial and institutional boundaries, the stadiums that emerged accrued sedimented layers of history and meaning, senses of topophilia and topophobia, that were integrated into a larger network of associated spaces and formed part of the histories of neighborhoods and regions of the city.[39] Linked with other spaces of masculine performance, soccer stadiums developed as vernacular public spaces that allowed for the expression of a highly localized urban identity. In a remarkably short time soccer games went from a novel leisure activity to a type of ritualized, intraurban warfare.[40]

The explosion of soccer between 1890 and 1930 positioned stadiums as venues for the expression of highly localized masculine solidarity that was not possible anywhere else. In the spaces of the tango bar and café, an individual's performance in relation to other men confirmed or denied acceptance as a singular man. In the stadium, however, a collective masculine performance was evaluated in relation to the action on the field and in the terraces in relation to an oppositional masculine collective. The gathering and confrontation of opposing groups of men produced ritualized conflict through which masculine supremacy was determined. With time, the stadium became the literal and metaphorical home of the collective, and the defense of this space by its possessors became increasingly important and violent.[41]

The most important factor in a club's longevity was the appropriation of urban space for soccer practice. Teams and clubs competed against other groups of men who were engaged in the same struggle, frequently over the same space. If we interpret the competition for urban space as a measure of masculinity, we can understand the process of stadium formation and the defense of that space through the game of soccer as a struggle for male dominance within the city. When soccer clubs were able to claim and modify geographic space, they asserted authority over it: constructing an arena ensured their prolonged existence. The ability of a team to succeed on the field affected its ability to recruit new members and fans, which in turn augmented the club's ability to consolidate control over urban space and invest in stadium infrastructure. The "home" of the stadium began to take on characteristics associated with the domestic sphere, and the fans became the "authentic" custodians of a highly localized identity. Thus the stadium became a place where masculine dominance of space was directly challenged by other groups of men. When a rival team and its supporters came to the stadium, the spatial dynamics of the game became a struggle for the appropriation of territory, movement within masculine hierarchies, and sociospatial supremacy in the city.[42] That is, teams were not only defending their goal and field, but their stadium, neighborhood, and collective identity. For club leaders and members, not to mention politicians and businessmen, the stadium effectively functioned as a *patria chica* that served to locate power, identity, and meaning.[43]

Within a short time, this masculine competition escalated from inter- and intra-barrio competition to the scale of the nation. International soccer matches positioned the stadium as an element of national public culture where "foreign forces" were "engaged in battle." In addition, stadiums became a spatial medium through which male identity and cultural power could be managed.[44] As happened in Brazil, Argentine competition against foreign teams was considered a test of national virility.[45] As early as 1916 Argentine fans set fire to a stadium during a game between Argentina and Uruguay, canceling the game they were losing. In 1924 the *clásico rioplatense* was again suspended after the public invaded the field. The match was replayed two days later but only after the installation of a two-meter-high fence around the field.[46] This was the first *alambrado olímpico*, now a commonplace architectural element of stadiums throughout Latin America.[47]

When teams representing Argentina took the field the stadium amplified masculine identification with the nation. When faced with an opponent that threatened to devalue the very maleness of the nation, threatening senses of virility and prowess, it is perhaps not surprising that violence was the result. The positioning of masculine virtues in soccer was exploited by politicians as a means of developing nationalist agendas.[48] Stadiums also crystallized more localized geographic identities. The first recorded instances of mortal violence between local teams occurred in 1932 during a game between River Plate and Racing Club, resulting in one death and a number of injuries.[49] However, given the very strong identities that had formed in relation to soccer stadiums, we can be almost certain that aggressive confrontations between fans were commonplace well before this date.

Similar to the processes in Rio de Janeiro, the codes and practices of the stadium extended to other public spaces. For instance, on July 30, 1930, thousands of men gathered in the Plaza de Mayo to listen to the radio broadcast of the World Cup Final between Argentina and Uruguay, transferring the codes of the stadium to the street. Uruguay won the match and the crowd turned violent, burning several Uruguayan businesses and badly beating Uruguayan nationals in the streets. For Argentines, the loss implied a lack of national virility, in the same way that losing to the Uruguayans provoked a crisis of national confidence in the Brazilians in 1950. The Argentine defeat was attributed to a superior Uruguayan masculinity, referred to as *la garra charrúa*, or Indian grip, and so devastated the masculine image of the Argentines that they did not send a first team squad to the World Cup until 1958, when they were again humiliated, this time by Czechoslovakia.[50]

While soccer in Argentina was internationally recognized for its excellence, the fear of emasculation on a global stage effectively eliminated the country's participation in World Cup competitions for several decades. As an informant of Archetti noted, "Football made it possible for us to be recognized as something in the world. An authentic masculine passion developed and, for many men, the majority of men, football became part of what I will call an internalized national identity. . . . Because of this, defeats and failures are especially painful for us."[51] Beginning in the 1910s and continuing today, the different manifestations of the Argentine National Team (La Selección) have been understood to reflect the masculine characteristics of the nation.[52] These sentiments originated in the burgeoning soccer spaces of the city in the early twentieth century and continue to inform the experience of soccer stadiums in the twenty-first century.

Violence has been a part of stadium cultures for millennia; it is not particular to Buenos Aires or Argentina. The Argentine historian Juan Jose Sebreli suggests that there is a direct correlation between sexual repression and stadium violence in Buenos Aires.[53] In addition to releasing sexual tensions, the stadium is a site for the release of emotional tensions that do not have other socially sanctioned outlets. Other studies have shown that soccer-related violence is carried out for a variety of reasons: excitement, frustration, celebration, competition, conflicts of interest, camaraderie, racial stratification, the production of spectacle intended for a wider audience, or as a reaction to social, economic, or political exclusion.[54] In addition to these reasons, stadium violence in Buenos Aires is a product of the historical development of urban space and the construction and defense of male territories.

La cancha de fútbol y la concha de tu madre[55]

Returning to the description of the soccer game at the beginning of the chapter, it is clear that one of the defining features of soccer games in Buenos Aires is the expression of violent, territorial, homophobic yet homoerotic sexuality. Most stadium cultures have elements of these tensions, but in Argentina they are stronger and more revealing of historical and cultural process. For instance, in the United States prepubescent boys might scream "You suck ref!" without understanding the act of fellatio. In Buenos Aires boys of the same age are likely to scream "¡Hijo de puta!" or "¡La concha de tu madre!" They might not understand the full implications of the words or even why they say them, but the explicit and accepted degradation of women takes the insult to another level.

In Argentina a soccer stadium is referred to as *la cancha*. This feminine noun is interchangeable with the masculine *el estadio* in popular discourse. Because the stadium is the literal and metaphorical home of the team and because the domestic sphere is strongly associated with the feminine, there is a logical extension of feminine attributes to the stadium. Given that soccer is a predominantly male practice, the labeling of stadiums as "canchas" indicates masculine control of a feminized space.[56]

The derogative term for a vagina in Argentine Spanish is *concha*. I suggest that the similarity between the word used for the stadium, the reproductive space of the club, team, and fan, and female genitalia, is not coincidental. The pervasive use of the phrase, "La concha de tu madre" in the *canchas* of Buenos Aires effectively eliminates the semantic differences between the two. If we position the game of soccer as the practice of defending one's reproductive space (*cancha*-space) against a masculine other, then the victory of an opposing team in one's *cancha* is a symbolic domination of *concha*-space. The tendency of *barrabravas* to remain in the stands for a longer period after their team has lost than if they had won is evidence that the *cancha* needs to be reclaimed following defeat.

The relationship between the *cancha* and the *concha* is embroiled in a paradox. Because of the contempt for femininity in the world of male sport women are degraded and opposing fans feminized in the stadium.[57] As the chant of the River Plate fans demonstrates, in order to assert one's masculine authority against other men, "Argentine soccer enthusiasts chant that the only *authentic* fans are those who fuck and tear open the anuses of all other fans."[58] This is consistent with David William Foster's historical examination of male and female cultural space in relation to tango wherein maintaining the primacy of heterosexual relationships defines the parameters of public behavior in Buenos Aires, yet in homosexual male relationships it is only the receptor of the sexual act whose masculinity is called into question.[59]

The openly homophobic stadium environment paradoxically encourages homosexual activity as long as it is suitably aggressive and degrading for the passive partner. The fear of being sexually violated by other men, if only symbolically, drives the aggressive behavior of the fans and players. This is particularly true if we accept Allen Guttman's suggestion that in Argentina the "soccer goal is not the symbolic vagina . . . but rather a symbolic anus, which must be defended from penetration by opponents of the defenders' own sex."[60] A large segment of the Argentine population believes that if one man sexually violates another he is not executing a homosexual act but rather a gesture of power. For this reason, among others, the *hinchadas* (fans) sing songs about anal rape.

The gestures of fans are also an important part of a "gender myth" that perpetuates male power.[61] The aggressive gestures associate masculinity with the ability to physically dominate one's opponent on the field, in the terraces, and on the streets. Those who perform the gestures are making a claim about their masculine attributes in the context of the stadium. In addition to signifying an ability to mete out and absorb pain, the gestures are a coded means of communication and intimidation that are frequently enough to convince the opponents that the battle is already lost. In the same way that the hierarchies and myths of the heterosexual world are reified in the masculine codes of the café and the tango bar—that is, a particular vision of masculinity is acted out in its appropriate space—so, too, are *porteño* masculinities enacted, contested, and confirmed in the stadium.

The *cancha* also refers to the space of the playing field. In the narrative that opened this chapter, the field is "clean" before the fans enter the stadium. As the players (paradigms of masculinity) enter the field flanked by scantily clad women (paradigms of femininity), the fans throw confetti and long, streaming rolls of paper onto the field. I interpret this as a symbolic soiling of the feminine *concha/cancha* with the metaphorical sperm of the crowd. It is not coincidental that the players emerge from phallic-shaped tunnels each of which has a vaginal-shaped opening at the end (from the inside, it appears as if one is running out of the womb into a blindingly bright world). Viewed from the stands, the tunnels appear to be phalluses ejaculating the reproductive elements (players) of the team onto the field. If we understand the locker room as the place where the reproductive agents of the team (players) prepare themselves, it is easy to understand the locker rooms as testicles. The spermlike emergence of the players onto the field is augmented by the spermlike emissions from the stands. The fans effectively claim the re-creative space of the field as their own. The rising tension of the game is punctuated by sexualized sounds emanating from the crowd. The collective release at the scoring of a goal is both functional and symbolic in that it spurs an orgiastic celebration and signals the violation of the protected sexual space of the opponent.

Women are, of course, present in the stands, yet their presence is not generally perceived as a threat to the masculinity of the men. This may be because women are not openly questioning the heterosexuality of the men and because the primary identities are understood as "us and them," not male and female. At play are oppositional masculinities into which women are partially incorporated. I suggest that women are only partially incorporated into the masculine "we" of the fans because they are generally denied full agency in the spectacle. There is a common assumption among men that women are incapable of understanding the significance of soccer because it is a game with which they have no direct (or expert) knowledge and experience.[62] The presence of women in a male-dominated space complicates the interpretation of the stadium that I have presented, yet as Archetti observed more than twenty years ago, "Soccer is a masculine discourse carried out in explicit sexual terms which moves from verbal to actual violence as insecure groups seek to define/maintain that male identity."[63] This identity is linked with multiscalar geographic processes and patterns of socialization that are spatially referred in the stadium.[64]

Conclusion

For more than a century, soccer stadiums have functioned as nodes in a network of masculine spaces that extend throughout Greater Buenos Aires and Argentina's urban system. From luxury boxes to sporting goods stores, world-class pitches to lumpy roadside fields, World Cup qualifiers to six-a-side games among friends, stadium cultures are ever-present in Argentina. The sixty-four professional soccer stadiums in Greater Buenos Aires are hosts to preternaturally strong identities rooted in class, labor, ethnicity, religion, individual and collective history, cultural tastes, lifestyles, and geography. These subcultural groups compete politically, economically, socially, and on the field of play. The codes, practices, and urban functions of soccer stadiums are complicated by the historical relationships between them and other spaces in the city: the residence or domestic sphere, the street, transportation networks, the workplace, the tango bar, the café, parks, and plazas. The simultaneous development of all these spaces forged a particular sense of *porteño* masculinity that is most virulently expressed today in the soccer stadiums of the city.

In addition to having more professional soccer stadiums than any city in the world, Buenos Aires has one of the highest incidences of stadium violence, with one hundred recorded deaths and innumerable injuries in the period 1958–1985.[65] Understanding the historical development of stadiums in the context of the gendered development and networking of urban space and culture in Buenos Aires is essential to making sense of the contemporary uses and function of stadiums and public space in the city.

Academic investigations have almost completely disregarded stadiums as elements of public space and culture in Buenos Aires, though, similar to churches, parks, plazas, streets, and shopping malls, they define public culture and shape the urban landscape. This absence has to do in part with the ubiquity of stadiums, which renders them invisible, and with traditional modes of academic investigation. This chapter has examined the rapid expansion of soccer as a popular sporting practice in the early twentieth century as evidence that there were a multiplicity of spaces dedicated to the performance and observation of masculine identities. There were of course formal spaces such as fields and stadiums for the practice of soccer, but, similar to the proliferation of spaces for Mesoamerican ball games, there were many times more informal spaces. We shall probably never know exactly where these spaces emerged, transformed, and disappeared, yet we must assume that they defined large areas of the urban and cultural landscape. The historical trajectory of the *potrero* contributed to the discourse of *porteño* masculinity and "reflects the power of liberty and creativity in the face of discipline, order and hierarchy"[66]—characteristics that continue to define twenty-first-century stadium culture in Buenos Aires.

Not only were stadiums constructed for the explicit purpose of staging ritualized confrontations between opposing masculine collectives; the codes and practices of these spaces extended into other areas of the urban environment. Thousands of men gathered in public squares to listen to radio broadcasts of the World Cup and thousands of people moving to and from stadiums occupied transportation lines and streets, which helped to integrate a rapidly expanding city. As in Rio de Janeiro, the diffusion of sport brought with it increased media attention; the production, distribution, and consumption of sporting goods; and the development of a locally specific vocabulary to describe a foreign game. The stadium was a venue for the expression of masculine solidarity that was not available in other social arenas. This masculine solidarity raises the possibility that the stadium was a space for the expression of an otherwise taboo sexuality.

While more comparative research is necessary, it appears that the relationships and sexual norms that developed in relation to the songs, lyrics, and spaces of the tango also developed, albeit differently, in the soccer stadium.

A fascinating project would be to compare the lyrics of soccer fans and tango in the first half of the twentieth century in terms of their portrayals of romantic love, passion, and sexual codes. My hypothesis for such a study is that tango and soccer lyrics describe a particular kind of heterosexual love that taken together form a composite picture of gender in Buenos Aires. In tango the male is in constant danger of rejection and subject to the power of the female. Though the male is assumed to be the dominant force in any heterosexual relationship, the possibility of inversion is ever-present in the tango because of the prospect of female rejection or another male assuming supremacy. This danger is also present in soccer, although it is expressed in a different way. If we substitute the female of tango with the soccer team (or even the stadium), we can better understand what banners in the stadiums define as an "inexplicable passion" that is equivalent to romantic love. By positioning the team as a female, the predominantly male fan base constructs a collective partner that can only betray them by losing on the field. Even if the team loses, the love for the club will endure because there is always the possibility of winning the next week, or the next year. There is also the possibility of asserting group masculinity by engaging in battle with the opposing fans or the police. The team represents an enduring, collective love that is ritually consummated in the stadium and permits males to openly show their emotions. In this sense it is much less risky than the kind of individual, heterosexual love expressed through tango. Soccer lyrics, much like tango lyrics, have space-specific meanings and target audiences who will understand and legitimate what the singer is communicating.[67]

The masculinities of the stadium, bordello, tango bar, and café are complementary yet differentiated in space. Each has its space-specific codes and expectations, is concerned with expressive sexuality, fear of rejection by females and violation or competition from other men, and speak to the need to assert one's self as a man in public space. However, only in the stadium is the integrity of maleness secure, through violence if necessary. This violence serves to legitimate masculine identities in the face of competition from other men. Given the overwhelming number of stadiums in Buenos Aires and the cultural centrality of sport, the connections between the stadium and the gendered spaces of the city are essential to understanding the historically continuous production of public space and sexual identity performance in Buenos Aires.

As stadiums proliferated in local contexts and occupied a more prominent cultural role in Buenos Aires in the early to mid-twentieth century, they assumed greater meaning for individuals, groups, and communities. It is clear that stadiums form an important component in the physical and

conceptual geographies of cities all over the world. The remarkable proliferation of soccer stadiums in Buenos Aires positioned these urban landmarks as prominent elements of the urban and cultural landscapes. The
broad popularity of soccer among all classes of *porteño* society ensured
that they became sites of capital accumulation and political interest, which
in turn increased their importance in the public life and culture of the city.
The language and the behavior of the stadium have informed and influenced the culture, lives, and identities of generations of *porteños* and continue as unmistakably central elements of *porteño* society.

Stadiums have been present in Buenos Aires since the development of
the Plaza de Toros in the neighborhood of Belgrano in 1791.[68] Today
Buenos Aires has the most vibrant stadium culture in the world. The
majority of urban research on Buenos Aires in the early twentieth century
investigates the domestic sphere, modernist reform projects, and the development of public space and transportation infrastructure, completely
ignoring one of the most important and common kinds of public space in
the city.[69] The proliferation of stadiums formed an integral part of Argentine conceptions of masculinity and nationhood and the development of
public space and culture in Buenos Aires. The next chapter examines the
contemporary geography of the city's many stadiums.

CHAPTER FIVE

Class and Conflict in the Stadiums of Buenos Aires

Soccer stadiums dominate the sporting landscape of Greater Buenos Aires, but Argentine athletic achievement is by no means limited to soccer. In December 2005 Argentina's national teams were ranked in the world's top ten in rugby, men's Davis Cup tennis, men's basketball, men's and women's field hockey, men's and women's volleyball, men's soccer, and had numerous world-class boxers.[1] If the international polo federation kept national rankings, Argentina would hold the top position without ever facing a serious challenge. This level of sporting success on the global stage suggests a pervasive, institutionalized culture of sport and a proliferation of sporting venues. Greater Buenos Aires, with one-third of the national population, is the epicenter of sporting life in Argentina, and its eighty stadiums structure urban life to a high degree. Each sport and its associated spaces have historically, geographically, and culturally distinct characteristics that together provide deep insight into the cultural landscapes of the city and nation.

This chapter examines and compares the intersecting and contrasting geographies of soccer, rugby, and polo stadiums in Greater Buenos Aires. Entering into *porteño* society through these stadiums allows me to argue that the different geographies of these stadium cultures define and describe larger economic and political worlds in Argentina that reveal class divisions and differing visions of the nation and the exercise of power. The relatively privileged social positions of rugby and polo tend to reify existing socioeconomic and political structures, whereas soccer tends towards a populist violence against the state that is unevenly managed by the governing classes. In addition to reflecting social structures, the stadium cultures of these three sports reveal divergent yet complementary nationalist

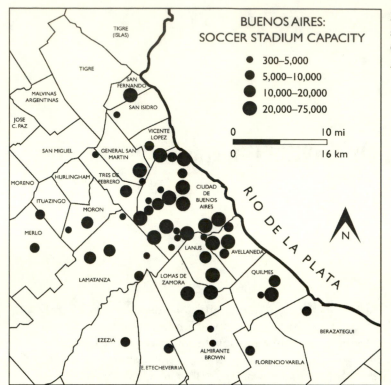

Map 5.1 Soccer stadiums in Greater Buenos Aires, 2008

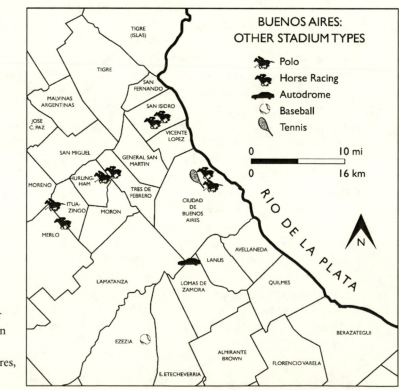

Map 5.2 Nonsoccer stadiums in Greater Buenos Aires, 2008

ideologies and class-based behavioral norms. In what follows, I examine the social and urban geographies of each stadium culture before comparing them in the context of class and conflict in early-twenty-first-century Buenos Aires.

Polo

Greater Buenos Aires has four major polo stadiums: Hurlingham Club, Campo de Polo Los Pinguinos, Club Militar de Polo San Jose, and Campo Argentino de Polo, also known as the "Temple of Polo." The largest, most public and well known of the four is the Campo Argentino de Polo, located on the Avenida Libertador, the main avenue that runs beside the Rio de la Plata in Buenos Aires. Inaugurated in 1928, the 30,000-capacity stadium is situated between the Jorge Newberry airport, the national racetrack, an expansive Lebanese–Argentine mosque complex, and the well-to-do residential neighborhood of Palermo. The stadium, owned by the Argentine military, sits on some of the most valuable land south of the Tropic of Capricorn and hosts the most prestigious event of the international polo circuit, the Argentine Open Polo Championship.[2]

Before exploring the geographic space of the stadium it will be instructive to begin with a brief history of polo in Argentina. Modern polo is a legacy of the British who began to play in colonial India in the 1860s after encountering it among local peoples. By the end of the nineteenth century, the British had introduced polo to Europe, Africa, the Caribbean, and North and South America. British expatriates played the first public game in Buenos Aires in 1884 on the infield of the 10,000-capacity horse-racing stadium of the Sociedad Sportiva. Despite its occasional appearance in the metropolis, polo matches at the turn of the twentieth century were not typically public events. The majority of practitioners were either in the military officer cadre or wealthy British landowners who played on their *estancias* in Buenos Aires and Santa Fe provinces.[3]

The processes of adaptation, hybridization, and identification with polo in Argentina are expertly documented by the anthropologist Eduardo Archetti.[4] Here it is sufficient to note that the British gradually lost institutional control as it was adapted and improved on by local players and highly skilled *pesiteros* (horsemen and trainers). The equestrian culture of the *gaucho* (romanticized cowboy figure of the Argentine pampas) augmented the appeal of polo, linking it to the traditional sport of *pato*.[5] The geographic expansion and subsequent adaptation of polo contributed to a hybridized national identity, taking the "natural" horsemanship of the Argentine gaucho and imbuing it with aristocratic, European airs. Polo was

Palermo Polo Grounds and Environs, Buenos Aires

Map 5.3
Palermo Polo
Grounds and
environs

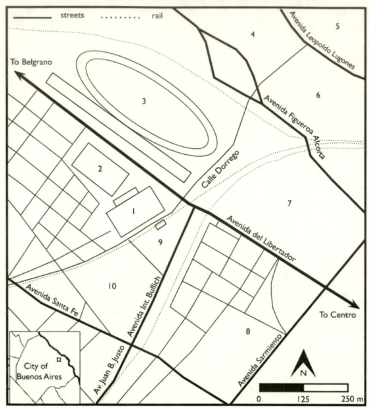

1 Palermo Polo Grounds, Field One
2 Palermo Polo Grounds, Field Two
3 Hippodromo Argentino
4 Planetarium
5 Domestic Airport

6 University Club of Buenos Aires
7 Park Space
8 U.S. Embassy
9 Islamic Cultural Center
10 First Infantry Headquarters

Photo 5.1 Palermo Polo Grounds, looking across field 2 to the southeast

Photo 5.2 Palermo Polo Grounds, looking across field 1 to the northwest

Photo 5.3 Palermo Polo Grounds seating section, main grandstand. The steeply inclined seats cost between $60 and $100 pesos; those on the other side of the field are $15 pesos.

the province of British and Argentine upper classes and became a nationalist symbol that fused cosmopolitan notions of modernity with the mythic, rural, and populist origins of the *gaucho*.

The introduction of polo to the Argentine army in 1894 as an exercise for the cavalry consolidated its early association with Argentine national identity. In 1908 a directive from the president instated polo as a mandatory practice for cavalry regiments, and for the next half a century military teams competed in open tournaments.[6] We can hypothesize that the associations between polo and military life served to structure a more generalized association between the sport and a masculine national identity. Polo, much as the military and the nation, became a repository of masculine ideologies. It is therefore likely that "unequivocal interpretations of masculinity and its attendant ideologies of heterosexism, sexism and homophobia" characterized political, social, and martial arenas while the practice of polo solidified their geographic networks.[7]

Whereas soccer developed almost exclusively as an urban sport, polo continued to be the sport of *estanceros* (wealthy landowners), who also wielded significant political influence in national government. One effect of polo's restrictive geographic and economic requirements was that the growth of polo clubs among the landholding elite and the expansion of polo within military ranks positioned the game as the preferred participatory sport of the Argentine ruling classes. The intermarriage of important landholding families helped to consolidate political power on a national level.[8] Not coincidentally, most of these families fielded polo teams. In addition to controlling the country, these families had the political power to control the rules of competition, the financial resources to create the best horses, and the leisure time to produce the best players. Despite the centrality of *estancias* to the development of the sport, polo became an important part of urban public culture in that it represented a "civilized" spectacle where the stadium functioned as a site and symbol of modernity and metropolitan (read: European) sophistication.

Argentine polo players took the raw material of the sport and adapted and improved on it until there developed a definable style to their play that was popularly understood to reflect the national character. This style, identified and propagated by the national press, was consolidated in particular times and places, such as when an Argentine team traveled to England in 1922, winning all of their contests. Even though the team was composed of players with English surnames, they represented an *estilo criollo*, or hybridized style, that confirmed a particular image of Argentine polo and of Argentina both at home and abroad.[9] The international successes of Argentine polo players made it that much easier to link the sport with the nation.

The two times (1924, 1928) that polo featured in the Olympics, Argentina won the gold medal. Since then Argentina has continued to produce the best polo horses, players, and teams in the world. Each one of these components is popularly attributed to the unique characteristics that derive from the cultural and geographic conditions of Argentina: the unflinching skill and bravado of the *pesiteros* and the large estancias of the pampas, which provide a symbolic and problematic connection of the provinces to the dominant capital city.[10] Following the building of the Palermo Polo Grounds in 1928, these identities and associations have been publicly performed and disseminated in the space of the stadium.

That polo continues to be an upper-class pursuit is confirmed by attending the Argentine Open Championships at the Palermo Polo Grounds.[11] The expansive grounds are ringed by wrought iron gates that bear the date and place of their manufacture: Liverpool, 1927. The stadium grounds are the headquarters for the Argentine cavalry and veterinary schools. Among the well-dressed crowd at the ticket windows, one is as likely to hear English and French as Spanish, confirming the international appeal of an event broadcast to 130 countries. Tickets for the main stand cost anywhere from 40 to 100 pesos (US$13–$33) and the entrance to the stands is marked by an oversized Rolex watch. Tickets for the long, ivy-covered bleachers on the south side of the stadium are relatively affordable at 15 pesos (US$5). The discrepancy in prices quickly separates socioeconomic groups.

Inside the stadium a veritable feast of consumerism takes place along tree-lined paths. Well-dressed women pass out samples of *yerba mate*, ESPN key chains, and pamphlets for Movicom, the Argentine subsidiary of Bell South. A large sign advertises a recent event: "El Ejercito con los chicos," the military with the children. Behind the goals at both ends of the stadium are large billboards advertising ESPN, Schweppes, Avis, Rolex, Stella Artois, Peugeot, Movicom–Bell South, MasterCard, *La Nación* (a conservative newspaper), and Pirelli, with the ominous English subhead, "Power is nothing without control." Behind the main stand, corporate sponsors set up tents to sell their wares. Young women beckon customers to subscribe to *La Nación*, buy Motorola phones, or try Stella Artois beer. There is also a store to buy the accoutrements of polo: shirts ($200 pesos), boots ($325 pesos), helmets ($150 pesos), *tacos* (mallets). Next to a display for the Llao Llao Hotel and Resort (US$200 per day) is a diminutive display for the Fundación de Alimientos de Buenos Aires (Food Bank of Buenos Aires) announcing the success of their milk donation project: 7,180 glasses. Underneath the bleachers are the headquarters of the Argentine Polo Association (APA), which leases office space from the military.

Polo is the fastest nonmotorized team sport in the world. Thundering hooves and thousands of pounds cover an immense playing space: 275 by 182 meters. The horses know the rules of the game as well as their riders. Highly trained and powerfully explosive, they are not for the casual rider at between $50,000 and $300,000 each. At this level players use between four and five horses a game and have fifteen or more in their stables. Some *estancias* maintain Web sites that catalogue the horses owned by the players.[12] This is a display of family wealth, grown in the pampas and exercised in the metropolis.

Binoculars are a must for polo, and many fans bring theirs to the stadium. High heels are common, as are large purses, jewelry, and expensive sunglasses—accoutrements that are ill advised at soccer stadiums. The police presence is minimal as the security risk is low. There is a sense of appreciation for the truly exceptional level of play. The crowd basks in the sun, applauds at the appropriate times, while here and there shouts of encouragement get swallowed up by the vast space of the field. A black banner with a red star taped to the top of the long stands reads: "Indios Chapeleufú II: Iglio Avela Presente." Chapeleufú I and II are the names of the Heguy family teams that competed for the 2004 Campeonato Abierto trophy and refers to the department of the province of La Pampa where their *estancia* sits. Chapeleufú is a name dripping with irony as it is taken from an indigenous ethnic group extinguished during the cavalry-driven genocidal wars of national consolidation at the end of the nineteenth century.

After a game punctuated with rolling applause and dramatic intakes of breath, fans in the cheap seats push aside low metal barriers and cross the field of play, making their way to the main stand. No one prevents them from doing this. Horses at full gallop cover these distances with ease, and walking across the grass gives one a sense of the relationship between bounded space and horsepower that defines the sport. More, by entering onto the field of play, spectators gain an uncommon sense of connectedness with the event and the space of the stadium. This connection partially dissolves notions of social hierarchy, integrating everyone into a consuming collective, allowing a freedom of association and movement that is dangerous, even deadly, in soccer stadiums. This is a secure world, buffered from the violence that characterizes Buenos Aires: a simulacrum of the comfortable, consumerist reality to which the middle classes aspire and the upper classes live.

The clothes, grooming, and general appearance of the polo crowd gathering behind the main stand give an impression of vitality and prosperity. This is the place to see and be seen while checking out the latest consumer

Photo 5.4 Players on horseback, Palermo Polo Grounds

Photo 5.5 $100 peso note. The relationship between the landholding class and the military in Argentina is partly expressed through polo. The pose of General Roca and his cavalry troops at the end of the "Conquest of the Desert" is not fundamentally different from that struck by polo players in the previous photo.

goods, making arrangements for that night's parties, or brushing shoulders with European royalty.[13] The daily struggles that define life for the majority of Argentines appear to be absent. Police are nowhere to be seen, the Rolex watches keep time, and $100 peso notes fill the corporate coffers.

Rugby

O rganized rugby in Argentina began in the 1870s, around the same time as soccer and polo. Again, it was the British who brought it to South American shores, but its diffusion was much more limited than that of soccer and its nationalist associations much more modest than polo. Rugby requires an open, grassy field adequate for tackling, long kicks, and lateral passing. This impeded its informal practice in dense urban areas and reduced its exposure to a general audience.

Throughout most of the twentieth century, rugby maintained its limited social and geographic positioning, namely that of the upper middle and upper classes in the private middle and high schools. As the wealthy moved out of the urban core, rugby went with them, and until quite recently the sport has been almost completely limited to the suburban Zona Norte. Until its professionalization in the mid-1990s, only the wealthy had enough leisure time to excel on an international level and cultural associations with the sport did not cut across class lines.[14] The institutional amateurism of the Unión Argentina de Rugby (UAR) encouraged many of the best Argentine players to move to European leagues where they gained valuable professional experience.

The sixth-place finish of Los Pumas, the nickname for the national rugby team, in the 1999 World Cup greatly increased media coverage and popular exposure to the sport. Now, rugby competes with basketball for the status of second most popular team sport in Argentina. Before 1999 there was no attempt to popularize rugby within Argentina through the media because there was not a sense of successful nationalist accomplishment that would draw a broader audience (thus generating more money for advertisers). While rugby is played in the major cities of Argentina and is expanding in popularity, its practice remains the province of the suburban upper middle and upper classes.[15]

A remarkable element of rugby's contemporary geography in Buenos Aires is that there are no major rugby-specific stadiums. While there are dozens of *fields* in the Zona Norte (and a scattered few in the South and West), some with capacities for thousands of spectators, for international matches the UAR leases a soccer stadium in the City of Buenos Aires.[16]

International rugby has what are called "test matches" that pit national

Estadio José Almaritani and Environs, Buenos Aires

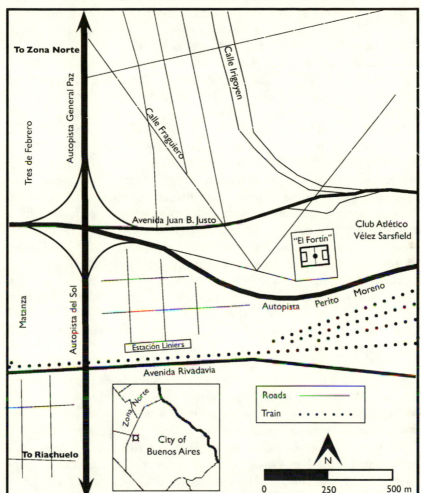

Map 5.4 Velez and environs, Buenos Aires. The Velez stadium is proximate to major transportation lines leading the middle- and upper-middle-class spectators back to the northern residential zones.

squads against each other in an environment that has little competitive meaning. Similar to "friendlies" in international soccer, test matches usually occur in the months leading up to a major international tournament. Beginning in 1932 with the visit of South Africa's national team and continuing into the 1970s and 1980s, the UAR most frequently leased the 24,000-capacity soccer stadium of Ferrocarril Oeste, located in Caballito, a middle-class club in the geographic center of the Ciudad de Buenos Aires. During the 1990s, the UAR shifted to the stadium of Velez Sarsfield or that of River Plate, both located at the outer edges of the City of Buenos Aires. In the twenty-first century the UAR appears to have settled on the Velez Sarsfield stadium as their "national ground." These stadiums were chosen for a variety of functional and representational characteristics that have to do with the social and cultural history of Buenos Aires, transportation infrastructure, and socioeconomic residential patterns.[17]

For instance, it is improbable that a rugby match would be contested in the stadiums of the Racing Club, San Lorenzo de Almargo, Huracán, or Boca Juniors even though they are some of the largest in the city. These stadiums are too far from the residential zones of rugby practitioners and spectators and are situated in zones of the urban matrix associated with lower socioeconomic classes. The middle- to upper-middle-class sensibilities of Caballito residents and members of Ferrocarril Oeste made their stadium a logical choice from the 1930s to the 1980s. As the middle and upper classes moved out of the city center for the Zona Norte, access to transportation lines, proximity to upper-class residential zones, and size and functionality became the primary characteristics for choosing a stadium. The River Plate stadium is on the northern edge of the City of Buenos Aires and that of Vélez Sarsfield on the western edge, both proximate to major transportation lines leading to the Zona Norte.

The presence of rugby in a soccer stadium dramatically transforms the sense of place typically associated with the stadium, as well as the semiotic codes, behavioral norms, and relationship of fans to police forces. While soccer, rugby, and polo are clearly commercial events, rugby is notable for the dominant presence of two foreign, corporate sponsors: Visa and Heineken. Rugby is the only sport in Argentina that allows its corporate sponsors to paint their iconography on the field of play. By claiming the field as a corporate domain, the entire event (spectators included) becomes associated with the symbols and values of the corporations, which have as their end goal the continued consumption of material goods. In this case Heineken represents a refined, expensive European taste that exists in opposition to the perception of the national taste as common (especially because the "national" beer, Quilmes, is strongly associated with the Argentine soccer team) and Visa represents a consumerist model with which many of the fans are very familiar. Ironically, yet sensibly, Argentine law prohibits the sale of alcohol in stadiums. In the same way that neighborhood banners represent the geographic identity of the soccer fan, the logos and symbols of the companies that sponsor rugby can be understood to represent the identities of its fans. These corporate logos are emblems of

Photo 5.6 Television at Velez. An enormous television screen is mounted on scaffolding at a Pumas test match.

Photo 5.7 A young man looking back at the television screen. When a large television is inserted into a stadium, it changes the behavior of spectators. Here a young man dressed in the national team shirt looks back at the television screen as the action happens in front of him. He is also striking the "hang on the fence" pose more characteristic of soccer stadiums.

a privileged minority associated with social and economic resources, a capacity for conspicuous consumption in an impoverished society, and a general sense of possession more than active participation.

Another important element of the rugby experience that transforms the soccer stadium is the temporary installation of a jumbo television screen. Most stadiums in Argentina are fairly minimalist; few have functioning scoreboards, and none have the large screens that Europeans and North Americans are accustomed to. Consistent with stadiums in other parts of the world, the live broadcast of events happening on the field of play shifts the fan from active participant to passive observer. The valorization of the stadium experience through television is revealed as a socioeconomic predilection in rugby. Television effectively transforms the traditional minimalist, participatory space of the Velez Sarsfield stadium into a space of passive leisure in the North American, Asian, or European mold. The effective redoubling of time and collapsing of space that instant replay brings to the stadium creates a more passive audience because it partly re-creates the comfortable home environment and conveys an illusion of power over the events on the field.

There is some evidence that rugby culture is changing to include a more active and passionate fan base. During a December 2004 test match against France, fans unfurled a huge Argentine flag emblazoned with a puma and "VISA", lit flares, and chanted as if they were at a soccer game. The group was small but very loud relative to the rest of the crowd. Their behavior was strangely in place *and* out of place. Their exuberant chanting, already spatially linked to the codes and practices of the soccer stadium, was a stark contrast to the more passive participation of the majority. The "soccerization" of the rugby crowd is evidence of its expanding popularity, which in turn is the result of increased media exposure that is positioning rugby as a more generalized expression of Argentine nationalism.

The lack of visible urban referents for rugby in Buenos Aires places the sport outside of mainstream culture. Although there are exceptions to the rule, rugby players are born and bred in the well-heeled neighborhoods of the Zona Norte, attend private schools in the British mode, and spend most of their rugby lives outside of the dense matrix of the City of Buenos Aires. They may tend to have a different vision of Argentina than those who do not have an interest in the sport. However limited, there is evidence to suggest that rugby has a central role in the idea of Argentina for its fans.

In March 2003, as the United States was conjuring reasons to invade Iraq, Los Pumas began an intensive training regimen with the Argentine Navy in preparation for the World Cup. The UAR invited the press to the "basic training"; the public was stunned by pictures of Los Pumas dressed in camouflage, wielding rifles, and crawling under barbed wire. The media reaction was predictably strong: "In an atmosphere full of the smoke of war, it appears that these are fragments of images from a nightmare that reinforces the physical force of elite athletes. Is it really necessary that the rugby players dress in combat gear? Is it really an opportune time for the UAR to diffuse these images now?"[18]

The UAR saw nothing unusual about the timing or the association of rugby players with the military as the drums of war were first fabricated, then beaten in Washington. Emilio Perasso, director of the UAR stated, "It is something we have been planning for months; we can't anticipate what is going to happen in the world. If they were playing rugby they would be wearing rugby shirts, but since they are doing this survival work they need military uniforms." A former Puma disagreed: "The team has a lot of problems in the scrums, the lines and scoring and this is not going to get fixed by participating in a *reality show*. It's also not the best time to be playing at soldier. Today a friend asked me if they were preparing to go to the Gulf."[19]

It is difficult to determine whether those in charge of the UAR were giving their tacit approval for war in Iraq or if they displayed a profound ignorance of symbolic relationships. Whatever one's opinion of the event, there is an indisputable coziness between the UAR and the Argentine military. The associations between rugby and the military were also underscored in the pregame presentation of a military band at a 2004 test match against France. As we shall see, it is nearly impossible that a similar presentation would occur at a soccer game.

Soccer

Attending a soccer game in Buenos Aires can be one of the most spectacular and vibrant urban experiences in the world. The pageantry and passion of the fans is matched by intense, physical, and highly skilled competition. Even lower division games are highly charged affairs with thousands of spectators waving flags, lighting flares, chanting, jumping, singing, and climbing barbed wire fences, as well as threatening rival groups and clashing with the police. Between 2003 and 2007 the national leagues were suspended on three occasions due to security concerns. Stadiums are closed with increasing frequency, and teams whose fans are considered too dangerous are forced to play matches behind closed doors, or at other stadiums. Violence is an ever-present, elemental aspect that is incorporated into the infrastructure and social organization of the city's sixty-four soccer stadiums. In the previous chapter we explored the origins of this violence as a product of competing masculinities. In what follows, we will examine the escalation and perpetuation of stadium violence as one outcome of shifting, historically situated social networks that bond stadiums to the larger society and vice versa. The overwhelming popularity of soccer in Argentina makes it impossible to describe these networks in their entirety, but by grounding this study in the space of the stadium, we can evaluate them in the spaces where they most frequently and dramatically intersect.

Like many of the stadiums in Rio de Janeiro, stadiums in Greater Buenos Aires are the property of social clubs. The clubs range widely in size, location, resources, and membership demographics. The stadium and the soccer team are the most public manifestations of the social club and are responsible for bringing in the majority of club receipts through cable television contracts, corporate sponsorship, the sale of players, championship royalties, and ticket revenue. The size and condition of a club's stadium is a direct reflection of its wealth and/or history. Membership in these independent clubs is open to the general public, and many offer a range of services in the *sede social*, or social center. *Socios* pay monthly membership dues and are granted access to the club's varied sporting, social, and educational resources. Some social centers such as those at Boca Juniors, River Plate, Ferrocarril Oeste, and Independiente are located next to or within their respective stadiums and provide tennis courts, swimming pools, dining rooms, and meeting space. Historically, many clubs have had to move their stadiums away from their *sede social* because of the high property values and demand for space within the City of Buenos Aires.

From their beginnings, soccer clubs and their stadiums played a central role in the social and political life in the neighborhoods in which they were formed. These historical relationships between clubs, local political figures, and national government have meant that stadiums generate and consolidate economic and political power. Because of their centrality in barrio life, stadiums became places for local politicians to gain visibility and to secure a solid voting bloc. Because club directors are democratically elected, becoming a club director is a political process in its own right that frequently results in involvement in the larger political world of Buenos Aires.[20]

Following the professionalization of Argentine soccer in 1931, the importance of the clubs in the economic and political spheres increased. Investing in stadium infrastructure, expanding the social club, and traveling abroad became ways of increasing a club's exposure and revenue.[21] While the clubs continued to be run by amateur, democratically elected directors, the economic and political influence of the clubs further centralized soccer in the cultural life of neighborhoods and the city at large.

Clubs associated with influential political figures could count on their financial assistance in building or improving their stadiums. This clientelism reached an apogee during Peron's first presidency when most of the city's major clubs had *padrinos* (godfathers) in high government positions. The rash of stadiums built with state sponsorship in the 1940s and 1950s is directly attributable to the relationships between national politicians and clubs.[22]

By the 1950s and 1960s the economic potential of soccer was beginning to dictate the management practices of club directors. The advent of televised games and the increase of high-value player transfers to European teams bolstered clubs' finances. This further encouraged the involvement of local political figures, and a club directorship was frequently a path to riches and a means of consolidating political power. In the local community, clubs augmented their neighborhood-based membership by expanding recreational and social facilities. As soccer grew on local, national, and global scales, these neighborhood-based clubs acquired more wealth and exercised more influence over their locales, which had the added effect of increasing local identification with teams and stadiums. Many clubs based development programs for young soccer players on European models, and, in the 1970s, larger clubs began to take responsibility for the education of their up-and-coming soccer stars.

During the military dictatorship of 1976–1983, clubs functioned as a bastion of democracy in a totalitarian environment. These civic entities provided some of the few spaces of free political association. And while there is not much empirical evidence to corroborate the idea, it is possible that social clubs were the loci of organized resistance to the military regime. On the other hand, it is widely suspected that the military regime used the *barrabravas* to organize against the Madres de Plaza de Mayo and to chant pro-government slogans during the 1978 World Cup.[23] The implication is that stadium cultures exercised an important political role in the production and contestation of public space.

Today the democratically elected leaders of clubs continue to be powerful social, economic, and political actors at the local and national levels. For instance, the president of Boca Juniors, Mauricio Macri, ran for the mayorship of Buenos Aires on the platform that he would be able to transform the city economically just as he had done with his private businesses and with Boca Juniors. Although he lost the 2003 election, he was successful in 2007. Macri has used the popularity of Boca Juniors to consolidate his political power and was a potential candidate of the center-right party in the 2007 presidential elections. The president of Chacarita Juniors, Luis Barrionuevo, is also a senator in the national congress and on one occasion refused to answer the questions of a federal judge regarding violence in soccer because he claimed he was being persecuted by former president Menem.[24]

Macri, Barrionuevo, and others like them are often long-standing members of the clubs they head and have a vested personal interest in their sporting, economic, and political successes. The involvement of high-level political figures in the running of social clubs, soccer teams, and stadiums frequently involves conflicts of interests, claims of corruption, and a lack of transparency in local and national governance.[25] This lack of transparency positions stadiums, as the most public and most profitable element of clubs, as sources of political influence on a national level.[26] There is growing concern that while many clubs are falling inextricably into debt, in part due to stadium violence, the directors are maintaining their wealth and privilege at the clubs' expense, a situation many see as a reflection of Argentine society at large.

If we look at what happens in the stadium as an allegory or metaphor for the larger society, some startling similarities appear. Stadiums were an integral component of modernity and industrialization and, in addition to reflecting national economic development, carried messages of hope and social progress. The rise of the import substitution industrialization (ISI) economy, which replaced the importation of foreign goods by creating internal industries and a national consumer base, corresponded with a spate of stadium building, abetted by prominent political figures. Beginning in the mid-1960s, the inability to manufacture expensive foreign goods marked the decline of the ISI model, which in turn spurred the emergence of military dictatorships. The repressive social climate of the dictatorships that left stadiums as some of the few venues for open resistance led to their becoming increasingly violent. This led to a militarization of stadiums and public space to meet the violent response of the disenfranchised to socioeconomic insecurity and political disenfranchisement. Far from being spaces of hope, stadiums became spaces of last resort, especially after other public spaces in the city were closed to open discourse. Thus the increase in soccer violence was a direct result of the decline of ISI and the rise of dictatorships. The implementation of violence as a response to political and economic instability is nothing new in Latin America, and stadiums are good barometers of social equilibrium.

During the 1990s, the historically situated identities that clubs represented appeared to be in crisis at the same time that their cultural centrality increased disproportionately. The Argentine sociologist Pablo Alabarces has suggested that this paradoxical crisis was a product of the explosion in the mediums of communication that displaced entrenched notions of class and substituted national popular culture with international popular culture. In this process, soccer, a fundamental object of global culture, has tended to amplify its limits of representation among all classes. However, in the same way that soccer has expanded its economic, geographic, and social reach, it has produced mechanisms of exclusion. The neoliberal regimes of the 1990s expelled large numbers of people from the market and increased socioeconomic disparities. The increased costs of tickets (and the cost of cable television) eliminated the traditional public from the stadium in droves, leaving the space to groups more intent on producing spectacle and participating in open conflict than watching a rule-governed contest.[27]

Following the economic and political crisis of December 2001, club membership began to decline precipitously as people cut back on expenses. Stadium violence escalated, with multiple deaths and scores of critical injuries in the early months of 2002. The devaluation of the Argentine peso effectively tripled the cost of membership, and the middle-class base of most clubs dwindled. Although club memberships have begun to rebound, the income from membership dues has not allowed smaller clubs to extricate themselves from grave financial difficulties. The financial association between soccer's governing institutions and mass-media outlets penalizes smaller clubs that compete in lower divisions. In order to make ends meet, small clubs must sell their best players to larger clubs, which then sell them to European, Mexican, or Brazilian clubs for millions of dollars. Smaller clubs with limited media exposure and player development programs have trouble paying the limited salaries of their players or maintaining their stadiums. This is consistent with the declining economic conditions of smaller clubs throughout Latin America and Europe.

Regardless of their financial condition, social clubs continue to be the locus of very powerful identity constructions for millions of people in Argentina. Routed through the soccer team and stadium, these identities are based in a number of different arenas: historical, familial, national, class, ethnic, neighborhood, and labor. Club loyalties form an integral part of personal identity in Argentina. Instead of saying one likes a team or is a fan of a team, one uses the immutable verb *ser*, to be. This implies that club affiliation is as unchangeable as gender, labor, national, or family identities.

Fan Hierarchies

There is a hierarchy of fandom in Argentina. The *barrabravas* occupy the top of the pyramid. As opposed to *simpatizantes* (sympathizers) or *hinchas* (literally, "someone who is pumped up"), *barrabravas* are professional fans and occupy a "reserved" space in the stadium. The term *barrabrava* is used to identify both individuals and the group, a semantic condition that conflates the two in the popular imagination. *Barrabravas* are the most powerful and visible elements of stadium culture in Argentina and are widely considered the most organized and violent fan groups in the world.

The *barrabravas* first came to prominence in the mid-1960s during a time of increased political violence in Argentina and represented the trib-alization of soccer supporters.[28] They became the loci of strong identity formations for socially, politically, and economically marginalized youth. In a hostile political environment that limited free association in public space, the traditionally carnivalesque environment of the stadium became a site of violent struggle between the state and disenfranchised members of society. In a very short time, the *barrabravas* developed symbiotic relation-ships with the clubs who came to depend on them for intra- and interclub political rivalries, economic stability through labor for the club, and pride in having the most vocal, colorful, and passionate group of supporters. Combined with the historical formations explored in the previous chapter, the increasing marginalization of large segments of the population and, the deterritorialization of the city as a whole, the stadium became one of the last bastions of social agency for hundreds of thousands of young men.[29]

A club director maintains political and economic, but not social, rela-tions with his *barrabrava*.[30] The *barrabravas* are hierarchical organizations of young, economically and socially disenfranchised men who are paid by the club in a variety of ways. Some members are given fictitious jobs in the companies of club directors, others are given tickets to sell on game days, while others have relationships with the stewards of the clubs and collect money from ticketless spectators who are then slid under the turnstiles. The *barrabrava* can also act in a more sinister fashion in the service of the club directors by disrupting rival club directors' businesses, causing politi-cal disruptions, or engaging in violent acts against rival *barrabravas* and the police. They are professional fans, operating within an institution of their own creation, financed by club management to act in their service.

Barrabravas wield disproportionate influence over the decisions and internal politics of the club and on occasion extract payment from coaches and players in return for their public support in the stadium. In November 2006 the *barrabrava* of Gimnasia de La Plata threatened to shoot their play-ers in the legs if they did not *lose* a game against Boca Juniors so that their city rivals Estudiantes de la Plata would not claim first place in the national league.[31] Some have suggested that because of their connections with club directors much of the activity of the *barrabravas* outside of the stadiums is politically motivated, adding an unpredictable and disruptive element to local and national politics.[32]

Relationships between club leaders and their *barrabravas* are very guarded, primarily because they involve national political figures and insti-tutionalized violence. Because of this it is unlikely that the details of the relationships between them will ever be fully brought to light. However, it is clear that the relationships between the clubs and their *barrabravas* are complex, paradoxical, and likely reflect the clientelistic networks that define politics in the city at large. The Argentine historian Juan Sebreli notes that the *barrabravas* of the 1970s were "ductile elements manipulated by totalitarian political interests that knew how to exploit juvenile anxieties."[33] It is unlikely that this situation has changed in recent years, especially with the expanded televisual reach of stadium events that amplifies the power and reach of the *barras*.

The clubs can not completely control the *barrabravas* because of the political, economic, and social weight that fandom carries in Argentina. It is a point of pride among club directors and fans to have a large, supportive *barrabrava* that can produce spectacles both in the home stadium and on the road. Clubs compete among each other in several spheres: on the field, economically, politically, and in the terraces. These competitions can be understood as metaphors for larger social struggles wherein large, organized, historically dominant social groups exercise control over smaller, vulnerable, but fiercely defended, neighborhood organizations.

Despite their apparent influence over players, coaches, and the internal function of clubs, the *barrabravas* are dependent on the space of the stadium to manifest their identities in public. Frequently, the only recourse to limiting their power is to close the stadiums and play games with no public or obtain injunctions limiting the ability of certain individuals to attend games. The *barrabrava* has a vested interest in maintaining the social order that permits the successful staging of sport while acknowledging through its actions that this very system creates the conditions of marginalization against which they are (unconsciously) protesting. It is fairly certain that the *barrabravas* are not actively aware of these paradoxes, as one rarely sees textual signs of political protest in the stadiums unless it has to do with retaking the Falkland Islands (Islas Malvinas) from Great Britain. The messages displayed on terrace banners have more to do with localized geographic identity, dedication to rock and roll, alcohol, cocaine, and marijuana, or vitriol aimed at the principal rivals of the club. The only political clout the *barrabravas* appear to exercise (consciously) is in the mutually dependent context of their clubs.

A *barrabrava* is a patriarchal, paramilitary society with specific codes, masculine norms, behaviors, and modes of accruing status within the group. There is a strict division of labor within the *barrabrava*: the youth rise up through the ranks by stealing the banners of opposing *barras*, showing courage in battle, stealing cars, or fighting with other ascendant members. Within this division of labor there are specific liaisons with the media, the police, and club management. Some members are purportedly involved in drug trafficking, others with the organization and production of group spectacle in the stands, and others are involved with arranging local, national, continental, and international transportation.

The constitution of a *barrabrava* membership is dependent on the team and its location within the city. Many individual *barrabrava* have little education and very limited economic opportunities.[34] Their marginalization limits social and economic agency, which, in a patriarchic and capitalist society, is a threat to their masculinity. Although the *barrabravas* have many middle-class members, the impoverished majority organize their lives around the one element of society in which they can be publicly seen, heard, felt, and understood: soccer. In this male-dominated world, women are almost wholly absent and cannot occupy *barra* space in the stands unless they are accompanied by male members.[35]

The loyalty commanded by *barra* leaders is very strong, and they engender cults of personality, which responds to ascendant members' desire to strengthen individual identity and strategic connections within the group. Though it has not been documented in Buenos Aires, we know from studies in other Latin American countries and North American urban gangs that there are initiation rites that youth must pass through in order to gain acceptance.[36] Once one has entered into the world of the *barrabrava* it is very difficult to leave. As one of my informants reported, "They were like a family to me. We ate together, went out together, and fought together. I was afraid that I was never going to get out, and I think the only way to make a clean break is to get married and start a family of your own. That's what I did and I can never go back."

For the *barrabrava*, socioeconomic marginalization is to a large degree reversed within the social structure of the stadium, as they command as much attention as the players on the field. In this sense their actions in the stadium (augmented through media) provide public agency in ways otherwise denied them. It is in this guise that stadium-centered violence demonstrates frustration with marginality, as well as produces an alternative social hierarchy. The stadium is the medium for the expression of those sentiments. The violence of the *barrabravas*, however, is distinct from the political violence that periodically shook Buenos Aires in the first years of the twenty-first century. For the *barrabrava*, the stadium may function as a refuge from the symbolic and structural impacts of neoliberal economic regimes and globalization. By offering a nonmodern refuge of strongly felt and vibrantly experienced collective identity, the *barras* offer a meaningful alternative to the increasingly harsh economic and social realities of Buenos Aires and Argentina.

The relationships among the scores of *barrabravas* in Buenos Aires are historically and geographically complex. The communal representations of the teams do not extend equally to the whole city but pertain to micro-communities associated with neighborhood stadiums. In recent years an overly generalized discourse has developed in relation to these micro-spaces within the city, associating certain zones with crime and danger, others with wealth and refinement. The barrio and club has become (for *hinchas* and *barrabravas*) a moral and spiritual reserve, an area of decon-tamination and a space constructed as a reserve of the local in the face of tensions associated with accelerated globalization and the changing dynamics of the city-space. Youth groups are more likely to assume this discourse and produce a metonym between the neighborhood, stadium, and notions of authenticity. That which is more local is considered more authentic, less commercialized, and less subject to the mercantile logics of global industrial culture.[37] When that authentic and territorial identity is threatened, as it is during every scheduled game of the soccer season, its defense frequently turns violent. As a lived experience, this provides a level of intensity that is removed from the clean logic of words.

There is an imaginary ranking among the *barras* that is considered a reflection of the relative masculine power that each *barra* wields. Those who are more violent or who support their teams with more observable passion rise up the ranking. They know that print and television media amplify their actions in the stadium and on the urban battlefield. In this ranking violent confrontations with the police bring the biggest number of points.[38] Some *barras* become known by the weapons they use: rubber mallets at San Lorenzo, group pummeling at Huracán, and umbrellas at Independiente.[39] Other *barras* are known for their loyalty, creativity, or strong organization. The competitions also extend beyond physical battles into the realm of spectacle production; the *barra* that can produce the wit-tiest and most creative display rises in the ranking even if they are not too good with their fists.

The word used to describe the level of toughness and dedication of soc-cer supporters is *aguante*, defined as both suffering patience and forceful vigor. This word can also be defined as an ability to act in space. The *barras* need to have the *aguante* to support their teams through defeat and defend the stadium and neighborhood through physical strength and symbolic actions such as graffiti.[40] This defense and conquest of territory involves strong organization, physical force and skill in street fighting, and the cun-ning to steal rivals' banners, as well as modes of intimidation that happen through chants, gestures, feints, and bodily movement in and around the stadiums. Through these codes and behaviors the *barras* show that they are ready for battle, that they have more *aguante* than their rivals. In many cases battles are won and lost through intimidation without necessitating

Photo 5.8 Mural at Estadio Islas Malvinas. This mural depicts some of the elements of "Aguante": strength, carnivalesque, luck, alcohol, drugs, rock and roll.

Photo 5.9 Bin Laden es de Sacachispas. Many of the *barrabravas* in Buenos Aires invoke Osama bin Laden on signs, murals, and graffiti. Bin Laden is taken to be the ultimate expression of callous violence—the fans adopt him as one of their own.

Photo 5.10 Foucault supports All Boys. The Estadio Islas Malvinas of Club Atlético All Boys resembles a prison as much as a place of leisure.

Photo 5.11 "They are watching us from heaven." Fallen members of the Argentinos Juniors' *barrabrava* are memorialized on the side of Estadio Diego Armando Maradona. Tellingly, there is a dot left after Mario Molina, anticipating the next name.

the hand-to-hand battle of the streets.[41] Friendships and antagonisms between *barras* are historically situated, yet shift according to present needs and values. It is not uncommon for *barras* that are on friendly terms to gather before their games to share a cookout.[42] In these instances the police are informed that they do not need a strong presence at the stadium.

Ironically, the *barrabravas* do not perceive themselves to be violent actors. Rather, they are forced into a position of acting violently against the "system." This narrative of victimization places their violent actions in a passive framework. They act, not unreasonably, as if they are barred from society and the only place they can express unquestionable authority is in the stadium. Any attempt to infringe on their right to act as they please in this space is met with a violent response. The internal hegemony of the terraces is echoed by the external coercion of the state.

The role of the Internet, television, radio, and print media in producing and projecting stadium identities has augmented in recent years. The proliferation of cable television has heightened the exposure of soccer, which has also led to an increase in print media coverage of sport. Soccer is front-page news every day. The availability of nearly constant soccer programming on television and exhaustive coverage in the daily press, coupled with an increase in violence in and around the stadium, has convinced many middle- and upper-class people to watch matches from the security of home or local bars and cafés. The more middle-class people stay away from the stadiums, the more they are likely to consume the performances of soccer teams and their *barrabravas* via television. This is not lost on the *barrabravas*, who stage elaborate, well-scripted performances that function to show up the other fan groups and to demonstrate their capacity for organizing impressive visual spectacles to local, national, and international audiences.[43] It is possible that many of these performances are designed and staged with the amplifying effect of the media in mind.

Although no one would assert that ritualized stadium violence is an acceptable societal norm, there is little mention in the daily press that this violence is a product of socioeconomic and political marginality. When soccer games turn deadly or result in the suspension of games, the attention is focused on the symptoms and not the causes of the violence. This implies a toleration of violence within certain bounds that recognizes the "need" for social expression of this kind. In a highly masculine culture with a long history of state-sponsored violence, the Argentine press does not give the impression that the combative norms of the stadium are conceptually or functionally aberrant but should be tolerated within certain bounds. Because stadiums are loci for the acting out of a larger social problem, the root causes of that violence are rarely addressed in public dis-

course. As we have seen, this violence had its origins in the gendered production of public space and in the larger socioeconomic and political situation of the country.

Soccer violence is considered in a different light from the urban political violence that has periodically gripped Buenos Aires since the 1950s.
Journalists and academics have focused on the latter to the near-total
exclusion of the former, although one is a product of the other. The lack of
attention paid to the root causes of stadium-related violence is in part the
product of a generalized academic aloofness in regard to sport.[44] It may
also be true that using violence to create an alternative social order has a
long history in Argentina and is something not commonly connected with
the space of the stadium.

The history of violence between *barrabravas* and between *barrabravas*
and the police increases on a weekly basis with casualties on all sides. The
sixty-odd *barrabravas* in Buenos Aires describe a phenomenally complex
web of political, economic, geographic, historical, and sporting relationships that taken together constitute an indisputably powerful and spectacular element of urban culture. In general, we can assert that the network of
stadiums and associated spaces that comprise the soccer world of Buenos
Aires touches nearly every social sector and elides the distinctions between
the public and private realms. Imbued with notions of masculinity,
wrapped in a discourse of violence, and supported by powerful economic
and political forces, soccer stadiums in Buenos Aires provide a window
into the functioning of society at large.[45] By entering into Argentine society
through them, we are faced with the essential contradictions and paradoxes of the nation.

Conclusion

In Argentina violence exists in daily life, not just in soccer. The majority of
this violence takes the form of social exclusion, expulsion from the labor
market and consumption, and the deterioration of public health and education. Though it may appear from the actions of soccer fans that there are
tendencies for the general population to engage in violent actions, the historical record indicates that the upper classes are more inclined to use
deadly force.[46] The use of force has rarely been in the personal context of the
soccer fan but rather using the guns of the military and police to act in the
interests of capital accumulation and the consolidation of political power.

The different geographic and social spaces of polo, rugby, and soccer in
Buenos Aires delimit complex and intersecting discourses of masculinity,
national identity, class, power, and social identity. Polo and rugby are

strongly associated with suburban residential zones, cultures of consumerism, foreign tastes, and the Argentine military. In both of these sports, conflict is limited to competition between teams on the field of play and localized geographic identities appear to be trumped by class concerns. By contrast, soccer pertains to all social sectors and involves multilayered conflicts and contradictions that frequently boil over into violent acts both inside and outside the stadium. Even where there is no direct physical confrontation between fans or between fans and police, soccer stadiums are cauldrons of passion where masculine, class, ethnic, and geographic identities clash in ritualized combat. Soccer stadiums are designed to control the transgressive behavior of the fans and function as militarized spaces policed by the lethal agents of the state. It is not coincidental that the *barrabravas* draw their members from the most marginalized social sectors—those groups that are perceived to be the greatest threat to social stability. Thus patterns of class and conflict are expressed in soccer stadiums while patterns of class and contentedness are expressed in rugby and polo.

The functional and symbolic relationships between the state, the military, and class in Argentina are differentially expressed in polo, rugby, and soccer stadiums. At the Palermo Polo Grounds, the advertisement of a day for the "children and the military" signifies a comfortable relationship between polo fans and the military officer class in Argentina. This is not surprising given that the military is a wealthy and prestigious institution in Argentina. The children-and-the-military event is a sign that the historically close associations between Argentina's governing classes and the military continue to be solidified and performed through the practice and experience of polo at the Palermo Polo Grounds. That the Argentine military maintains its own polo stadium and is the owner of the Palermo Polo Grounds is further evidence of these associations.

Class conflict is not evident within the space of the polo stadium but is an implicit element of the culture and geography of the sport. Capitalism is inherently violent as it creates mechanisms of social and spatial exclusion that are enforced through the power of the state and the ordering of urban space. Because polo requires high levels of capital and extensive leisure time the stadium can be considered a symbol and locus of these exclusionary mechanisms. That the polo stadium is a site for the expression of capital accumulation, social privilege, and political power is beyond doubt. Competitions between polo fans happen in other social arenas, not in the stadium. The Palermo Polo Grounds are a node in a network of spaces where the governing classes of Argentina gather to celebrate their mutually assured victories.

In rugby the pregame presentations of military bands and the 2003 military training exercises of Los Pumas indicate similar relationships, although they are not as pervasive or historically situated. The relatively light police presence at international test matches stands in stark contrast to the overwhelming show of force in the same stadium for soccer games. During test matches, the militarized infrastructure (paddocks, fences topped with barbed wire, crush barriers) of the Velez Sarsfield soccer stadium is unnecessary to control a crowd that is not faced with significant numbers of opposing fans. The old adage that "rugby is a hooligans' game played by gentlemen and soccer is a gentlemen's game played by hooligans" speaks to the physical violence of rugby that precludes the fans from engaging in violent behavior themselves. While in the stands, fans can watch their sporting representatives sacrifice their bodies on the field of play. The players are effectively soldiers of the middle and upper classes.

In rugby, because the stadium is full of people from a limited range of the socioeconomic spectrum there is no built-in mechanism to trigger violence between fans. In addition, conflict against the state would be out of place because fans are drawn from the classes and professions that represent and create the state: bureaucrats, managers, and white-collar suburban dwellers that form the consumerist, capitalist class. They likely perceive themselves to be upwardly mobile, take their vacations in Florida and Europe, and have a favorable vision of U.S. and British culture. Associated with the military and suburban residential zones, violence among rugby fans is no more conceivable than among golf or Formula One racing fans in North America or Europe.

Soccer can be understood as ritualized combat that enflames passions and encourages an essentialized conception of the "other," even though that "other" is frequently a mirror image. The militarization of stadium space indicates a level of authoritarian social control and reactive aggression that is designed to contain social unrest. Because fan identities are rife with geographically and historically situated identifications as well as sectarian antagonisms towards other teams the passions generated by this sense of belonging and opposition, as well as the virulent rhetoric of fandom, allow the stadium to take on the role of a transcendent space, where the fans are more important than the players on the field or the directors in the VIP section.[47]

Rather than the game's rule-based ideology, the *barrabrava* offers a vision of the world that explodes rules and their human costs. It is a form of place-specific romanticism; a very masculine utopia of brute force and clannish intensity.[48]

The real, physical battles that occur both inside and outside soccer stadiums between police forces and fans, between rival groups of fans, and between two groups of fans and the police can be understood as an attempt to suspend the dominant social order. These battles are not just staged for the media. But to what end then? It is possible that soccer violence could be a form of social expression, wrapped inside a crisis of legitimacy. However, it is also true that the stadium is a platform for powerful political and media interests that have a vested interest in manipulating and amplifying violent behavior for a larger audience.[49] Thus the soccer stadium is where the social order is simultaneously contested and reaffirmed. Media broadcast both rule-based and anarchic spatiality in a single "package" for viewers to interpret according to their tastes and social positions, while the police battle marginalized male youth for control of urban space.

Society permits a certain disruption of the social order in the soccer stadium. This is natural given the historical nature of the stadium as a liminal space where transgression and social inversion are the norm. However, when the behaviors of the stadium spill out into the public space of the streets society demands a different order. This order does not allow the barrabrava full social agency. The stadium is the only place where they have a voice, and they dare not overturn the order that sustains it, even though their violent actions always threaten to do so.

The social, political, and spatial realms of Buenos Aires' stadiums constantly change, along with the city and society at large. In recent years there has been a proliferation of institutional and legal changes in regard to stadium culture.[50] These policies and tactics have begun to address issues of stadium management, safety, access, and accountability. Examining legal codes, government subsidies, and the political machinations that structure stadium space would reveal valuable insight into the political culture of Buenos Aires and Argentina. Much of this information is tightly guarded and will take a brave and well-connected investigator to tease out the details.

An anthropological approach to the barrabrava can only be accomplished with prolonged exposure to these groups. Understanding their internal functioning, codes, values, geographies, and the reasons for joining them would reveal important clues about the relationships between urban space, subcultural groups, identity formation, and urban governance. Clearly, this is dangerous territory that requires an extensive system of informants, contacts, and safeguards. It is unlikely that exploring the inner workings of the barrabravas could be safely accomplished by a foreign researcher.

Taken together, the spaces of soccer, rugby, and polo trace the urban and rural histories of Argentina: national consolidation, class differentiation, economic integration and development, the development of urban space, the uneven exercise of political and economic power, social violence, residential segmentation, racism, patriarchy, and sexism. The stadiums of Greater Buenos Aires are anchored in these larger themes, but they also reflect local histories and function as sites and symbols of power and identity for millions of people. On game day, the stadium comes to life and enters into public consciousness. When it is empty, the stadium is far from quiet—its very presence connects us to the histories and cultures of the city.

CHAPTER SIX

Comparative Cultural Urbanism

Stadiums communicate across space and time, linking us to
the past and future in a cauldron of the present. As elements of urban cultures all over the world, stadiums are lenses through which we can interpret, compare, and understand each other. Each stadium is ensconced in
its locale and cannot help but tell us about the people who build, use, or
experience it. Taken as interlocking bits contained within larger social, economic, political, and geographic networks, stadiums describe patterns and
flows that move from the tailgate party to the transnational corporation.
The inherent complexity of stadiums permits varied interpretations of
similar phenomena at multiple scales.

As I explained at the beginning of this book, I have taken very different
methodological and thematic approaches to the stadiums of Rio de Janeiro
and Buenos Aires. In Rio de Janeiro we followed the geographic and social
trajectories of four stadiums in a circumscribed geographic area near the
city center. Each told us very different yet intersecting stories that revealed
some of the larger socioeconomic, political, and geographic patterns and
processes in the city and nation. Understanding the different and shifting
ways in which the same stadiums have influenced urban space and culture
over time gave us insight into the geographic and sociocultural complexities of Brazil's most famous city.

In Buenos Aires we undertook a historical examination of urban space
in order to understand why and how soccer stadiums are such emotionally
and sexually charged environments. In the modern context, we examined
three different kinds of stadiums in order to explain class divisions and
conflicts within the city and nation. We saw how the very different social
and geographic worlds of polo, rugby, and soccer touch on all segments of

Argentine society while remaining exceptionally distinct. Taken separately, these three sports and their stadiums reveal a limited view of Argentina's capital city. Together, they form a composite picture that more fully describes contemporary society.

The differences in focus and methodology are primarily a result of the different geographic conditions and stadium cultures of each city. In Buenos Aires the overwhelming number of stadiums made deep investigation of a particular stadium problematic as it would have limited a broader analysis of stadiums in the larger culture. Also, the stadium cultures of polo, rugby, and soccer are so distinct that to focus on a particular kind of stadium would have ignored the relationships between them. In Rio de Janeiro the broad diffusion and limited importance (beyond the neighborhood level) of many of the city's stadiums encouraged a deeper reading of stadiums in a restricted geographic area. The shifting positions of Rio's soccer stadiums in local, national, and international contexts also argued for a spatially and historically continuous focus.

My decision to treat sexuality and masculinity in Buenos Aires but not in Rio de Janeiro was motivated by stadium demographics and cultural norms. In Argentina the presence of women in the stadium is statistically insignificant, whereas in Brazil women are full agents in stadium spectacles, forming between 10 and 20 percent of an average crowd. It is no secret that sexuality in Brazil is very different from that in Argentina and no surprise that this is directly observable in their respective stadiums. The dynamics of sexuality and gender performance in Brazilian stadiums are complex, but they are not a central element in the production of stadium identities.

Conversely, my decision to treat race in Brazil but not in Argentina was motivated by the centrality of race in Brazilian national consciousness. Although Argentina carries a myth of racial homogeneity that is as strong (and incorrect) as Brazil's myth of a racial democracy, the power of race to define categories of class and national belonging is much stronger in Brazil. Though it is always a temporary condition, soccer in Brazil tends to eliminate notions of race and class: by pulling on the same jersey there is a literal incorporation into the body of the team and the mass of the crowd. Identity is routed through the colors of the team, not skin. Outside of the stadium context, the sad reality of racism continues to define Brazilian society.

By way of reconciling these different methodologies and foci, I want to briefly revisit the historical geography of stadiums in both cities. Then I compare and contrast the stadiums in terms of organization and governance as well as the ways in which cultural meanings are expressed by and through them. I conclude by reinserting the stadiums of Rio de Janeiro and Buenos Aries into a global context, arguing that by maintaining a consistent spatial focus over time, the stadium provides a unique comparative window that can be used in a variety of urban and cultural contexts.

Comparative Overview

Despite their obvious physical and cultural differences, patterns of Iberian colonialism, economic development, migration, and urban planning shaped Rio de Janeiro and Buenos Aires in remarkably similar ways. When the first stadiums appeared in the late nineteenth century, both cities were the capitals and dominant urban centers of their respective countries but relatively small and "underdeveloped" in comparison to European and North American cities. The growth of foreign mercantile interests in South America brought industrial technologies that accelerated the inclusion of Brazil and Argentina, Rio de Janeiro and Buenos Aires, into the world economic system.

The growth of export-oriented industries, coupled with rural to urban migration and European immigration, exploded the boundaries of the colonial city along modern transportation lines while residential densities, land values, and informal settlements increased in the urban center. In a response to rapid urban growth the governing classes in each city structured urban reforms on a Parisian model, shaping the future development of the urban environment according to the dictates of capital accumulation and perceptions of Eurocentric cosmopolitanism. Installation of broad avenues, port reforms, and sanitation projects combined with a "scientific" application of urban design to shape the future city. Whereas Rio de Janeiro faced increasing competition from São Paulo and would eventually lose its economic primacy, economic wealth and political power concentrated in Buenos Aires at the expense of a more geographically even national development.[1]

In both cities, the development of institutionalized sport was a by-product of inclusion in the global economy. The presence of British merchants, engineers, laborers, sailors, and technicians brought modern sporting cultures to both cities around the same time, although slightly earlier in Buenos Aires. The British and their creole business partners established private social clubs where they could exhibit their sophisticated tastes and habits, creating a sociospatial system wherein rigorous pursuit of leisure occupied a central position. Notions of leisure and the use of sport as a civilizing mechanism had broad effects on culture, especially among the upper classes.[2] In both Rio de Janeiro and Buenos Aires the first stadiums were associated with Jockey Clubs—spaces and practices of modernity that confirmed cultural associations with Europe.

The development of stadiums and sporting cultures in both cities occurred simultaneously with the restructuring of the urban environment, the development of modern public space, and an emergent civil society. Stadiums were linked with other spaces of modernity focused on public space associated with the state, neocolonial commerce, tourism, and Europhile high culture.[3] As we have seen, the first sporting clubs in each city were provinces of the elite and early stadiums developed alongside restricted social clubs. Throughout Latin America early modern notions of public space were exclusive, and the poor were more likely to experience urban reforms as corrective rather than integrative measures, such as when local governments demolished popular living quarters and informal settlements under the pretext of eliminating disease. Stadiums, akin to government buildings, wide commercial avenues, or plazas in elite residential neighborhoods, were not initially intended for a broadly conceived public.

The adaptation of soccer by the popular classes in the first decades of the twentieth century was what ultimately spurred the proliferation of stadiums in both cities. We can judge from the number of teams, leagues, and stadiums relative to the overall population that the influence of sport on city space was fairly extensive, not just in terms of formal spaces such as stadiums, but also in terms of the presence of innumerable informal spaces. As practice expanded among the middle and lower classes, it formalized in the context of neighborhood-based social clubs that developed "home grounds." These fledging stadiums functioned in relation to other spaces such as the workplace, street, parks, cafés, beach (in Rio), bars, and bordellos as more truly public spaces where a broader range of the socioeconomic spectrum could gather. As soccer leagues gained formal institutional structures, stadiums became a necessary requirement for teams to participate in league competitions and began to host ever larger crowds, attracting media attention and becoming urban spectacles and landmarks in their own right.

Soccer became the sport of the masses in Buenos Aires and Rio de Janeiro between 1910 and 1930.[4] As both cities grew at unprecedented rates and stadiums proliferated, the upper classes moved into positions of management and financial directorship as they abandoned the practice of the sport, though they continued to participate in polo, cricket, rowing, and horse racing. By the 1930s Brazil and Argentina (and Uruguay) had emerged as world soccer powers and the stadiums (architecturally similar to British, Italian, and Spanish soccer stadiums) attracted enormous crowds where fan violence was increasingly common.[5] The growing popularity of soccer frequently transferred the codes of the stadium to the street, and in both cities it was common for tens of thousands of people to gather in public spaces to listen to broadcasts of soccer games during major international competitions such as the South American Championship or the World Cup. Tens of thousands filled the stadiums of each city on a weekly basis, producing ritualized urban spectacles between competing groups of men and generating profits for teams. It was also in this era that stadiums became instruments of political power and control. Though the geographic processes associated with this development are undertheorized in the historical context, the stadiums in both cities became an integral component of urban public culture. Masculine, national, class, ethnic, and racial identities all found a home in the stadium.[6]

From the 1930s onwards, national political figures in Brazil and Argentina used stadiums as a venue for the consolidation of power. State-sponsored stadium projects were viewed as "progressively modern"—outward symbols of the technological and organizational capacity of the state. In Brazil Getúlio Vargas used the Estádio São Januário and São Paulo's Estádio Municipal (Pacaembú) to disseminate political ideologies. In Argentina the Perón family (among others) utilized sport and stadiums to consolidate their popular appeal.[7] Stadium architecture became more monumental and less intimate, shifting from closed rectangles to the large ovals favored in Germany and Italy (especially after the 1936 Olympics).

The professionalization of soccer in the 1930s (Buenos Aires 1931, Rio de Janeiro 1933) ensured that the stadium would be a site of profit and a source of diversion for the urban masses. Instead of being places that reaffirmed elite values, as they had been in the early part of the century, it was the capitalist, political, and working classes that had their values reaffirmed in these ceremonial centers. By the 1940s hundreds of thousands of people attended stadiums on a weekly basis; politicians at all levels of government could not afford to ignore them as mechanisms for economic and social control. Moreover, the international successes of these neighborhood-based teams from Rio de Janeiro and Buenos Aires fostered the development of national identities in relation to the space and codes of the stadium and provided a coherent national narrative in societies without many nationalist traditions.[8]

While Rio and Buenos Aires continued to expand demographically and spatially, at the neighborhood level stadiums helped to organize territorial and group identity and became part of the conceptual geographies of urban residents. The identities that formed in relation to stadiums provide a fairly accurate picture of the divisions within the society as a whole.[9] In Rio these identities tended to form along race, labor, and class lines, yet became more generalized as stadium-based identities spread beyond the immediacy of the locale (principally through radio broadcasts). In Buenos Aires strong divisions continued to exist along geographic (neighborhood), labor, class, and ethnic lines. In both cases the stadiums were masculine domains and *patrias chicas* that linked the local to the national and the global through sport. They also functioned as a kind of domestic space in the public realm—venues for men to openly express emotions in a communally held space, the defense of which became increasingly important.

Although present as early as the 1910s and 1920s, violence was not an endemic characteristic of stadium cultures in either city until the late 1960s and early 1970s. This is the epoch in which organized fan groups appeared (*barrabravas* in Argentina and *torcidas organizadas* in Brazil). Thousands of unemployed, underemployed or otherwise disenfranchised youth began to form cohesive groups in support of their team. These collectives, organized as paramilitary gangs or urban tribes, began to exert political and economic influence in the clubs. The increasing polarization of social classes coupled with a lack of social agency on the part of the working class left the stadium as one of the few places in society where the disenfranchised could exercise collective and individual agency in the face of social and political repression. The space of the stadium became a stage for the acting out of larger social problems through ritualized and organized violence.[10]

Much as the Greens and the Reds had done in the chariot racing stadiums of third-century Constantinople, organized fan groups began to wield political and economic influence beyond the limited sphere of the stadium and the club.[11] Throughout the 1980s their increased agency prompted the state to amplify control over the stadium with military forces of their own; violent conflicts among and between police and *barrabravas* and *torcidas organizadas* became routine. Clubs were forced to militarize their stadiums while police attempted to control the streets around them. The violence that these groups continue to exercise against each other can be understood as a competition for scarce resources and an assertion of social agency abetted by preternaturally strong yet visibly threatened identities, particularly among young men. The national and local police forces in Rio de Janeiro and Buenos Aires are not hesitant to use lethal force to control stadium environments displaying their own institutional cultures. In both countries people are forced to reconcile their strong emotional associations with soccer with the violence of the stadium. The problems of the Latin American mega-city—violence, decaying infrastructure, corruption, militarization, exclusion, territorialization of public space, and social fragmentation—are compactly and ritually enacted, presented, and broadcast in the stadium.

Today, because of their generalized insecurity and increasing age, stadiums have come under increasing public scrutiny in Brazil and Argentina. Issues of public safety, governance, and stadium management are discussed in local, national, and international contexts. The staggering violence associated with stadiums, particularly in Buenos Aires, is embroiled in a discourse that dehumanizes the people who engage in it. This discourse effectively eliminates the need to address the underlying social conditions that generate gang warfare. Violence is an all too common aspect of life in these cities and the stadiums—sites of socioeconomic, political, and cultural convergence—tend to amplify (or in some cases, obfuscate) larger social problems.

Public space in Latin America functions as a mediating mechanism between society and the state and makes visible political expressions of citizenship through multiple forms of association and conflict.[12] Stadiums in both Buenos Aires and Rio de Janeiro act as quasi-public spaces that function in the public realm and are connected materially and symbolically to other public spaces. Much like post–World War II urban renewal projects in the United States, when national governments built stadiums in periods of national optimism and industrial growth, stadiums represented progress and stability. The generalized failure to create prosperous, democratic societies has left stadiums as symbols of decline, socioeconomic polarization, and decaying social infrastructure. Ironically, the wildly uneven distribution of wealth in Brazil and Argentina has left stadiums as some of the few remaining public spaces where a wide range of social actors regularly converge. As such, they are connected to the production and reproduction of public space within each city. As Buenos Aires and Rio de Janeiro become increasingly fragmented and less public, the stadiums of each city will be barometers of larger social issues, and the ways in which they are managed and experienced will tell us about the fate of public space and public life in Latin America.

Major Differences and Similarities

This book has demonstrated that stadiums are privileged sites to examine the ways in which two very different societies organize space, express unequal relationships of power, and use public space as a means to attain or contest the advancement of social and political goals. In addition to serving as stages for the acting out of larger social and spatial relations, stadiums are symbolic representations of these processes. That is to say, even when they are empty, stadiums communicate meaning in the larger context of the cultural landscape. It is through examining the signification systems of landscape that larger discursive frameworks are revealed.[13] Therefore, by examining the ways in which the stadiums of Rio de Janeiro and Buenos Aires are distributed, organized, and governed, we are exposed to the institutional and political frameworks that structure sociospatial relations in the larger society.

Location

In both Buenos Aires and Rio de Janeiro, stadiums have been forced to the fringes of the metropolitan regions, although there are some notable exceptions.[14] The large architectural footprint of stadiums necessitates a significant capital investment in property, taxes, and maintenance; because stadiums open their doors so infrequently they are more suited to less valuable plots of land. This is consistent with historical processes of stadium development and redevelopment in many countries.

The spatial logics of the real estate market, the architectural exigencies of international sport, and the difficult financial situations of many smaller clubs have resulted in the demolition or modification of stadiums in both cities. For instance, in 2001 the América Football Club of Rio de Janeiro sold its centrally located stadium to developers who razed it to build a shopping mall on the property. América F.C., which had been located in the same spot for eighty-five years, made enough money from the sale to construct a more modern, yet fairly modest facility in the poor northern suburbs of the city. Similarly, the sporting and residential facilities for the 2007 Pan American Games were built on greenfield sites far from the urban center, yet close to the booming upper-middle-class suburb of Barra de Tijuca whose residents can afford to attend the games. The João Havelange Olympic Stadium is located in the working-class suburb of Engenho do Dentro, a site chosen for its low land values and proximity to major highways. The 2006 renovation of the Maracanã was a response to FIFA's requirement for stadiums that host international matches to be all-seater. The reforms were partly an attempt to bring Brazil's most famous stadium back into the global sporting realm in anticipation of the 2014 World Cup.

The historical record in Buenos Aires also indicates that many teams have had to move their stadiums on more than one occasion. However, it is also true that the logics of the real estate market do not always apply to soccer stadiums. This is perhaps the only place in the world where two stadiums with capacities of more than 50,000 (Racing and Independiente) are situated three blocks apart. In the middle of the worst economic crisis in twenty years, Argentinos Juniors, a relatively minor club, built a new 28,000-capacity stadium (Estadio Diego Armando Maradona) in a mid-

Vamos defender o Maracanã

A cultura carioca corre perigo. O Maracanã, inaugurado em 16 de julho de 1950 está seriamente ameaçado de demolição. Querem um novo estádio com capacidade apenas para 30.000 pessoas, que excluiria desta forma o principal personagem: o torcedor popular.

Dizem que o Maracanã está ultrapassado, que não tem condições para abrigar as Olimpíadas ou uma possível Copa do Mundo em 2012. Nós temos condições de equipar o Maracanã com todas as qualidades necessárias à sua modernização.

Muitas obras de arte, monumentos, praças, ruas e a própria natureza da nossa cidade já foram destruidos em vão, motivados unicamente pela ganância de políticos e empresários inescrupulosos.

O Presidente da CBF é quem propõe a implosão deste estádio que é simbolo da paixão nacional, da cultura carioca e referência mundial. Isso nós não vamos permitir!

Além de uma grande campanha popular, proporemos a LEI DE PROTEÇÃO AO PATRIMÔNIO HISTÓRICO E ARTÍSTICO CARIOCA – material e imaterial. Além de salvarmos o Maracanã, seremos capazes de preservar as Folias de Reis, o Jongo, a literatura de Cordel, a nossa natureza e todos os monumentos e manifestações culturais da Cidade do Rio de Janeiro.

PARTICIPE DA CAMPANHA
IPANEMA: R. Visconde de Pirajá, 207 sl. 204 Tel: 2522-2375
CENTRO: R. Senador Dantas, 75 sl. 1701 Tel: 2220-6686
ENDEREÇO ELETRÔNICO: dalva@dalvalazaroni.com.br | www.dalvalazaroni.com.br

Photo 6.1 Maracanã and Cristo. This political pamphlet was distributed by Mayor Cesar Maia during his successful 2004 campaign. It depicts the statue of Cristo Redentor embracing the Maracanã, thus bringing together the religious and the secular, the masculine and the feminine, and globally recognizable icons of Rio de Janeiro. The text promises a fight to preserve Rio's cultural heritage.

dle-class neighborhood in the City of Buenos Aires. Similarly, Atlanta F.C. is undertaking multimillion-dollar stadium renovations in the middle-class neighborhood of Villa Crespo. How these stadiums are financed is a closely guarded secret.

Many of the smaller clubs located in the City of Buenos Aires, especially those like Excursionistas and Defensores del Belgrano, located in the upper-middle-class neighborhood of Belgrano, are under pressure to sell their stadiums for the development of shopping malls or condominium complexes as América F.C. did in Rio de Janeiro. It is also true that stadiums located in the urban periphery such as San Telmo F.C. and Dock Sud are forced to choose between paying player salaries and maintaining their stadiums. The result is that stadiums fall into further disrepair as club management struggles to find effective financial solutions. More investigation is needed to understand the differences between successful and unsuccessful survival strategies of these smaller clubs.

Security and Governance

Stadiums in both cities are under pressure from the governing institutions of sport and local and national governments to install closed circuit television to aid in crowd surveillance and control. One major difference is that smaller clubs and stadiums in Rio de Janeiro are almost completely dependent on political patronage and membership dues, not gate receipts or television revenue, for survival. The institutional structures of soccer in Brazil are only strong at the national level; teams that participate in the second and third divisions of the national tournament or that only compete in state tournaments basically function as developmental teams for larger clubs.[15] While this is partly true in Buenos Aires, teams that compete in the lower divisions there have intense fan support and historically situated rivalries within the city that stimulate media interest and attract fans to the stadium in far greater numbers than in Rio de Janeiro. Yet these clubs are also under increasing financial pressure worsened by the violent behavior of the very fans that make the stadium such a dynamic environment.

The relative positioning of Buenos Aires and Rio de Janeiro in their respective national contexts has important implications for the ways in which stadiums are organized and integrated into the urban fabric. Because Buenos Aires dominates the economic, political, and cultural spheres of Argentina, local events are placed in a national context. Thus the governance and control of stadium space on a local level is inexorably linked to the national. This is not necessarily the case in Rio de Janeiro, which has lost economic and political power to São Paulo and Brasilia but has retained much of its cultural influence. The declining economic and sporting fortunes of Rio de Janeiro's four major teams and the solidification of the Brazilian national league have reduced the relative importance of Rio de Janeiro in terms of Brazil's soccer culture. However, Rio de Janeiro is still home to the CBF, which moved from its downtown offices to a palatial office complex in Barra de Tijuca in 2002: a reflection of larger social trends among Rio's upwardly mobile. In contrast, the AFA headquarters are in downtown Buenos Aires near the seat of national government: a symbolic and functional position that highlights the relationships between national politicians and soccer teams.

The influence of local, state (or provincial), and national governments on stadiums in each city differs, yet both organizational systems reflect the inherent complexities of stadium management structures that create vacuums of responsibility for what happens inside and outside the gates. The administrative model of stadiums in Buenos Aires is fairly homogeneous, whereas that of Rio de Janeiro is more variable.

In Buenos Aires all soccer stadiums are the property of the social clubs to which they pertain, while the military owns and manages several polo stadiums. As historically continuous and influential elements of civil society, social clubs are quasi-public entities that influence social relations at the neighborhood and metropolitan scale. All clubs have a *sede social* that may or may not be part of a stadium complex. Similar to other privately owned spaces of public entertainment such as theatres, stadiums are subject to municipal building codes, permits, and inspections. They also need to meet security criteria determined by the AFA in conjunction with the federal government. Policing of stadium space is contracted (and paid for) by the club to security forces that may be drawn from the federal police (PFA) or Buenos Aires provincial and municipal police who operate in conjunction with club directed surveillance operators. Thus no one entity is ultimately responsible for what happens in and around soccer stadiums.

In Rio de Janeiro smaller stadiums and clubs abound, but lower division games are not attended with the intensity that they are in Buenos Aires. I have never witnessed anything more than the intimation of violence inside any stadium in Rio de Janeiro, and only on rare occasions have I witnessed violence directed at opposing teams and their fans outside a stadium. This is not to suggest that violence is not a pervasive part of the soccer world in Rio de Janeiro; it is. However, the police presence in and around the stadiums is so heavy that the *torcidas organizadas* arrange for their ritualized confrontations in other parts of the city (much as has happened in Britain). These are very real battles, and group members are sometimes killed or wounded. For instance, in September 2004 a *torcida organizada* of Vasco da Gama incinerated a bus of São Paulo's Corinthians Fiels da Gavota *torcida organizada* with several Molotov cocktails. This would perhaps not have been so extraordinary except that the bus was parked in front of the Military Police headquarters for the neighborhood of São Cristóvão.

In Argentina, the *barrabravas* appear to have more influence over stadiums, clubs, and teams than their counterparts in Rio de Janeiro. The leaders of the largest *barrabrava* are well-known public figures. In November 2006 the leader of Boca Juniors' *barrabrava* received much-publicized visits in jail from some of the Boca players. One reason for this discrepancy is that in Buenos Aires there is only one *barrabrava* associated with each team and internecine conflicts happen within it. In Rio de Janeiro each club has multiple *torcidas organizadas* that compete for political and economic favors from the club. The larger the *torcida organizada*, the more political clout it can wield in club elections, assuming that most of its members hold voting rights in the club. *Torcidas organizadas* that have fallen out of favor with the club management typically stage public protests by hanging their banners upside down, or do not occupy the stands behind their banners during a game. The underlying reasons for the structural differences between Argentine and Brazilian fan groups are unclear. Because these groups form such an integral part of the stadium cultures of both cities they warrant further, yet cautious, attention from researchers.[16]

In Rio de Janeiro the state government owns and manages (through SUDERJ) the Maracanã, the Estádio Caio Martins in Niteroi, and the stadiums constructed for the 2007 Pan American Games. The ownership and management structures of privately owned stadiums (such as the São Januário) are not significantly different from those in Argentina. Local government is responsible for organizing traffic control, providing for additional public transportation, and street policing. The difference in Brazil is that soccer's governing bodies (FERJ and CBF) contract the Military Police to provide riot squads, mounted police, and attack dogs, lessening the financial burden on clubs.

The transparent corruption of the soccer world in Latin America has generated a series of reforms in recent years. The FERJ is now required by law to publish detailed records of gate receipts, and the AFA has begun to publish attendance data for league matches on a weekly basis. It is impossible to know if the numbers provided by these organizations are accurate as the *torcidas organizadas* and *barrabravas* are given hundreds, sometimes thousands, of free tickets to games. Thus historically accurate data for stadium attendance are difficult to come by. Even if they were correct, they would not reflect the amount of money coming into club coffers, or where that money is directed.

In both Brazil and Argentina, national governments have passed specific laws and created special judicial bodies that address stadium-related violence. They have also passed laws protecting clubs from bankruptcy. A more thorough exploration of the political economy of stadiums in both cities would be fascinating but potentially difficult to carry out because of the closed nature of social clubs and the opaque management practices of national soccer federations.

In addition, national governments in both countries have created specific prosecuting units and police forces to deal with stadium-related violence, treating it as a special legal category.[17] In Argentina sport-related criminal prosecutions are ineffectively incorporated into existing institutional frameworks of justice, although the Kirchner government created the CoProSeDe (El Comité Provincial de Seguridad Deportiva / Provincial Committee of Sports Security) to control and prosecute stadium violence in Buenos Aires. This institution has resorted to closing stadiums, fining clubs, and barring visiting fans, or particular fans, from attending games.[18]

In Brazil the implementation of the Law of the Fan in 2001 guaranteed stadium-goers certain rights and made specific provisions for illegal activities that occur in and around the stadium. In response to the violence associated with soccer matches Brazilian state and national governments have formed special prosecution units and installations within stadiums themselves. In both cities the implementation of laws designed to combat violence address the symptoms but not the causes of socioeconomic polarization and its attendant lack of social agency.[19]

Despite the relative levels of violence in each city, stadiums appear to be safer in Rio de Janeiro than they are in Buenos Aires. The generalized insecurity that pervades all aspects of daily life in Rio de Janeiro is largely absent from the stadium. Rio's stadiums are among the most militarized, policed, and controlled environments in the city, and it is principally due to poor management that violence and disorder emerge as problems. In Buenos Aires, generally considered a less violent city than Rio, there is no escaping violence in and around the stadiums. Even third and fourth division games, with fewer than one thousand fans in attendance, have the potential for confrontations between rival *barrabravas*. The police are ever present, well armed, and battle tested, yet they are also a potential threat to spectator safety.

The involvement of national-level political figures in the ownership and management of teams and stadiums ensures the sociopolitical opacity of the soccer world. In both cities the stadium sits at the intersection of the public and private realms, between private management and public governance, state control and civic organization. As public spaces are frequently the stages on which political and social struggles are acted out, the stadiums of these two cities give us important insight into how public space is controlled, contested, and organized. The long history of violence in Latin American urban public spaces is typically associated with repressive political regimes or a generalized level of violence on city streets. Given that stadiums are quasi-public spaces, their intersection with larger networks of public space complicates existing theoretical models. These models have been satisfactorily developed in North American and European contexts but have not yet received dedicated attention from African, Latin American, Middle Eastern, or Asian urban scholars.

Stadiums in Latin America are too variable to be classified schematically. The diverse locations, architecture, histories, sizes, and unpatterned connections to the city make it difficult to generalize. A basic rule is that the larger the stadium, the more easily it connects with the urban environment, drawing people to it. Stadiums such as the Bombonera or the Maracanã are global icons that attract tens of thousands of tourists a year. Others are virtually unknown to people who have lived their whole lives in the city. Some stadiums are ensconced in neighborhoods such that their exterior walls merge seamlessly with apartment buildings and houses. Others are built on marginal land away from centers of population but are well served by public transportation. Detailed documentation of the connections between stadiums, public spaces, and their relative strength over time is beyond the scope of this investigation. I hope that the unanswered questions this book has raised will generate research dedicated to the architectural, urban, and social histories of stadiums in Latin America.

The Uncertain Fate of Social Clubs

Sporting clubs in Latin America have functioned as important elements of urban civil society since the late nineteenth century. The associations between clubs, neighborhoods, and stadiums continue to be strongly felt, perhaps more so in Buenos Aires than in Rio de Janeiro. Even as their emergence was a product of global flows, these community spaces of broad-based social interaction have been reincorporated into a global system of sport production that threatens the existence of the clubs themselves. The institutional frameworks that structure the relations of economic production in regard to sporting clubs reveal the ways in which globalizing processes are articulated, interpreted, and managed at the local level.

In terms of sport, both Argentina and Brazil are export economies. The migration of soccer players from Brazil and Argentina to foreign clubs began in the 1930s and has had debilitating effects on local leagues in both cities.[20] Today there are somewhere between five thousand and six thousand Brazilians playing professional soccer outside of Brazil and perhaps a thousand Argentine *fútbolistas* ply their trade abroad.[21]

Increasing numbers of Brazilians and Argentines play basketball, volleyball, and rugby in foreign leagues. Local clubs simply cannot afford to compete with the wages offered in places like Saudi Arabia, England, or Japan, although the recent economic upturn in Brazil has allowed some clubs to develop and retain more star soccer players.[22] Moreover, the exigencies of the global economy have had an impact on the ability of smaller clubs to maintain their previous roles as sites of social integration and community interaction.

The social and economic insecurities of smaller clubs in Buenos Aires and Rio de Janeiro are in part a result of the global expansion of cable television services. As in Europe and North America, the greatest source of revenue for teams is no longer drawn from club memberships, ticket sales, or player transfers but from the sale of sponsorship rights and cable television contracts. Teams in the top division earn huge sums while the lower division teams that feed them suffer. Falling from the first to the second division can mean financial and sporting ruin for clubs as they cannot afford to pay their top players competitive wages.[23] In Argentina the games that determine relegation and promotion are highly charged and frequently result in violence between opposing fans.

The exodus of quality players to larger clubs with bigger payrolls makes it ever harder for small clubs to reach the top flight and secure the royalties associated with expanded television coverage and advertising rights. These conditions have negatively affected social programs at clubs, and many have been forced to curtail the activities they provide for their members. These pressures also prohibit clubs from repairing or improving their stadiums or providing adequate security.

The impact of television has changed the nature of sports spectatorship throughout the world, but in Buenos Aires it has not significantly changed the overall numbers of people who go to the stadium. According to one study, 78 percent of club *socios* say that they prefer to go to the stadium rather than watch a game on television. Of these people 82 percent say that they watch games other than those of their team at least once during the week. Surprisingly, 36 percent say that they bring their spouses and children to the stadiums. This suggests that more people are watching stadium events than ever before and that the stadiums function as important vehicles of socialization.[24]

In Brazil membership at large clubs has remained more constant, but the exodus of middle- and upper-class residents to condominium complexes in the southern suburbs is withering an important membership demographic. These newly suburbanized residents form social clubs within the condominium complexes themselves, further isolating them from the neighborhood-based social interaction provided by traditional clubs. While some see this as evidence of further social fragmentation and polarization, others see it as a logical and necessary response to an increasingly violent urban environment.

A related effect of the decline of smaller, traditional clubs is that more professional players are coming from the middle and upper middle classes. It is these players that have access to the institutional frameworks from which world-class athletes frequently emerge. Provided with the calories, equipment, coaching, and spaces to play, they are more likely to develop their talents within a system of sport production that identifies, creates, and cultivates soccer talent at an early age. Players from lower socioeconomic classes are forced to invest a higher percentage of financial resources to compete for professional wages within the clubs. The dominant ideology of sport offers a slim chance of success while consigning the majority to socioeconomic marginality.

Given that the smaller stadiums of Rio de Janeiro play a more limited public role than similar stadiums in the Argentine capital, it is ironic that Rio de Janeiro has a much stronger institutional structure for organizing its clubs. The Federação de Clubes e Associações do Estado do Rio de Janeiro (Federation of Clubs and Associations of the State of Rio de Janeiro, FCAERJ) provides an institutional framework for improving and supporting social clubs. This nongovernmental organization is funded by the clubs themselves and serves as a liaison between the clubs and the city government of Rio de Janeiro. It has developed programs that function as mechanisms for social interaction, infrastructure development, and community cohesion between its members. FCAERJ sponsors programs for the elderly and teenagers, assists smaller clubs to develop their social and athletic centers, and attempts to lessen the social, economic, and political distances between large and small clubs. This has been accomplished through grants, organizing interclub competitions, and opening communication lines between the clubs and with government agencies. This is a very positive development and one that is consistent with other community-based social organizations in Rio de Janeiro.

In Rio de Janeiro there are also mechanisms through which social clubs are integrated into community organization and governance structures. For example, the Associação do Moradores do São Cristóvão (Residents' Association of São Cristóvão) holds a monthly meeting at which local businesspeople, and representatives from the local hospital, schools, and other community organizations gather with the Military Police to discuss pertinent neighborhood issues: prison breaks, the danger faced by schoolchildren crossing the street, incidents of robbery and violence, and upcoming community events. The goal of the association is to facilitate communication between the Military Police and neighborhood residents regarding the structure and control of neighborhood space. A common complaint of neighborhood residents is the lack of investment in community projects from the municipal government, which creates a sense of isolated struggle against the violence and disorder that characterizes much of Rio de Janeiro. Though they do not always attend, the presidents of São Cristóvão's sporting clubs, C.R. Vasco da Gama, São Cristóvão F.R., and São Cristóvão Imperial, are expected to participate in these meetings.

For most social clubs in Buenos Aires, soccer is the raison d'etre. All

professional soccer teams are organized through the AFA, an institution
that the larger clubs have historically dominated. Although neighborhood
organizations in Buenos Aires are very active and the city of Buenos Aires
has an institutional organization for sporting clubs, the integration of clubs
in a metropolitan context is lacking. Most smaller clubs continue to draw
on local residents for dues-paying members, while the "Big 5"—River
Plate, Boca Juniors, San Lorenzo del Almargo, Racing Club, and Velez Sarsfield—have local, regional, and national followings.

Although more research needs to be done regarding the relationships
between social clubs, stadiums, and the general functioning of civil society
in Latin America, it is clear that clubs and their stadiums have traditionally
served as centers for social integration, neighborhood-based activities, and
identity formation. Soccer teams and stadiums are the most visible elements of the clubs and are a source of pride and historical continuity. By
observing the structures and institutional frameworks of the clubs, we can
better understand the ways in which national and global geographic
processes manifest at the local level.

Memory, Representation, and Meaning

Social memory, representation, and meaning are three interrelated structures that can be read in the cultural landscape.[25] The intersections of
historical events, contemporary realities, and visions for the future shape
the meanings and textures of places. Stadiums are places in their own right
but also define the space around them to a large degree. Thus the characteristics and textures (i.e., that which defines place) of neighborhoods, districts, and cities are shaped by stadiums. In the introduction we explored
the ways in which the stadium functions as a "sacred space." Here we will
look at some of the ways in which stadiums anchor meaning and memory,
as well as the ways in which they represent social relations at various scales.

The Estádio Jornalista Mario Filho (Maracanã) functions as an iconographic national symbol in the geographic core of Rio de Janeiro. In chapter 2 we explored the significance of the Maracanã and the loss of the 1950
World Cup final in relation to the development of Brazilian national identity. More than half a century later, the memory of this defeat continues to
be lived through the stadium's sky blue exterior. There is no apparent
treaty or agreement binding the SUDERJ to maintain the exterior of
Brazil's most famous stadium as a tribute to the loss. Consistent with
Foote's analysis of sites of national tragedy, it is likely that the Maracanã
functions as a shrine that "celebrates the covenant of nationalism in the
landscape" and that the sky blue exterior produces a "historical conscious-

Photo 6.2 Vasco foot soldier. This statue stands between the soccer stadium and the swimming complex at C.R. Vasco da Gama. It memorializes the participation of Brazilian forces fighting in World War II. This is one of a multitude of statues at the club, each one memorializing the relationships between the club and Brazilian national history or renewing associations with Portuguese ethnicity.

Photo 6.3 Garrincha and a fan at the Maracanã. "The joy of the people," Mane Garrincha was one of Brazil's best players, possessed of phenomenal dribbling skills. Garrincha played for Botafogo his entire career. Some Botafogo fans rub his head for good luck before games.

ness [that] is less a matter of objective reality than it is a retrospective invention conditioned by the ideological imperatives of contemporary society."[26] This ideological imperative is further expressed through the symbolic positioning of the stadium near the Quinta de Boa Vista, the former seat of the Portuguese empire, which serves to integrate the colonial and contemporary landscapes of Brazil.

In Buenos Aires stadiums frequently provide cues to the ways in which society copes with violence and tragedy. For instance, the Estadio Antonio Vespucio Liberti (El Monumental de Núñez) was the site of Argentina's victory in the 1978 World Cup final during a repressive military dictatorship and is considered the "home ground" of the Argentine national team. In July 2003 the AFA hosted a game commemorating the twenty-fifth anniversary of the Argentine victory. The game was attended by tens of thousands of people, but many tens of thousands more consciously stayed away because they associated the event and the space of the stadium with the military dictatorship and the "dirty war." By staging a commemorative event in the Monumental, the AFA was viewed by many as continuing the troubling association between soccer, the stadium, and political violence.

Photo 6.4 Bombonera mural. This mural, painted on the side of the Bombonera, depicts daily life in the Boca district. The port area is in the background, and the children of immigrants play soccer in the streets. Many stadiums in Latin America have murals and paintings depicting team and neighborhood histories. These are central places in cities, creating and reflecting urban life.

Photo 6.5 El Monumental. Named for a former president of River Plate in 1979, the Monumental is considered the "national" stadium of Argentina. Three of its four sections of stands are named for military officers. The advertising is typical of most stadiums in Latin America.

BUENOS AIRES NORTE

Photo 6.6 El Monumental postcard. This postcard positions the Monumental of River Plate as an urban amenity in the north of Buenos Aires. There are hidden, oppositional messages at play here wherein the north is rich and leisurely and the south is poor and working class. Such broadly conceived notions of place help to define the sectarian antagonisms of soccer teams and stadiums in Buenos Aires.

For many others, particularly fans of River Plate, El Monumental does not carry these negative associations, suggesting that the stadium may also function as a container of social memories that "cannot be forgotten but should not be remembered," revealing the conflicting discourses present in the cultural landscape.

Another troubled memory associated with El Monumental occurred on June 23, 1968, when seventy-one Boca Juniors fans were crushed to death as they tried to exit through the infamous Puerta 12. Following the tragedy, the numbered doors of the stadium were changed to letters, a clear case of "obliteration" wherein sites of tragedy are eliminated from the landscape. Despite the permanent removal of this door from the stadium and the relabeling of all the other entrances, Boca Juniors' fans continue to memorialize the tragedy by grabbing a testicle ("dar un huevo") when they pass by, confirming Foote's observation that "obliterated sites stand out as much as sacred places."[28]

As constitutive elements of cultural landscapes in Latin America, stadiums are "communicative devices that encode and transmit information," providing insight into political discourses, cultural values, the organization of social space and meanings associated with place.[29] While larger stadiums in Latin America tend to have local, regional, and national associations, smaller stadiums function as sites and symbols of heritage, identity, and meaning for limited local communities.

An example from Buenos Aires is the stadium Dr. Osvaldo F. Baletto of San Telmo F.C., located in the neighborhood of Isla Maciel in the southern zone of Avellaneda. San Telmo F.C. was formed by immigrants from southern Brazil and Uruguay in the neighborhood of San Telmo in 1904. The marginal socioeconomic position of the immigrants forced them to move their stadium and club on several occasions; they were finally able to appropriate some of the least environmentally desirable land in the city. Inside the stadium is a mural that depicts an early-twentieth-century Carnival celebration in Buenos Aires: black and mulatto men and women are singing, dancing, and playing *candomblé* music in the neighborhood of San Telmo. This scene is more commonly associated with Brazil and Uruguay than Argentina, and the mural is a reminder of the ethnic, class, and national origins of the club. Although many of the current club members (about four hundred) are not familiar with the historical origins of the club, the continued association of San Telmo F.C. with marginalized social actors and immigrants is a source of identity and pride for the club and the local community, one of the poorest in Buenos Aires. Thus the stadium of San Telmo F.C. acts as part of a larger signifying system through which a "social system is communicated, reproduced, experienced and explored."[30]

Photo 6.7 Jairo and Ceres. Political propaganda left over from one of Jairo's campaigns for state deputy. Behind the stadium is state housing that Colonel Jairo militated for when in office. The slogan reads: "Always be true to yourself" [Vote Jair].

Photo 6.8 Jairinho and Ceres. Exterior wall of Ceres F.C. stadium. Jairinho is running for the same political office held by his father. The text below the photos reads: "The doctor who is going to care for Rio."

The rhetoric of landscape in Rio de Janeiro allows for an examination of stadiums as sites for the consolidation of political and economic power. Because identity is affected by our sense of location in space and time developing an understanding of how political power is expressed and consolidated in the stadium aids in deciphering the identities and meanings associated with these elements of the cultural landscape.[31]

Many smaller stadiums in Rio de Janeiro represent the *pátria chica* of local political figures. For example, the suburban stadium of Ceres F.C. is plastered with the image of "Jairinho" (Jairo junior). Jairo's father served on the Rio de Janeiro city council for many years and used the space of the stadium to consolidate political power in the neighborhood. The stadium is surrounded by government housing constructed through Jairo's political influence. Since the retirement of his father, Jairinho has been using the soccer team and the space of the stadium to court votes among local residents in his own bid for elected office. Metropolitan law prohibits the use of stadiums for political propaganda, even though the practice is quite common. The Ceres stadium is part of a larger signifying system that uses the ideologies and semantic fields associated with sport to mask the stadium-based consolidation of economic, social, and political power on the neighborhood and metropolitan, regional, and national scales.

Sporting cultures generally have strong historical associations that are anchored in the place of the stadium. Similar to other public spaces, the stadium structures broad-based social interactions and functions as a "repository of history" that is an ever present element of the urban environment. Given the historical nature of stadiums and their use as sites of secular pilgrimage, it is perhaps not surprising that John Bale suggests they "build on nostalgia as an antidote to modernity," providing an escape into an idealized world.[32] The development of museums within stadiums, therefore, incorporates the processes of memorialization and identity formation and creates a condition in which the stadium represents, contains, produces, and reproduces historical meaning. These meanings, in turn, are presented to tourists as authentic representations of cultural heritage.

In North America and Europe there are innumerable tourist guides to stadiums and arenas. Although there are not yet guidebooks to the stadiums of Buenos Aires and Rio de Janeiro, stadiums have been on travelers' itineraries for some time, and stadiums occupy an important place in the imaginary city. In both cities there are an increasing number of services dedicated to providing tourists with a stadium experience. On the beaches of Rio individuals canvass the beach passing out pamphlets for guided tours to soccer games at the Maracanã. Throughout Buenos Aires soccer tour pamphlets are prominently displayed in hotel lobbies. Stadiums are part of the global image of Rio, much less so of Buenos Aires, even though the latter has many more stadiums.

In Rio de Janeiro the Maracanã has been a centerpiece of the conceptual landscape of the city since the stadium was constructed in 1950. The Maracanã marks the northern limit of the "tourist city," and in 2004 SUDERJ charged more money to visit the stadium as a tourist than to enter the stadium as a fan (R$13 vs. R$10). In 2000 FIFA, SUDERJ, and the city of Rio de Janeiro began construction on the International Soccer Hall of Fame to be housed within the stadium. After completing an elaborate glass facade, the museum project has stalled, yet the selection of the Maracanã as *the* representative site for the global memory of soccer testifies to the powerful meanings associated with the stadium. The stadium will host its second World Cup final in 2014.

Social clubs that sponsor professional soccer teams at all levels in Rio de Janeiro have displays dedicated to their sporting conquests that memorialize past glories. Many of these are no different from what one sees in the halls of athletic departments at high schools and colleges in North America. In the case of the Estádio São Januário, the trophy room is quite elaborate as C.R. Vasco da Gama has won innumerable local, national, and international tournaments. While Vasco does not yet charge admission to its trophy room, there are plans to develop a museum dedicated to the São Januário and the sporting and social history of the team. Rio's other large clubs (Flamengo, Fluminese, and Botafogo) also have elaborate museum-like displays in their social centers.

The trend towards museumization is also present in Buenos Aires. Boca Juniors established an extensive, well-polished museum in 2001. Its cross-town rivals, Club Atlético River Plate, have begun construction of a museum within its stadium.[33] As in Rio de Janeiro, most of the clubs in Buenos Aires have some kind of historical display that commemorates club victories in a wide variety of sports. There is usually a wall dedicated to photos of past presidents of the club and bronze busts of prominent former officials. Unsurprisingly, these displays are dominated by the accomplishments of men, although women's sports are generally included in the trophy cases.

Because the stadium is a principal site of collective memory in urban societies, the placing of museums in stadiums is eminently logical. As Latin American clubs look for ways to get more economic return from their stadiums we can expect a proliferation of museums, restaurants, meeting rooms, and generalized rental of stadium space. These processes are already well under way in Europe and North America, which continue to provide the models for stadium development in Latin America. Examining and comparing the ways in which societies commemorate and memorialize their histories in their stadiums will be fascinating comparative research.[34]

Each stadium has strong geographic and social ties to a local community and informs the larger cultural landscape. These are but a few examples of the ways in which clubs and stadiums function as sites and symbols of social memory, representation, and meaning in the two cities. The importance of these places in the lives of local people emerges out of historical continuity, community identity, and a collective experience of place that cannot be separated from urban, cultural, and historical contexts.

Stadiums and Globalization, a Very Likely Theory

Much of what I have discussed in the preceding pages has dealt with globalizing forces as they are expressed at the local level. The word *globalization* has been used so often in the past twenty years that it has become a nearly meaningless trope for interpreting the inevitable processes of cultural change. As we have seen throughout this book, globalization is not new, nor is its current expression in Latin America particularly accelerated. The impacts of global capital and culture were just as profound at the end of the fifteenth and nineteenth centuries as they are at the beginning of the twenty-first—if anything, the exchanges between Latin America and the rest of the world have become more even. However hackneyed *globalization* has become as a descriptive term, it is still a useful paradigm for discussing patterns and processes of change at multiple scales.

It should come as no surprise that the countries with the most modern and most expensive stadiums in the world are those that hold the greatest economic, political, and military power: G8 nations top the list; Australia, Saudi Arabia, Mexico, Brazil, Venezuela, Argentina, and South Africa constitute a second tier. While China and India have scores of stadiums, their sporting infrastructures are just beginning to reflect the pace and scope of industrial modernization and its attendants. The facilities built for the 2004 Asian Football Championship and the 2008 Beijing Olympics were the first stadium modernization projects in China since the end of the Cultural Revolution and were self-consciously produced as representations of the technological, economic, and organizational capacities of the Chinese nation.

The United States is far and away the world leader in stadiums, in per capita, total number, variety, and total money invested. Even relatively small cities like Lincoln, Nebraska, Ann Arbor, Michigan, and Clemson, South Carolina, have stadiums with capacities in excess of 85,000—larger than any stadium in Argentina, France, or Germany. In the United States emerging sun-belt and declining rust-belt cities have used stadiums as a tool to attract highly mobile national and international capital or as a means of renovating decaying city centers. Suburbs of Dallas, Chicago, Los Angeles, Raleigh, Denver, and Salt Lake City have built soccer-specific stadiums that cater to wealthy, white suburbanites but also attract recent immigrants from Latin America who are finding a familiar mechanism to connect with and create community in a new home.

Professional sport in the United States follows the same model as society at large whereby public money is used to subsidize large corporate interests—using public dollars for private profit. The accelerated corporatization of U.S. society in the 1990s was echoed by the selling of stadium naming rights to corporations, a maximization of the economic utility of stadium space that effectively routes public memory through corporate iconography. These trends have started to take hold in Canada, Australia, Britain, and Germany—emerging wherever and whenever capital has transformed societies in ways similar to the United States.

Yet it is not only a generalized level of capitalist development that transforms a nation's stadiums. The movement of global capital in search of profit through stadium building is well developed, though underchronicled. Starting with Seoul 1998, cities and countries that have hosted the Olympics or World Cup have had ultramodern stadiums inserted into their midst, sometimes as an expression of emergent development, other times as a result of political machinations, and others as a result of rapacious global accumulation regimes. Thus global capital has plopped world-class facilities into corners of the world like Segouipo, South Korea; Salt Lake City; Lillehammer, Norway; and Braga, Portugal, placing high-tech stadiums in places better suited to low-maintenance, low-capacity facilities. Sometimes stadiums appear in recognized global cities like London, Sydney, Los Angeles, and Berlin, or regional centers such as Istanbul, Miami, Caracas, Atlanta, and Barcelona. In the case of Barcelona, the Catalonian government used the 1992 Olympics as an opportunity to redesign and re-present the city to the world; an exceptional event that continues to define images of the city.[35] Most other cities that have built stadiums in search of mega-events have not fared as well—the most spectacular financial failure being Montreal's 1976 Olympic Stadium, which is still being paid off. The 2007 Pan American Games in Rio de Janeiro were a litmus test of that city's capacity to safely and efficiently host large-scale international events in anticipation of the 2014 World Cup and 2016 Olympics.

If we think about stadiums in terms of world systems theory, using core and periphery as opposite poles, the unequal patterns of development and underdevelopment espoused by those theories emerge. For instance, stadiums in Asunción, Paraguay, are not as modern as those in Buenos Aires, nor are those in Buenos Aires as modern as those in London. Paraguay is an economic hinterland of Argentina, and Argentina of Britain. Similarly, stadiums in Abilene, Texas, are not as architecturally sophisticated as those in Dallas or Houston. The concentration of economic and political capital in urban centers is expressed in part through the stadiums that they contain. Rome had the 50,000-seat Colosseum; provincial Gaul's biggest coliseum could hold 5,000.

The increased economic functionality and architectural rationality of stadiums built in the last decade of the twentieth century and the first decade of the twenty-first has been carried off by a handful of global firms. These firms, such as HOK Sport, self-consciously produce "signature architecture" that will create metonymic relationships between the stadium and its host city. While this is a welcome change from the stadium designs of the 1960s and 1970s, the "themeing" of the stadium has distanced the interaction of the fan and place, "catering to customers" in place of "pertaining to fans." There is a cookie-cutter sameness to many of these new stadiums, particularly in the United States, where maximization of profit begins in the parking lot and the swift and efficient delivery of goods and services is relentless. In many of these new stadiums, particularly those in Britain, standing is forbidden and repeated offenders are removed for not keeping themselves in their place. Regulations for stadium behavior are exhaustive and read more like a correction facility's strictures than one would expect for a place of leisure.

The stadiums of Latin America have yet to undergo the kind of coporatization, rationalization, and profit maximization of their cousins in North America and Europe. While global corporations such as Nike, Adidas, Budweiser, Coca-Cola, Panasonic, and Toyota make their presence felt through massive advertisements on stadium walls, jerseys, sponsorships, and points of sale, there is a relative absence of consumerism in Latin American stadiums. There is an intensely felt sense of belonging to place, to stadiums, their teams and communities, that defines the geographic lifeworlds for tens of millions throughout the region.

There have been significant recent stadium developments in Latin America that deserve dedicated attention. Between 2005 and 2007 Venezuela spent nearly a billion dollars renovating and building stadiums for the Copa America and the state and city of Rio de Janeiro spent in excess of $700 million in preparation for the Pan American Games. While not all of this investment was directed towards stadium infrastructure, these events were used to achieve political and social ends. By beginning in the stadiums built for these events and working outwards, we will be able to understand the political motivations, cultural messages, and social meanings that sustain them.

The Conclusion of the Conclusion

Meaning, representation and heritage, organization and governance, and local responses to globalizing forces are interrelated and overlapping themes that inform the stadiums of Rio de Janeiro and Buenos Aires.

REVISTA LANCE A MAIS

A REVISTA DO **LANCE!**
ANO 5 // NÚMERO 216
DE 16 A 22 DE OUTUBRO DE 2004

PARTE INTEGRANTE DO DIÁRIO LANCE! AOS SÁBADOS. A PARTIR DE TERÇA-FEIRA, VENDA AVULSA A R$ 3,50

A fúria de Kanaan
Campeão da IRL, piloto critica governo por não tê-lo homenageado

Trilha de sucesso

Transparência
Segurança
Futebol-empresa →

Guarde a tabela do Campeonato Holandês

Novos estádios ←

Entenda as mudanças no futebol de Portugal e como o Brasil pode encurtar a distância rumo a uma organização moderna do esporte

FALA, CLODOALDO! Após os seis ouros na Paraolimpíada, nadador recebe chuva de convites para dar palestras

ISSN 1676-1537

Photo 6.9 Path to Success. The caption at the bottom left reads: "Understand the changes in Portuguese football [for Euro 2004] and how Brazil can begin to modernize its sports organizations." The three words on the road sign are *transparency, security, football-business.*

The complex geographic, political, economic, and cultural networks that extend from the stadium will never be understood in their entirety. However, by situating stadiums as points of entry into cultural landscapes, we can enter, interpret, and contextualize the myriad systems and processes that sustain them.

At first glance, the stadium cultures of Buenos Aires and Rio de Janeiro indicate relatively homogeneous landscapes. However, as we enter into them we see that they are as distinct as the cities themselves. When we move deeper, we understand that each stadium operates at variable scales and pertains to a geographically situated subculture. Even though these subcultures are highly variable, the common urban and cultural functions of stadiums are so crystallized that they can be used to compare social structures and political organization; the use, production, reproduction, and transformation of public space; narratives of identity; and historical trajectories in global and urban systems.

I have attempted to give a balanced vision of the stadium, although in the case of women's perspectives I fear that I have fallen short. Part of the reason for this failure is that, "with notable exceptions, works that study Latin American female athletes are brief, isolated, come as part of works more generally devoted to men and are often sexist, or at least condescending, in tone."[36] The same can be said of female perspectives and relationships to the stadium. In Buenos Aires women are generally not interested in soccer and rarely go to the stadium. This is not the case in Rio de Janeiro, where women debate soccer as fiercely as men and are full agents in the stadium spectacle. Women rise to positions of power with the *torcidas organizadas* and are directly involved in the transmission of team allegiances to their children. I believe I have hit upon the reasons for these differences in terms of the development of gendered space and sexuality in Buenos Aires, but there are probably contradictory or complementary explanations that will build on what I have presented here.

There are myriad unanswered questions that await responses in the coming years: Will women carve out more space in the stadiums of Buenos Aires? What are the relationships between organized fan groups and team management? Will the overwhelming corruption of Latin American stadium cultures change? How will local and national governments move to deal with the violence and social disorder associated with the stadium? What will be the fate of the many smaller stadiums in each city? Will the stadium become a site of social transformation, or will violence escalate until the stadium can no longer function in the public realm? How will larger social changes be expressed through the architecture, management, and cultural practices of the stadiums in each city? Will Brazil be able to pull its stadiums together in time for the 2014 World Cup? How will the ability, or inability, of Brazil to host a global mega-event affect Latin America?

Going back to the ball courts of pre-Columbian America, stadiums have been present in the region for millennia, yet scholars have almost completely ignored them as places and spaces of cultural production. The vast numbers and inherent complexity of stadiums allow researchers to approach them from a number of different methodological, ideological, and disciplinary perspectives. It is by positioning stadiums within larger historical, cultural, and spatial domains that the essential interconnectivity of cultural phenomena can be brought to light. By entering into Latin American cultures through the stadium, we are exposed to the intersecting networks that combine to create the textures and meanings of place. Frequently acting as facades of sophistication, stadiums are some of the most intense and visible places in any city, and what happens there can be deadly, invigorating, tragic, enlightening, and mundane. Stadiums are everywhere; understanding them brings us closer to understanding our commonalities, differences, and shared human qualities.

Stadiums in Rio de Janeiro, 2007

Owner	Stadium	Capacity	Year Built
América Football Club	Edson Passos	8,000	2002
Associação Atlética Portuguesa	Luso Brasiliero	30,000	1965
Bangu Athletic Club	Silveira Filho	15,000	1947
Bonsuccesso Futebol Clube	Leonidas da Silva	9,000	1936
Botafogo de Futebol e Regatas	General Severiano	3,000	1912
Campo Grande	Italo del Cima	18,000	1960
Centro de Futebol Zico	Antunes	5,000	2003
Ceres Futebol Clube	João Francisco dos Santos	3,000	1933
Clube de Regatas do Flamengo	José Bastos Padilha	8,000	1938
Clube de Regatas Vasco da Gama	São Januário	40,000	1927
Everest Atlético Clube	Ademar Bebiano	3,000	1953

Owner	Stadium	Capacity	Year Built
Fluminese Football Club	Manoel Schwartz	8,000	1919
Jacareparagua F.C.	Jacareparagua	5,000	
Madureira Esporte Club	Aniceto Moscoso	10,000	1941
Mesquita F.C.	Nielsen Lousada	4,000	
Olaria Atletico Clube	Mourão Vieira Filho	11,000	1947
Raiz da Gavea	Maravilha	9,500	
Rodoviario Pirai Futebol Clube	Ênio Simões	3,000	
São Cristóvão de Futebol e Regatas	Figueira de Melo	3,500	1914
Tomazinho Futebol Clube	Josias José da Silva	4,000	
União Esportiva Coelho da Rocha	José Amorim Pereira	5,000	
Universidade Estácio de Sá	Estácio de Sá	6,000	2005
SUDERJ	Jornalista Mario Filho	79,000	1950
SUDERJ	Caio Martins	12,000	1941
City of Rio de Janeiro	Hipódromo da Gavea	80,000	1875
SUDERJ	Olímpico João Havelange	45,000	2007
City of Rio de Janeiro	Sambódromo da Marquês de Sapucaí	100,000	1984
City of Rio de Janeiro	Autódromo Nelson Piquet	60,000	1977

Clubs and Stadiums in Buenos Aires, 2007

Club/Stadium	Capacity	Club Foundation
Acassuso	1,000	9/7/1922
All Boys	12,000	3/15/1913
Almagro	19,000	1/6/1911
Almirante Brown	10,000	1/17/1922
Argentino (Quilmes)	12,000	12/1/1899
Argentino de Merlo	9,000	8/30/1906
Argentinos Juniors	24,800	8/15/1904
Atlanta	34,000	10/12/1904
Atlas	300	8/17/1951
Autódromo Municipal	45,000	N/A
Banfield	33,351	1/21/1896
Barracas Central	2,500	4/5/1904
Berazategui	5,000	9/19/1975
Boca Juniors	57,395	4/3/1905
Campo Argentino de Polo	15,000	1927
Campo de Polo Los Pingüinos		1925
Canuelas F.C.	2,000	1/1/1911
Centro Social y Recreativo Español	34,500	6/24/1934
Chacarita Juniors	24,300	5/1/1906
Claypole	1,300	10/1/1923
Club Atlético Brown	4,000	1952
Club Atlético V. Ballester		N/A
Club Deportivo Español	30,000	9/3/2003
Club Militar de Polo San José		1940
Colegiales	4,500	4/1/1908
Comunicaciones	3,500	3/15/1931
Defensa y Justicia	8,000	3/20/1935

Club/Stadium	Capacity	Club Foundation
Defensores del Belgrano	8,300	5/25/1906
Defensores Unidos	6,000	7/14/1914
Deportivo Armenio	8,000	11/2/1962
Deportivo Italiano	8,000	5/7/1955
Deportivo Laferrere	5,000	7/9/1956
Deportivo Merlo	5,000	10/8/1954
Deportivo Morón	19,000	6/20/1947
Deportivo Paraguyo	N/A	8/15/1961
Deportivo Riestra	3,000	2/22/1931
El Porvenir	14,000	9/12/1915
Estadio Nacional de Béisbol	3,000	1953
Estudiantes de Buenos Aires	16,500	8/15/1898
Excursionistas	6,900	2/1/1910
Fenix		4/25/1948
Ferrocarril Oeste	24,268	7/28/1904
Ferrocarril Urquiza	500	5/21/1954
Flandria	5,000	2/9/1941
General La Madrid	3,000	5/11/1950
Hipódromo Argentino	100,000	1876
Hipódromo de San Isidro	60,000	1935
Hipódromo de Trote		1968
Huracán	48,314	11/1/1908
Hurlingham Club		1888
Independiente	52,823	1/1/1905
Ituazingo	3,300	4/1/1912
J.J. Urquiza	4,000	6/8/1936
Jockey Club de Buenos Aires		4/15/1882
Lanus	44,000	1/3/1915
Leandro N. Alem	4,000	5/10/1925
Liniers	5,000	7/2/1931
Los Andes	35,000	1/1/1917
Lugano	1,500	11/18/1915
Luján	2,500	4/1/1936
Nueva Chicago	28,500	7/1/1911
Platense	31,000	5/25/1905
Quilmes	33,000	11/27/1887
Racing	64,161	3/25/1903
Riestra	3,000	1/22/1931
River Plate	76,687	5/25/1901
Sacachispas	4,000	10/17/1948
San Lorenzo	43,480	4/1/1908
San Telmo	9,000	3/5/1904

Club/Stadium	Capacity	Club Foundation
Sarmiento	18,000	1951
Sportivo Barracas	5,000	10/30/1913
Sportivo Dock Sud	5,500	9/1/1916
Temperly	18,000	1/1/1912
Tigre	30,000	8/3/1902
Tristan Suarez	5,000	8/8/2004
Vélez Sársfield	49,540	1/1/1910
Victoriano Arenas	1,500	1/2/1928
Villa San Carlos	2,000	4/25/1925
Yupanqui	200	10/12/1935

Time Line, Brazil

1888	Brazil abolishes slavery.
1889	Brazilian Republic proclaimed.
	Charles Miller returns to Brazil from Europe.
	Charles Miller starts soccer team at São Paulo Railway.
1897	Oscar Cox organizes first soccer team in Rio de Janeiro after returning from studies in Switzerland.
1902	Fluminese Football Club founded, Rio de Janeiro.
	Rio Cricket Club stages soccer game in honor of the coronation of Edward VIII.
1904	Botafogo Football Club founded, first Brazilian-only team.
1908	First English and Argentine teams visit Rio de Janeiro as part of "National Exposition of Modernity."
1914	Pitch invasions at Botofogo cause public scandal and implementation of private police forces at many Rio stadiums.
1916	Estádio Figueira de Melo inaugurated.
1917	Estádio das Laranjeiras inaugurated.
1918	Figueira de Melo inaugurated.
1919	Third South American Championship, Rio de Janeiro.
1920	King Albert of Belgium visits Rio de Janeiro.
1922	Brazilian Centennial Exhibition.
	Fifth South American Championship.
	Zinucati.
1924	Vasco da Gama wins Rio league with blacks and mulattos in team; São Cristóvão finishes second.
	Rio leagues split into AMEA and LMDT.
1925	Jockey Club replaces Derby Club as Rio's principal horse-racing track.

1926	São Cristóvão wins AMEA.
1927	Estádio São Januário inaugurated with Brazilian president Washington Luis in the stands. Vasco loses 5–3 to Santos.
1928	First stadium lights in South America installed in São Januário.
1930	First World Cup in Montevideo, Uruguay wins.
1934	Soccer professionalizes in Brazil. Italy wins World Cup.
1938	Brazil finishes third at World Cup in Chile. Italy wins.
1946	Brazil chosen to host fourth World Cup.
1949	Maracanã construction begins in August.
1950	Maracanã opens on June 18.
	July 16, World Cup Final: Uruguay 2, Brazil 1.
1958	Brazil wins World Cup.
1962	Brazil wins World Cup.
1970	Brazil wins World Cup.
1994	Brazil wins World Cup.
1997	Maracanã capacity reduced from 179,000 to 119,000.
2002	Brazil wins World Cup.
2004	Brazil beats Argentina in Copa América final.
2006	*Geral* eliminated. Maracanã capacity reduced to 79,000.
2007	Brazil emerges as only South American candidate to host 2014 World Cup.
	Rio de Janeiro hosts Pan American Games.
	Brazil beats Argentina in Copa América final.

Time Line, Argentina

1876	Hipódromo Argentino inaugurated.
1884	First polo game in Buenos Aires.
1891	First soccer league disputed in Buenos Aires.
1899	River Plate Rugby Championship begun.
1900	First Uruguay vs. Argentina soccer game.
1904	British soccer teams visit Buenos Aires.
1900–1907	Local leagues expand to have more than 350 teams. Polo becomes mandatory training for cavalry regimens.
1916	Fans set fire to stadium during Argentina vs. Uruguay match.
1924	Argentina wins gold medal in polo at Paris Olympics.
1928	Palermo Polo Grounds inaugurated. Argentina wins second Olympic gold.
1929	Argentina finishes second in 1930 World Cup, loses to Uruguay 2–1.
1931	Professionalism accepted in soccer.
1930–1950	State-sponsored stadium-building projects increase.
1968	71 Boca Junior's fans crushed to death at River Plate. Rise of *barrabravas* as major stadium force.
1978	Argentina wins World Cup under suspicion of tampering by military dictatorship.
1986	Argentina wins World Cup with Diego Maradona as captain.
1990s	Neoliberal economic regimes bring false prosperity to Argentina. Low levels of mortal stadium violence.
1996	Los Pumas finish sixth at Rugby World Cup National coverage of rugby increases.
2001	Argentine economy collapses in December. Five presidents take office in 21 days.

2002	Escalation of stadium violence.
	Argentina crashes out of World Cup in first round.
2003	National soccer leagues suspended due to fan violence.
2004	National soccer leagues suspended due to fan violence.
2006	National soccer leagues suspended due to fan violence.
	Argentina loses in quarter-final of World Cup.
2007	Argentina loses to Brazil in Copa América final.
	Boca Juniors president Mauricio Macri becomes mayor of Buenos Aires.
	Boca Juniors *barrabravas* chief jailed.

notes

Chapter One

1. FIFA, www.fifa.com, accessed Sept. 1, 2005; IOC 2005; United Nations 2006.

2. Of course, not every politically organized territory has a stadium. Territories belonging to indigenous communities in North America (reservations in the United States, Nunivut in Canada) or to indigenous groups in Australia and the Americas are not as likely to have stadiums, although they do have folk games. This is a reflection of the continuation of traditional cultures not associated with the sporting cultures of industrial capitalism and global economic systems.

3. Gaffney and Bale 2004.

4. Durran 1970, 263.

5. Gebhard 1992; Miller, Coulson, and Helmut 1988.

6. Swaddling 1999.

7. Guttmann 1978; Olivova 1984.

8. MacAloon 1981.

9. Guttmann 1978, 1986; Futrell 1997; Cameron 1976; Olivova 1984.

10. Guttmann 1978, 24.

11. Futrell 1997; Inglis 2000.

12. Guttmann 1986, 23.

13. Mumford 1961; Butzer, pers. com., Feb. 14, 2005.

14. Scheffler 1985; Quirarte 1970; Guttmann 1978; Leyenarr 1978.

15. Wallerstein 1984; Tranter 1998; Thrift 1999; Pred 1984; Bale 1982; Bowden 1995.

16. Bowden 1995, 99–107.

17. Hardin 1968.

18. Bowden 1995, 82–96.

19. Holt 1988.

20. This pattern repeated itself in the twentieth century with the political, economic, and military influence of the United States in East Asia, the Caribbean, and parts of Latin America.

21. Bale 2000; Bowden 1995.

22. The period of decline began earlier, but it took some time for the stadiums to follow.

23. Euchner 1993; Danielson 1997; Noll and Zimbalist 1997.

24. King 1998; Weiner 2000; Danielson 1997; Benson 1989; Bale and Moen 1995. Portugal built or remodeled twelve stadiums for Euro 2004 to come into accordance with FIFA and UEFA regulations. Austria and the Czech Republic are doing the same for Euro 2008.

25. The instances of corporate stadium names are increasing in the United Kingdom and Canada (JJB Stadium, Reebok Stadium, Emirates Stadium, Rodgers Centre).

26. See Bale 2000, for an excellent review of different landscapes of sport.

27. On Copacabana Beach in Rio de Janeiro, temporary metal stadiums are constructed to host professional beach volleyball and beach soccer events. They are constructed in three to four weeks and hold between five thousand and eight thousand spectators.

28. There are a number of books dedicated to stadium architecture and large stadium design firms like HOK+Sport, a billion-dollar enterprise. See Sheard 2001, 2005; Inglis 1990, 1996.

29. Adams 2005, 25. Adams undertakes an excellent examination of the individual as an extensible agent. Because architecture communicates messages and stadiums are very large nodes in communications networks, it seems logical to apply theories of extensibility to buildings. Stadiums, skyscrapers, communications buildings, and financial markets all merit more attention in this regard.

30. Bowden 1995, 116.

31. It is difficult to distinguish between memorials and monuments, as both are created to "keep alive" or "commemorate" the memory of a person or event. For a sampling of geographic work on monuments and memorial landscapes, see Duncan 1990; Zukin 1991; Findlay 1992; Foote 1997; Cosgrove and Daniels 1988; Atkinson and Cosgrove 1998; Hayden 1995.

32. Foote 1997, 29.

33. Stadiums fulfill and/or describe all of Lynch's (1964) urban categories: paths, edges, districts, nodes, and landmarks.

34. Cosgrove 1984, 15.

35. Mumford 1961.

36. One of the claims to fame of the University of Nebraska–Lincoln's Memorial Stadium is that on game days it becomes the third largest city in the state.

37. Appadurai (1996) refers to the media-based formation of meaning as a "mediascape," which Adams (2005, 17) characterizes as "landscapes of media access and meaning."

38. www.rapidnet.com/~jbeard/bdm/psychology/jk/jk/htm. Accessed Oct. 14, 2005.

39. *Houston Chronicle*, Jan. 25, 2004.

40. Turner 1973, 195.

41. For an interesting discussion on the use of time-geography to analyze sport, see Moore et al. 2003.

42. MacAloon 1984, 3.

43. Following Lynch (1972), those inside the stadium are both *behavioral insiders and existential insiders*, while those watching on television or standing outside the gates are *vicarious insiders*. All types are *empathetic insiders*.

44. Foucault 1977, 200–201.

45. Foucault 1977, 202–203.

46. Foucault 1977, 203.

47. Guttmann 1996, 59.

48. Massey 1994.

49. Pronger 1990, 79.

50. Guttmann 1996, 67.

51. Pronger 1990, 82.

52. Gruneau 1999, 30.

53. Zirin 2005.

54. Scarpaci 2005; Herzog 2006; Low 2000.

55. Thinking in terms of political movements and the democratic public sphere in Latin America, Avritzer (2002, 76) envisions a category of *hybrid public space* defined by "penetration of the public into the public, non-plural popular identities, and private claims mechanisms rather than collective association." This may also be a useful categorization of stadium space but is too enmeshed with the development and functioning of the public sphere to be used in this case.

56. This discussion will not treat the critical theoretical underpinnings of the *social production of space*. For more about these theories, see Lefebvre [1973] 1991; Gottdeiner 1985; Harvey 1989; Gregory 1994.

57. Scarpaci 2005, 32.

58. Low 2000, 51.

59. Meade 1997, 45-55; Avritzer 2002, 77–79.

60. Scarpaci 2005, 12–20.

61. The conceptual city can be defined as the city that exists in the imagination. That is, knowing that certain spaces and places exist, whether or not one uses them, informs one's consciousness of the city. This was particularly important to the social and urban engineers of fin-de-siècle Latin America, which wanted to demonstrate to locals and European visitors their cosmopolitanism.

62. Godfrey 1991.

63. Scarpaci 2005, 13–14.

64. *Estádio* is the Portuguese spelling of stadium, *estadio* (without accent) the Spanish.

65. Browder and Godfrey 1997, 13.

66. Scarpaci 2005.

67. Low 2000, 47.

68. Rosenthal 2000, 36.

69. Jones 2004.

Chapter Two

1. Moura 1998, 17.

2. Mason 1995, 19.

3. Taylor 1998, 26.

4. Mascarenhas 2002, 119.

5. Fernandes and Negreiros 2001, 416.

6. See Bourdeiu 1984.

7. Pereira 2000, 27.

8. Bale 1994.

9. Pereira 2000, 31.

10. For a discussion of other cities in Latin America, see Arbena 2002; Stein 1988; Allinson 1978.

11. Pereira 2000, 68–71; Rodrigues [Filho] 1964, 90.

12. Capoeira is a Brazilian martial art characterized by fluid, playlike movements. It emerged in the sixteenth century among Afro-Brazilians along the Atlantic coast.

13. Mason 1995; Taylor 1998; Galeano 2002.

14. Appadurai 1996; Futrell 1997.

15. Graham 1988.

16. Kern 1983.

17. www.uroegon.edu/~serg.ok/brasil/bzpeople.htm. Accessed January 15, 2006.

18. Pereira Passos might be the only mayor to ever have a football club named after him: Pereira Passos F.C. played in Rio's second division in the 1920s. See Pereira 2000, 239.

19. Abreu 1987; Cardoso 1996; Graham 1988.

20. Godfrey 1991, 1999.

21. Anderson 1983; Hobsbawm and Ranger 1983.

22. Perlman 1976; Graham 1988.

23. Best XI teams comprised the best eleven players of a given geographic area taken from various club teams. Typically formed for one or two matches, Best XI teams were not considered "official" representatives of Brazil.

24. Pereira 2000, 106.

25. Anderson 1983; Hobsbawm and Ranger 1983.

26. Pereira 2000, 108.

27. The generalized processes of soccer club formation were foundation, move and improve, buy space, build stadium, consolidation and solidification, institutionalization.

28. The cost of tickets to the games was prohibitively high for many: "equivalent to a kilogram of *bacalau* [traditional meal of salted cod], two tickets for the cinema or a monthly newspaper subscription" (Pereira 2000, 136).

29. Special thanks to Dr. Bert Barickman for his help in researching this building.

30. Pereira 2000, 137.

31. Pereira 2000, 157.

32. Rodrigues [Filho] 1964, 30; italics denotes English words in the original text.

33. Pereira 2000, 300–305; see also Bellos 2000, 77–79.

34. Pereira 2000, 314.

35. São Cristóvão is called the "Imperial Neighborhood" because of the extended tenure of the Portuguese royal family in the Quinta de Boa Vista. When the Portuguese fled Lisbon ahead of Napoleon, they established the Royal Court in Rio de Janeiro and built a palace in São Cristóvão on the Quinta de Boa Vista.

36. Graham 1988.

37. Quadros 2004, 31–34.

38. *O Correio da Manhã*, Apr. 24, 1916.

39. This era marked the beginning of a powerful discourse in Brazilian society that positions sport as a mechanism to escape socioeconomic marginality. The spectacular

success of Brazilian soccer players and teams on an international level is, among other things, a product of this discourse. In my opinion, this insidious regime allows for the continued socioeconomic marginalization of a large percentage of the population that feeds the global production of sport, which in turn generates massive profits for multinational corporations, club directors, and the directors of national and international soccer federations.

40. Ferreira 2004, 44.

41. Rodrigues [Filho] 1964, 119–123.

42. In 1920 the first division was divided into "A" and "B" categories. Vasco participated in the "B" division from 1920 to 1922 and was champion in 1922. The team was promoted to "A" for the 1923 season and won. F. da Costa Ferreira, pers. com., 2006.

43. Filho intimates that Vasco came to represent an essentialized, menacing "other" to the elites: "It didn't matter much that Vasco, with its whites, mulattos, and blacks was brazilianizing the sport. The players of Morais e Silva [the street intersection where the Vasco ground was located] lost their nationality and turned into Portuguese. No one could say that the big clubs were against the small clubs or against the blacks. They were against the Portuguese, who had altered the status quo" (Rodrigues [Filho] 1964, 122).

44. Ferreira 2004, 94.

45. Pereira 2000, 100.

46. The construction was carried out by a Danish firm, and the architectural specifications for the interior of the stadium and field were taken from the German Sport Federation. Malhano and Malhano 2002, 141.

47. Pereira 2000, 338.

48. Moura 1998, 20–23.

49. Rodrigues [Filho] 1945, 2–3.

50. Malhano and Malhano 2002, 225.

51. "The capital of the Republic could not be behind São Paulo in anything. Rio de Janeiro needed a big stadium to show up the Pacaembú" (Moura 1998, 26).

52. The public financing of the project "reinforced the symbolic identity of the stadium with the generalized development of Brazil and represented the monumentalization of the national development project and consolidated the relationship between the public and the government working together for the betterment of Brazil" (Moura 1998, 36–37).

In the decades to come, politicians sponsored hundreds of stadium projects throughout Brazil. By the 1970s Brazil had seven of the ten largest stadiums in the world. A town might not have running water, schools, or transportation infrastructure, but if a local politician could deliver a 100,000-seat stadium . . .

53. Moura 1998, 26–36.

54. The Derby Club was Rio's first stadium, built around 1850. It was abandoned when the Joquei Club was built on the shores of Lagoa de Rodrigo Freitas in 1913, just north of the (then) southern suburb of Ipanema.

55. Moura 1998, 38–40.

56. This date coincided with the third anniversary of the administration of Mendes de Morais, the mayor of Rio de Janeiro, who was obviously keen to have the completion of the stadium associated with his government (Moura 1998, 43).

57. *Jornal do Sports*, June 17, 1950.

58. www.rsssf.com/tables/49safull.html. Accessed Sept. 15, 2006.

59. Moura 1998, 114–120; quote on p. 115. Cosgrove and Daniels (1998, 30) say that public monuments "intended to encapsulate an imagined national spirit or identity, seek to materialize ideas of the sacred, the mystical and the transcendental." This served to heighten the magic and potential of the pregame moment.

60. Bellos 2002, 54–55.

61. Moura 1998, 80.

Chapter Three

1. Lever 1983, 75.

2. See Fernandes 1974; Vinnai 1975; Paoli et al. 1982; Ramos 1984; Pimenta 1995; Lopes 1995; Henrique de Toledo 1996; Gama 1996; Pineto 1997; Damo 2002.

3. See DaMatta 1982, 1990.

4. DaMatta 1985.

5. DaMatta 1985, 25.

6. A *carioca*, strictly defined, is someone who was born in Rio de Janeiro. Loosely defined, it is anyone who lives in the city of Rio de Janeiro.

7. This was the morning of August 15, 2004.

8. Ronaldo Luiz Nazario de Lima is one of the most famous Brazilian soccer players of his generation. "Ronaldo" began his professional career at Flamengo but was unable to afford the bus fare and started playing at F.R. São Cristóvão. From there, he was sold to Cruziero in Belo Horizonte, then moved to PSV Eindhoven in Holland, Inter Milan, and, finally, Real Madrid. A fixture in the Brazilian national team for the past ten years and the all-time leading goal scorer in the World Cup, Ronaldo's emergence as a star at F.R. São Cristóvão remains a source of pride and inspiration for the club.

9. Perlman 1976; *O Globo*, July 13, 2005.

10. I put *hooligans* in quotation marks to highlight the difference in social organization and structure between Brazilan fan groups and others. The word *hooligan* implies football-related violence that is present in many sporting cultures. *Torcidas organizadas* is literally translated as "organized twisters." A full explanation of their role in the Brazilian stadium warrants a book in its own right.

11. Assaf 1997; www.fferj.com.br.

12. Brazil has three divisions in the national system. The first and second divisions are fairly consistent with the rest of the world in that they have a clear system of promotion and relegation between them and each division has twenty teams. The bottom six teams in the second division are relegated to the third. The third division has sixty-four teams that pass through three rounds of competition before a playoff determines which teams ascend to the second division. A team can enter into the third division by winning their state tournament or by being put forward by the state federation. In 2006 the teams from Rio de Janeiro that participated in the Brazilian third division were América F.C., Americano F.C., Madureira S.C., and A.D. Cabofriense, all of which compete in the first division of the Rio state tournament. So in order for São Cristóvão F.R. to enter a national competition, they must win the second division state tournament and finish in the top half of the first division state tournament and

be able to prove to FERJ that they have the facilities and financial capacity to comply with the regulations set forth for the Brazilian third division as set forth by the CBF.

13. The club's Web site, www.saocristovaofr.com.br, has a detailed history of Ronaldo's appearances, goals, and other statistics. (Web site accessed May 30, 2007.)

14. The stadium has hosted some curious matches: S.C.F.R. against Dinamo Zagreb in 1953, Brazil in 1964, Nigeria in 1979, and United Arab Emirates in 1988.

15. http://esporte.uol.com.br/futebol/ultimas/2004/10/04/ult59u87819.htm. Accessed Sept. 26, 2006.

16. Soares and Lovisolo 2003.

17. The neighborhood Vasco da Gama was created in 2003 through the efforts of a Vascaino city councilman in an attempt to curry favor with local voters. See Ferreira 2004 for a full account.

18. Vasco has the third largest fan base in Brazil after Rio's Flamengo and São Paulo's Corinthians.

19. See Bellos 2002 for a full-flavored sample.

20. *O Globo*, May 11, 2007. http://oglobo.globo.com/esportes/mat/2007/05/11/295715035.asp.

21. The details of membership benefits and activities can be found on the club Web site: www.crvascodagama.com.

22. Casaca 2007, 3.

23. Guieros, *O Globo*, July 2, 2004, 38.

24. *O Globo*, July 1, 2004.

25. Guieros, 38.

26. Gueiros, 38

27. The Guarda Municipal is responsible for controlling traffic flow to and from the stadium.

28. *O Globo*, Oct. 7, 2004.

29. Moura 1998, 35–37.

30. At the time of writing. After construction of the facilities for the 2007 Pan American Games the number will likely be much higher. The number 1,380 was just for the Maracanã complex in 2004.

31. Following the construction of a stadium in Volta Redonda, located midway between São Paulo and Rio de Janeiro, the municipality of Volta Redonda began to court Fluminese and Flamengo, paying the teams 100,000 reales for playing Brazilian league games there. This has proved enormously successful for the city and the teams.

32. Botafogo also plays in a SUDERJ-operated stadium, Caio Martins, which is located across the Bay of Guanabara in the municipality of Niteroi.

33. "Stadium of Plastic," *O Globo*, Sept. 17, 2004, 17.

34. Interview with Sergio Emilião, Oct. 2004.

35. Dee Oliveira and Graça 2004.

36. *O Globo*, July 11, 2004, 51.

37. *Desportes*, July 11, 2004, 1.

38. Azeredi 1930; Caldas 1990; Gama 1996; Ramos 1984, 1990.

Chapter Four

1. *Barrabravas* are organized fan groups. They are discussed at length in Chapter Five.

2. La Doce means "the twelfth," a reference to the eleven players on the field and the twelfth in the stands. It is unclear whether this number was chosen because of the death of seventy-one Boca Juniors' fans at door 12 of River Plate's stadium in 1968.

3. *Xeneixe* is taken from the name of the Italian dialect spoken in the Genoese region of Italy from where many immigrants to the Boca district came.

4. Gandara 1997.

5. "El que no salta es maricón."

6. "Whoever doesn't jump is English." This is chanted by thousands of people who jump up and down in the stands. The last word is frequently replaced by whatever derisive nickname the other team has, or by "maricón" (fag) or "militar" (soldier).

7. Mangan, Lamartine, and DaCosta 2001; Arbena 1988; Giulianotti 1999; Archetti 2003.

8. Holt 1988.

9. www.palermonline.com.ar/noticias001/nota536_hipodromo .htm. Accessed Oct. 7, 2006.

10. Sebreli 1983; Frydenberg 1999.

11. Scher and Palomino 1988, 24; Chepenekas, D'Addario, and Vivori 1997; Mason 1995, 2.

12. Giulianotti 1999; Sebreli 1983.

13. Arbena 1988; Taylor 1998.

14. Frydenberg 1999. For a more complete history of the early years of soccer in Argentina see Mason 1995, 1–8. Similar to what happened in Rio de Janeiro, Argentine teams played against visiting English teams, which served to heighten nationalist sentiments in relation to soccer and stadiums. In 1905 ten thousand people gathered in the Palermo stadium of Sociedad Sportiva to watch the Alumni team of Buenos Aires play against Nottingham Forest of England. This was by far the largest crowd to ever watch a sporting event in South America.

15. Scher and Palomino 1988, 21–22.

16. E. Archetti, pers. com., Nov. 14, 2003; Frydenberg 1999; Scher and Palomino 1988; Mason 1995.

17. Gorelik 1998.

18. Scher and Palomino 1988, 23.

19. Scobie 1974; Needell 1995; Foster 1998; Rosenthal 2000.

20. Foster 1998; Bao 1993.

21. See Scobie 1974; Gorelik 1998.

22. Frydenberg 1999, 8–9. I have yet to map these networks but intend to do so in the near future as I collect more data.

23. Conversely, among rural migrants, women were predominant, although their numbers did not compensate for the imbalance created by international immigrants. See Guy 1991.

24. Guy 1991, 5.

25. Jelin, pers. com., Oct. 2006; Archetti 1998, 159; Guy 1991, 204–205.

26. Rosenthal 2000, 58.

27. Archetti 2003, 223.

28. Foster 1998, 69.

29. Rosenthal 2000, 58.

30. Archetti 2003; Foster 1998.

31. Bao 1993.

32. For an examination of the homosexual spaces of early-twentieth-century New York, see Chauncey 1994.

33. Equal rights of citizenship were extended to all women in 1947 (Bao 1993).

34. I assume the near-total absence of women in the practice of the sport, although it would appear that they were brought into the realm of the soccer stadium through their associations with men in tango bars (Archetti 1998, 171). Even today women's soccer is a rarity in Buenos Aires, and given the cultural conditions in the early twentieth century we can describe the phenomenon as a nearly exclusive male domain. As Arbena notes, "The soccer ritual, for all its changes regarding women, remains a process of social reproduction of male dominance" (Arbena, Abreu, and LaFrance 2002, 224). While the social clubs associated with soccer teams may have provided space for female recreation and socialization, women's activities were never represented in stadium space.

35. *Cagón* literally means "shithead" but is translated as "coward."

36. Giulianotti 1999, 8.

37. Archetti 1998. A common appellation for Diego Maradona, Argentina's most well known and notorious soccer player, is *el pibe de oro*, or the golden boy.

38. Archetti 1998, 233–235.

39. Topofilia and topofobia are, respectively, love and fear of place (Tuan 1974, 1977).

40. Of course, the symbolic warfare of the stadium eventually extended to the nation-state itself. See Agostino 2002.

41. Alabarces 2000, 216.

42. Alabarces 2000, 219.

43. The intersection of stadiums, soccer, and politics in Argentina merits more attention than I can give it here. There are a number of excellent books on the subject, almost all of them in Spanish. See Sebreli 1983; Scher and Palomino, 1988; di Gano 2005.

44. Archetti and Romero 1994, 232.

45. Mayochi 1992.

46. *Clásicos* are the equivalent of "Derby" matches in Great Britain. Though there is no equivalent term in North America, a *clásico* is a team's biggest rivalry. In Buenos Aires, the Superclásico is between River Plate and Boca Juniors. On a continental scale, the Superclásico is between Brazil and Argentina. The *clásico rioplatense* refers to the Rio de la Plata, which separates Argentina and Uruguay.

47. Sebreli 1983, 106.

48. Archetti and Romero 1994, 228–229.

49. Sebreli 1983.

50. Bayer 1990; Archetti 1998, 109. Czechoslovakia beat Argentina 6–1 in the opening round.

51. Archetti 1998, 110.

52. Archetti 1997, 99.

53. Sebreli 1983, 99.

54. Alabarces 2000; Giulianotti 1994; Buford 1992; Gruneau 1999; Dunning 1999.

55. "The soccer stadium and your mother's cunt."

56. The extension of the stadium into the domestic sphere via radio and television may provide yet another form of escape or an assertion of male-specific epistemologies in an otherwise "feminine" space.

57. Guttman 1996, 147.

58. Guttman 1996, 77.

59. Foster 1998.

60. Guttman 1996, 139–140.

61. "The mythic world of gender power . . . acknowledging or accepting the power that has been invoked by the interpretation of a gesture as masculine is a matter of faith in the gender myth" (Pronger 1990, 51–52).

62. Binello et al. 2000.

63. Archetti 1985, 40.

64. Gil 2002.

65. Romero 1986. Data for the period 1986–2007 are unavailable, yet following the collapse of the Argentine peso in 2001 the Clasura tournament of 2002 began a period of increased mortal violence in and around the stadiums.

66. Archetti 1998, 158.

67. Foster 1998, 61.

68. Buenos Aires City Government, 2006. www.buenosaires.gov.ar. Accessed Nov. 1, 2006.

69. Guy 1991; Scobie 1974; Needell 1995.

Chapter Five

1. Rankings taken from the Web sites of international federations.

2. The stadium is also used for concerts, field hockey, and *pato* contests.

3. Archetti 2003, 121–127.

4. Archetti 2003.

5. *Pato* is considered the "national game" of Argentina. It is similar to polo in that the players are on horseback, but instead of hitting a ball, they try to throw a duck through a suspended ring. The contemporary version does not use a live animal but an oddly shaped ball with wicker handles.

6. Archetti 2003, 124.

7. Foster 1998, 69.

8. Archetti 2003, 148.

9. Archetti 2003, 131–137; Asociación Argentina de Polo 2005.

10. I suggest that this relationship is problematic because of the dominant role that Buenos Aires has played in Argentine history, frequently acquiring economic and political power at the expense of the provinces. The uneven geographic development of Argentina has engendered a lasting conflict between city and country, between the metropole of Buenos Aires and the rest of the country. For further reading, see Schumway 1991.

11. These observations are taken from numerous visits to the Palermo Polo Grounds when there were no games and from the final game of the Campeonato Abierto in 2004.

12. See, e.g., www.heguypolo.com/caballos.php.

13. As I did with Sarah Ferguson, Duchess of York.

14. Spinetto 1992.

15. Llistosella 1977; Spinetto 1992; T. Guterman, pers. com., July 17, 2004. There is some evidence that rugby is making inroads to the city. Club Atlético Nueva Chicago

started a rugby team in 2004 in the decidedly urban neighborhood of Mataderos.

16. Refer to chapter 1 for the distinction between a field and a stadium.

17. Much as the worlds of soccer and polo are spatially connected with particular spaces and places throughout the world, so too rugby has its own geography. The principal rugby-playing nations of the world are European and/or English speaking and the game has not been as successfully hybridized in Argentina as have polo and soccer. Thus identification with rugby implies an association with particular geographies and cultures: England, Wales, Ireland, Scotland, South Africa, Australia, New Zealand, France, and Italy.

18. "La guerra de los Pumas," *Diario Clarín*, Mar. 20, 2003.

19. "La guerra de los Pumas," *Diario Clarín*, Mar. 20, 2003; italics indicate words in English in the original.

20. Duke and Crolley 2001, 101.

21. Boca Juniors made a tour of Europe in the 1930s, winning most of their games. It was also common in this era for English teams to tour Buenos Aires and for Rio de Janeiro to compete against local teams.

22. Duke and Crolley 2001, 104.

23. The full details of the involvement of the military government and the 1978 World Cup are as well documented as they are frightening. See Scher and Palomino 1988, 147–175; Mason 1995, 66–76; Taylor 1998, 59–75; Giulianotti 2002, 100–106; Duke and Crolley 2001, 111–114; Arbena 1990.

24. www.clarin.com.ar. Accessed Apr. 12, 2003.

25. Sebreli 1983; Duke and Crolley 2001.

26. Scher and Palomino 1988.

27. Alabarces 2000, 215.

28. Archetti 1985; Scher and Palomino 1988; Alabarces 2000; Duke and Crolley 2001. This was also the period in which the *torcidas organizadas* of Brazil came to prominence.

29. Deterritorialization is a process in which the city as a whole becomes unbounded. The increased fluidity of formerly fixed boundaries allows for an accelerated movement of goods and people that has the generalized effect of reducing historically rooted associations with the place of the neighborhood.

30. Each team has one *barrabrava*. This is different from the structure of *torcidas organizadas* in Brazil, where each team has competing groups that are vying for political and economic favors from the club. The internecine competition between a team's various *torcidas* in Brazil is contained within the singular entity of the *barrabrava* in Argentina.

31. Estudiantes went on to win the championship for the first time in twenty-six years.

32. Duke and Crolley 2001.

33. Sebreli 1983, 35.

34. One of the boasts of Boca Juniors' *barrabrava* El Doce is that hardly any of its members have finished primary school.

35. Binello et al 2003, 42.

36. Rodgers 1999.

37. Alabarces 2000, 218.

38. Alabarces 2000, 220.

39. Romero 1986; Sebreli 1983.

40. Gandara 1997.

41. Alabarces 2000, 224; Romero 1986.

42. The Web site www.barrasbravas.com.ar is dedicated to the histories, relationships, and culture of *barrabravas* throughout Argentina and is an excellent reference for those who wish to know more about this world.

43. The *barrabravas* of Argentina are known around the soccer world. The transmission of soccer games from Buenos Aires to Europe is one of the primary mechanisms through which stadium behaviors are diffused among fan groups. The innovations of the Argentine fans frequently manifest themselves in Italian or Spanish stadiums the following week (T. Guterman, pers. com., July 17, 2004). A well-known anecdote is that some Mexican soccer teams hired members of Argentine *barrabravas* to travel to Mexico to organize their fans. The Argentines were incredulous that the teams did not provide financial assistance to their fan groups. An increasingly common element of Mexican stadiums is the long vertical banners that demarcate space for the *barrabravas*. In Mexico, however, the crowd is much more sedate and violence among fans is a rarity. There is also a popular television show in Argentina called *Aguante*. The weekly program showcases *barrabravas* from around Argentina (though mainly Buenos Aires) and makes consistent claims for peace in the stadiums.

44. Alabarces 2000, 213–214.

45. Though the majority of *barrabravas* are men, women are also present among them. Binello et al. (2003, 36–39) suggested that it through the mass-mediafication of soccer that women are able to manifest themselves more visibly in soccer culture. If their place in the spectacle is as an object of the masculine gaze, women appear to use this as a means of appropriating space in the soccer world. However, the "majority of the feminine images that are presented by the media of women in stadiums meet a double condition: sensuality and exoticism. This signifies that not all of the women present in the stadiums [during the 1998 World Cup] were captured by the cameras, but only those that met these two conditions" (37). Thus the media contribute to a gendered construction of stadium space wherein women are valorized for their sexual characteristics and not for their ability to participate as full agents in the spectacle. In many instances, women are brought to stadiums by their brothers or boyfriends and participate in the carnival staged by the *barrabrava*.

46. Alabarces 2000, 225; Archetti 1985.

47. Giulianotti 2002, 97.

48. There are dozens of disturbing videos of soccer-related violence in Argentina available on YouTube. Simply do a search for "violencia Argentina fútbol" to get a sample.

49. Alabarces 2002, 83.

50. In 2003 the Kirchner government created a special prosecution unit to investigate sports-related crimes as well as the Sports Security Secretariat that is headed by a former referee. In 1994 the Law on Sports Event Violence required that club directors provide the identities of the leaders of their club's *barrabrava*. This law is rarely complied with and makes prosecuting individuals for stadium-related violence difficult. The institutional framework of the Asociación de Fútbol Argentino is also inadequate for prosecuting *barrabrava*. The evasion of laws, the complicity of directors, and the power of *barrabravas* create a situation in which no one takes responsibility for the violence.

Chapter Six

1. For a more profound comparison of the urban history and morphology of Buenos Aires and Rio de Janeiro, see Needell 1995; Outtes 2003.

2. Meade 1997; Archetti 1995; Elias and Dunning 1986.

3. Needell 1995, 535.

4. Archetti 1998b; Braceli 2001; Cunha 1994; Hamilton 2001.

5. Uruguay was the first international soccer power. The *albiceleste* (sky blue) won the Olympic tournaments in 1924 and 1928 and the inaugural FIFA World Cup in 1930. Uruguay did not participate in the 1934 and 1938 World Cups; thus their fans could claim that they were consecutive four-time World Champions after beating Brazil in 1950.

6. Murad 1996.

7. Dieguez 1985; Helal 1997; Scher 1996.

8. Soares 2000; Archetti 1997.

9. Lever 1983.

10. E. Archetti, pers. com., Nov. 14, 2003; Aidar, Leoncini, and Oliviera 2000; Carrano 2000; Ciria and Ritter 1984; Parrilli 1997; Pimenta 2003.

11. Cameron 1976.

12. Gorelik 1998, 19.

13. Duncan 1990; Cosgrove 1984.

14. For instance, the Palermo Polo Grounds is one of the few stadiums that occupy space in the dense residential core of Buenos Aires and the Estádio das Laranjeiras has survived in its current locale for more than ninety years.

15. Currently, no Rio teams are in the Brazilian second division. Only Portugesa A.A. and América F.C. compete in the Brazilian third division.

16. In both cities entering into the world of the soccer gangs is dangerous and requires careful networking, an absolute mastery of colloquial speech, and protection from the gang leaders. In my opinion, entering into these micro-societies can only be accomplished and should only be attempted by local investigators who have preestablished relationships with the groups. For a running start at these groups, see Damo 2002; Helal 1997; Gil 2002; Alabarces 2003; Archetti 1992; Betti 1997.

17. In Brazil the 2002 Law of the Fan was intended to make soccer's governing institutions more responsive to and responsible for fan security. The Pelé Law, created when Pelé was Extraordinary Minister of Sport in the Cardoso government, was intended to make clubs more transparent in their financial dealings. The CoProSeDe in Argentina is a special legislative branch created under the Kirchner government with the express intent of solving the problems of violence and corruption in Argentine soccer.

18. In one case more than sixty police accompanied seventeen members of Boca's *barrabrava* to an away game at Racing.

19. Pimenta 2003; Santos 2003.

20. Lanfranchi and Taylor 2001, 69–110.

21. Bellos 2002; Foer 2004; Harpers Index, www.harpers.org/archive/2007/07/0081097, July 2006.

22. For instance, the Corinthians Football Club of São Paulo was recently infused with tens of millions of dollars from a multinational consortium based in England.

The club purchased several Argentine stars and won the Brazilian league in 2005.

23. This is especially true in Brazil where television coverage of the second and third divisions is virtually nonexistent.

24. *Diario Olé*, Dec. 9, 2004.

25. Cosgrove 1984; Duncan 1990; Tilley 1994; Hoelscher 1998; Flores 2002.

26. Foote 1997, 267–268.

27. Foote 1997, 208.

28. Foote 1997, 25.

29. Duncan 1990, 4.

30. Duncan 1990, 17.

31. Harvey 2001, 124.

32. Bale 1994a, 70. This is one reason that sports pages are so intentionally apolitical. When politics that contravene nationalist sentiment or challenge the status quo are inserted into the stadium, the response is usually quite virulently negative.

33. The staff of the Estadio Monumental conducted 53,760 guided tours in 2004 (*Diario Clarín*, Jan. 2, 2005, 76). This same article claims that the Estadio Monumental received "exactly 1,340,771 people in 2004." As with all stadiums, it is nearly impossible to count how many people enter. This number does not take into account employees, club members who enter and leave on a daily basis, concessions workers, game officials, and so on. The cumulative number of people who use the stadium in a given year is probably in the neighborhood of 1.7 million.

34. My initial research has discovered, unsurprisingly, that these museums are heavily male referred. In the "official" historical presentations of clubs (Botafogo, Flamengo, Fluminese, Vasco, Boca Juniors) there is an almost complete absence of women. The only references to women are the display of trophies won by female athletes.

35. Kennett and de Moragas 2006.

36. Arbena, Abreu, and LaFrance 2002, 226.

Bibliography

Abreu, M. A. 1987. *Evolução urbana do Rio de Janeiro*. Rio de Janeiro: IPLANRIO/ZAHAR.

Adams, Paul. 2005. *The Boundless Self*. Syracuse, NY: Syracuse University Press.

Agostino, Gilberto. 2002. *Vencer O morrer: Futebol, geopolítica e identidade nacional*. Rio de Janeiro: MAUAD.

Aidar, Antônio Carlos K., Mario Pereira Leoncini, and João José de Oliviera. 2000. *A nova gestão do futebol*. Rio de Janeiro: FGU.

Aiken, Susan, Ann Brigham, Sallie Marston, and Penny Waterstone, eds. 1998. *Making Worlds: Gender, Metaphor, Materiality*. Tucson: University of Arizona Press.

Aitchison, Cara Carmichael. 2003. *Gender and Leisure: Social and Cultural Perspectives*. London: Routledge.

Aitchison, Cara Carmichael, Nicola E. MacLeod, Stephen J. Shaw, eds. 2001. *Leisure and Tourism Landscapes: Social and Cultural Landscapes*. New York: Routledge, 2001.

Alabarces, Pablo. 2003. *Fútbologicas: Fútbol, identidad y violencia en América Latina*. Buenos Aires: CLACSO.

——, ed. 2000. *Peligro del gol. Estudios sobre deporte y sociedad en América Latina*. Buenos Aires: CLASCO.

Alabarces, Pablo, and Maria Graciela Rodriguez. 1996. *Cuestion de pelotas*. Buenos Aires: Atuel.

——. 1999. "Football and Fatherland: The Crisis of National Representation in Argentinian Football." *Culture, Sport, Society* 2 (3).

Alabarces, Pablo, Roberto di Gano, and Julio Frydenberg, comps. 1998. *Deporte y sociedad*. Buenos Aires: Editorial Universitaria de Buenos Aires.

Allinson, Lincoln. 1978. "Manchester and São Paolo; Problems of Rapid Urban Growth." In *Association Football and the Urban Ethos*, edited by R. L. Jones and J. D. Wirth. Palo Alto, CA: Stanford University Press.

Anderson, Benedict. 1983. *Imagined Communities*. New York: Verso.

Appadurai, Arjun. 1996. *Modernity at Large*. Minneapolis: University of Minnesota Press.

Araujo, Sebastião. 2000. Futebol e imigração. São Paulo: IDESP.

———. 2001. *O radio, o futebol, a vida*. São Paulo: SENAC.

Arbena, Joseph. 1988. *Sport and Society in Latin America: Diffusion, Dependency and the Rise of Mass Culture*. New York: Greenwood Press.

———. 1990. "Generales and Goles: Assessing the Connection between the Military and Soccer in Argentina." *International Journal of the History of Sport* 7 (1): 120–130.

———. 1999. *Latin American Sport: An Annotated Bibliography, 1988–1998*. Westport, CT: Greenwood Press.

Arbena, Joseph, and David LaFrance, eds. 2002. *Sport in Latin America and the Caribbean*. Wilmington, DE: Scholarly Resources.

Arbena, Joseph, M. A. Abreu, and David LaFrance. 2002. "In Search of the Latin American Female Athlete." In *Sport in Latin America and the Caribbean*, edited by Joseph Arbena and David LaFrance. Wilmington, DE: Scholarly Resources.

Archetti, Eduardo. 1985. "Fútbol, violencia y afirmación masculina." *Debates en la Sociedad y la Cultura* 2 (3): 38–44.

———. 1992. "Argentinian Football: A Ritual of Violence?" *International Journal for the History of Sport* 9 (2): 209–235.

———. 1995. "In Search of National Identity; Argentinian Football and Europe." *International Journal of the History of Sport* 12 (2): 201–219.

———. 1997. "The Moralities of Argentinian Football." In *The Ethnography of Moralities*, edited by Singe Howell. London: Routledge.

———. 1998a. *Masculinities: An Anthropology of Football, Polo and Tango*. Oxford: Berg.

———. 1998b. "El potrero y el pibe: Territorio y pertenencia en el imaginario del fútbol argentino." *Nueva Sociedad* 154: 101–119.

———. 2003. *Masculinidades: Fútbol, tango y polo en la Argentina*. Buenos Aires: Editorial Antopofagia.

Archetti, Eduardo, and Amilcar Romero. 1994. "Death and Violence in Argentine Football." In *Football, Violence and Social Identity*, edited by Richard Giulianotti. London: Routledge.

Armstrong, Gary, and Richard Giulianotti. 1997. *Entering the Field: New Perspectives on World Football*. New York: Berg.

———. 1999. *Football Cultures and Identities*. London: Macmillan.

———. 2001. *Fear and Loathing in World Football*. New York: Berg.

Asociación Argentina de Polo. 2005. "Asi fue como lo vieron los periodistas especializados." *Centauros* 25: 1.

Assaf, Roberto Clovis Martins. 1997. *Campeonato carioca: 96 anos de historia: 1902–1997*. Rio de Janeiro: Irradiação Cultural.

Atkinson, David, and Denis Cosgrove. 1998. "Urban Rhetoric and Embodied Identities: City, Nation, and Empire at the Vittorio Emanuele II Monument in Rome." *Annals of the Association of American Geographers* 88 (1): 28–49.

Avritzer, Leonardo. 2002. *Democracy and Public Space in Latin America*. Princeton, NJ: Princeton University Press, 2002.

Azeredi, Fernando. 1930. *A evolução do esporte no Brasil (1822–1922)*. São Paulo: Melhores Momentos.

Bale, John. 1980. "Football Clubs as Neighbors." *Town and Country Planning* 49: 93–94.

———. 1982. *Sport and Place: A Geography of Sport in England, Scotland, and Wales*. Lincoln: University of Nebraska Press.

———. 1984. *Sports Geography*. London: Spon.

———. 1993a. "The Spatial Development of the Modern Stadium." *International Review for the Sociology of Sport* 28 (2): 121–133.

———. 1993b. *Sport, Space and the City*. New York: Routledge.

———. 1994. *Landscapes of Modern Sport*. Leicester: Leicester University Press, 1994.

———. 2000. *Sportscapes*. Sheffield: Geographical Association.

———. 2003. *Sports Geography*. 2nd ed. London: Routledge.

Bale, John, and Philo Chris, eds. 1999. *Body Cultures: Essays on Sport, Space, and Identity*. London: Routledge.

Bale, John, and Mike Cronin, eds. 2003. *Sport and Postcolonialism*. Oxford: Berg.

Bale, John, and Joseph Macguire. 1994. *The Global Sports Arena: Athletic Talent in an Interdependent World*. London: Frank Cass.

Bale, John, and Olaf Moen, eds. 1995. *The Stadium and the City*. London: Keele University Press.

Bao, Daniel. 1993. "Invertidos Sexuales, Tortilleras, and Maricas Machos: The Construction of Homosexuality in Buenos Aires, Argentina, 1900–1950." *Journal of Homosexuality* 24 (3): 183–219.

Bayer, Osvaldo. 1990. *Fútbol argentino: Pasión y gloria de nuestro deporte mas popular*. Buenos Aires: Editorial Sudamericana.

Bellos, Alex. 2002. *Futebol: The Brazilian Way of Life*. London: Bloomsbury.

Benson, Michael. 1989. *Ballparks of North America: A Comprehensive Historical Reference to Baseball Grounds, Yards and Stadiums, 1845 to Present.* Jefferson, NC: McFarland.

Betti, Mauro. *Violencia em campo.* 1997. Ijuí, Brazil: Unijuí.

Binello, Gabriela, Mariana Conde, Analia Martinez, and Maria Graciela Rodriguez. 2000. "Mujeres y fútbol: Territorio conquistado o a conquistar?" In *Peligro del gol: Estudios sobre deporte y sociedad en América Latina,* edited by Pablo Alabarces. Buenos Aires: CLASCO.

Bourdieu, Pierre. 1984. *Distinction: A Social Critique of the Judgement of Taste.* London: Routledge.

Bowden, Martyn. 1995. "Soccer." In *The Theatre of Sport,* edited by Karl Raitz. Baltimore, MD: Johns Hopkins University Press.

Braceli, Rodolfo. 2001. *De fútbol somos: La condición argentina.* Buenos Aires: Editorial Sudamericana, 2001.

Brailsford, Dennis. 1991. *Sport, Time and Society: The British at Play.* London: Routledge.

Brittan, Arthur. 1989. *Masculinity and Power.* Oxford: Basil Blackwell.

Browder, John, and Brian Godfrey. 1997. *Rainforest Cities: Urbanization, Development and Globalization of the Brazilian Amazon.* New York: Columbia University Press.

Brown, Adam. 1998. *Virtual Fandoms.* New York: Routledge.

Bruhns, Heloisa Turini. 2000. *Futebol, carnaval e capoeira.* Campinas, Brazil: Papirus.

Bueno, Fernando. 2000. "Violencia no futebol." Ph.D. dissertation, Pontifícia Universidade Católica de São Paulo.

Buford, Bill. 1992. *Among the Thugs.* New York: W. W. Norton.

Burns, E. Bradford. 1978. "Cultures in Conflict: The Implication of Modernization in Nineteenth-Century Latin America." In *Elites, Masses, and Modernization in Latin America, 1850–1930,* edited by E. Bradford Burns and Thomas E. Skidmore. Austin: University of Texas Press.

Caldas, Waldenyr. 1990. *O pontape inicial: Memoria do futebol brasiliero (1894–1933).* São Paulo: IBRASA, 1990.

Cameron, Alan. 1976. *Circus Factions: Blues and Greens at Rome and Byzantium.* Oxford: Clarendon Press, 1976.

Cardoso, Adauto Lúcio. 1996. *Dualização e reestruturação urbana: O caso do Rio de Janeiro.* Rio de Janeiro: DP&A.

Carrano, Paolo, and Caesar Rodrigues. 2000. *Futebol: Paixão e politica.* Rio de Janeiro: DP&A.

Chauncey, George. 1994. *Gay New York: Gender and the Making of the Gay Male World, 1890–1940.* New York: Basic Books, 1994.

Chepenekas, Gabriel, Fernando D'Addario, and Luis Vivori. 1997. *Sábado:*

La historia del fútbol de Ascenso. Buenos Aires: Plan 9 Ediciones.

Ciria, Alberto. 1984. "From Soccer to War in Argentina: Preliminary Notes on Sports-as-Politics under a Military Regime (1976–1982)." In *Latin America and the Caribbean: Geopolitics, Development, and Culture*, edited by Arch R. M. Ritter. Ottawa: Canadian Association for Latin American and Caribbean Studies.

Clarke, Stewart. 1999. *The Homes of Football: The Passion of a Nation.* London: Little, Brown.

Cosgrove, Denis. 1984. *Social Formation and Symbolic Landscape.* Madison: University of Wisconsin Press.

Cosgrove, Denis, and Stephen Daniels. 1998. *The Iconography of Landscape.* Cambridge: Cambridge University Press.

Coulson, William, and Helmut Kyrieleis, eds. 1992. *Proceedings of an International Symposium of the Olympic Games, 5–9 September 1988.* Athens: Deutsches Archaologisches Institut Athena.

C.R. Vasco da Gama. 2007. *O São Januário aos 80 anos.* Rio de Janeiro: Casaca.

Cunha, Loris Baena. 1994. *A verdadeira historia do futebol brasiliero.* Rio de Janeiro: ABRADE.

Cunningham, Susan, and Janet Momsen. 1987. *Gender and Industrialization in Brazil.* London: Hutchinson Education.

DaMatta, Roberto. 1982. *Universo do futebol.* Rio de Janeiro: Edições Pinakotheke.

———. 1985. *A casa e a rua: Espaço, cidadania, mulher e morte no Brasil.* São Paulo: Brasiliense.

———. 1990. *Carnavais, malandros e herois.* Rio de Janeiro: Koogan.

Damo, Arlei S. 2002. *Futebol e identidade social: Uma leitura antropologica das rivalidades entre torcedores e clubes.* Porto Alegre, Brazil: Editora da Universidade.

Danielson, Michael. 1997. *Home Team: Professional Sports and the American Metropolis.* Princeton, NJ: Princeton University Press.

de Oliviera, Claudio, Henrique Machado, and Milton Coelho de Graça. 2004. "O perfil do tordedor carioca." Laboratorio UniCarioca de Pesquisas Aplicadas, Rio de Janeiro.

di Gano, Roberto. 2005. *Fútbol y cultura política en la Argentina.* Buenos Aires: n.p.

Dieguez, Gilda Corp. 1985. *Esporte e poder.* Petrópolis, Brazil: Editora Vozes.

Duke, Vic, and Liz Crolley. 2001. "Fútbol, Politicians and the People: Populism and Politics in Argentina." *International Journal of the History of Sport* 18 (3): 93–116.

Duncan, James. 1990. *The City as Text: The Politics of Landscape Interpretation in the Kandyan Kingdom.* New York: Cambridge University Press.

Dunning, Eric. 1999. *Sport Matters: Sociological Studies of Sport, Violence and Civilization.* London: Routledge.

Durran, S. A. 1970. *Gran enciclopedia del mundo.* Rio de Janeiro: Durran.

Dyck, Noel, and Eduardo Archetti. 2003a. "Playing Football and Dancing Tango: Embodying Argentina in Movement, Style and Identity." In *Sport, Dance, and Embodied Identities,* edited by Noel Dyck and Eduardo Archetti. New York: Berg.

———, eds. 2003b. *Sport, Dance and Embodied Identities.* London: Berg.

Elias, Norbert, and Eric Dunning. 1986. *Quest for Excitement: Sport and Leisure in the Civilizing Process.* Oxford: Basil Blackwell.

Euchner, Charles. 1993. *Playing the Field: Why Sports Teams Move and Cities Fight to Keep Them.* Baltimore, MD: Johns Hopkins University Press.

Fernandes, Ana Cristina, and Rovena Negreiros. 2001. "Economic Developmentalism and Change within the Brazilian Urban System." *Geoforum* 32: 415–435.

Fernandes, Mario do Carmo. 1974. *Futebol: Fenómeno lingüistico.* Rio de Janeiro: Pontifícia Universidade Católica de Rio Janeiro.

Ferns, H. S. 1966. *Gran Bretaña y Argentina en el siglo XIX.* Buenos Aires: Solar/Hachette, 1966.

Ferreira, Fernando da Costa. 2004. "O Bairro Vasco da Gama: Um novo bairro, uma nova identidade?" Master's thesis, Federal University of Rio de Janeiro.

Findlay, John. 1992. *Magic Lands: Western Cityscapes and American Culture after 1945.* Berkeley: University of California Press.

Flores, Richard. 2002. *Remembering the Alamo: Memory, Modernity, and the Master Symbol.* Austin: University of Texas Press.

Foer, Franklin. 2004. *How Soccer Explains the World.* New York: HarperCollins.

Foote, Kenneth. 1997. *Shadowed Ground: America's Landscapes of Violence and Tragedy.* Austin: University of Texas Press.

Foster, David William. 1998. *Buenos Aires: Perspectives on the City and Cultural Production.* Gainesville: University of Florida Press.

Foucault, Michel. 1977. *Discipline and Punish.* New York: Vintage.

Frydenberg, Julio. 1999. "Espacio urbana y la práctica del fútbol, Buenos Aires, 1900–1915." *efdeportes* 13 (1): 1–40.

———. 2001. "Los clubes del fútbol argentino en crisis: Diagnósticos y soluciones." *efdeportes* 6 (33).

Futrell, Allison. 1997. *Blood in the Arena*. Austin: University of Texas Press.

Gaffney, Christopher. 2002. "Soccer and the Geographic Construction of Identity: A New England Case Study." Master's thesis, University of Massachusetts–Amherst.

Gaffney, Christopher, and Gilmar Mascarenhas de Jesus. 2005. "O estadio de futebol como espaço disciplinar." *Esporte e Sociedade* 1 (1).

Gaffney, Christopher, and John Bale. 2004. "Sensing the Stadium." In *Sites of Sport: Space, Place, Experience*, edited by John Bale and Patricia Vertinsky. London: Routledge.

Galeano, Eduardo. 2002. *Soccer in Sun and Shadow*. New York: Verso.

Gama, Walter. 1996. *Aspectos socioculturais do futebol*. São Paulo: ECA-SP.

Gandara, Leila. 1997. "Las voces del fútbol: Análisis del discurso y cantos de cancha." *efdeportes* 17 (1): 1–20.

Gandara, Leila, and Sebastian Codeseira. 2000. "Graffiti, fútbol e identidad." *efdeportes* 5 (22).

Gebhard, Elizabeth. 1992. *The Early Stadium at Isthmia and the Founding of the Isthmian Games*. Athens: Deutsches Archaologisches Institut Atehena.

Gianole, Manuel. 1996. *Torcedor de futebol e o espectáculo da arquibancada*. São Paulo: EEF-ESP.

Gil, Gaston Julian. 2002. *Fútbol e identidades locales*. Buenos Aires: Mino y Davila.

Giulianotti, Richard. 1999. *Football: A Sociology of the Global Game*. London: Polity.

———. 2002. "Supporters, Followers, Fans and Flaneurs." *Journal of Sport and Social Issues* 26 (1): 25–46.

Giulianotti, Richard, Norman Bonney, and Mike Hempworth. 1994. *Football, Violence and Social Identity*. New York: Routledge.

Godfrey, B. J. 1991. "Modernizing the Brazilian City." *Geographical Review* 81 (1): 18–35.

———. 1999. "Revisiting Rio de Janeiro and São Paulo." *Geographical Review* 89 (1): 94–122.

Gordon, Barclay. 1983. *Olympic Architecture*. New York: John Wiley and Sons.

Gorelik, Adrian. 1998. *La grilla y el parque: Espacio público y cultura urbana en Buenos Aires, 1887–1936*. Quilmes, Argentina: Universidad Nacional de Quilmes.

Gottdeiner, Mark. 1985. *The Social Production of Urban Space*. Austin: University of Texas Press.

Graham, Sandra. 1988. *House and Street: The Domestic World of Servants and Masters in Nineteenth-Century Rio de Janeiro.* Austin: University of Texas Press.

Gregory, Derek. 1994. *Geographical Imaginations.* Oxford: Blackwell.

Groth, Paul, and Todd Bressi. 1997. *Understanding Ordinary Landscapes.* New Haven, CT: Yale University Press.

Gruneau, Richard. 1999. *Class, Sports, and Social Development.* Champaign: University of Illinois Press.

Guedes, Simon. 1998. *O Brasil no campo do futebol.* Niteroi, Brazil: Eduff.

Gueiros, Pedro Morra. "O caos total que as autoridades não enxergam," *O Globo.* 2 July 2004.

Guttmann, Allen. 1978. *From Ritual to Record: The Nature of Modern Sports.* New York: Columbia University Press.

———. 1986. *Sports Spectators.* New York: Columbia University Press.

———. 1988. *A Whole New Ball Game: An Interpretation of American Sports.* Chapel Hill: University of North Carolina Press.

———. 1996. *The Erotic in Sports.* New York: Columbia University Press.

Guy, Donna. 1991. *Sex and Danger in Buenos Aires: Prostitution, Family and Nation in Argentina.* Lincoln: University of Nebraska Press.

———. 1992. "'White Slavery,' Citizenship and Nationality in Argentina." In *Nationalisms and Sexualities,* edited by Andrew Parker. London: Routledge.

Hamilton, Aidan. 2001. *Um jogo interamente diferente. Futebol: A maestria brasileira de um legado britânico.* Rio de Janeiro: Griphus.

Hardin, Garrett. 1968. "The Tragedy of the Commons." *Science* 162: 1242–1248.

Harvey, David. 1979. "Monument and Myth: The Building of the Basilica of the Sacred Heart." In *Annals of the Association of American Geographers.* 69 (3): 362–381.

———. 1989. *The Condition of Post-Modernity.* Oxford: Basil Blackwell.

———. 2001. *Spaces of Capital: Towards a Critical Geography.* New York: Routledge.

Helal, Ronaldo. 1997. *Passes e impasses: Futebol e cultura de massa no Brasil.* Petropolis, Brazil: Vozes.

Henrique de Toledo, Luiz. 1996. *Torcidas organizadas do futebol.* São Paulo: Editora Autores Associados/ANPOCS.

———. 2002. *Lógicas no futebol.* São Paulo: Hucitec/Fapesp.

Herschmann, Micael. 1993. *Lance de sorte: O futebol e o jogo do bicho na belle epoque carioca.* Rio de Janeiro: Diadorim.

Hayden, Dolores. 1995. *The Power of Place: Urban Landscapes as Public History.* Cambridge, MA: MIT Press.

Hobsbawm, Eric, and Terence Ranger. 1983. *The Invention of Tradition.* Cambridge: Cambridge University Press.

Hoelscher, Steven. 1998. *Heritage on Stage: The Invention of Ethnic Place in America's Little Switzerland.* Madison: University of Wisconsin Press.

Holt, R. J. 1988. "Football and the Urban Way of Life in Nineteenth-Century Britain." In *Pleasure, Profit, Proselytism: British Culture and Sport at Home and Abroad, 1700–1914,* edited by J. A. Mangan. London: Frank Cass.

Inglis, Simon. 1990. *The Football Grounds of Europe.* London: Collins Willow.

———. 1996. *Football Grounds of Great Britain.* London: Collins Willow.

———. 2000. *Sightlines: A Stadium Odyssey.* London: Yellow Jersey Press.

Iwanczuk, Jorge. 1992. *Historia del fútbol amateur en la Argentina.* Buenos Aires: Ed. Sports.

Jones, Gareth. 2004. "A Geo-politics of Latin American Cities." Paper presented at Mellon Conference, "The End of Public Space in the Latin American City?" University of Texas at Austin, Mar.

Kennett, Christopher, and Miquel de Moragas. 2006. "Barcelona 1992: Evaluating the Olympic Legacy." In *National Identity and Global Sports Events,* edited by Alan Tomlinson and Christopher Young. Albany: State University of New York Press.

Kern, Stephen. 1983. *The Culture of Time and Space, 1880–1918.* Cambridge, MA: Harvard University Press.

King, Anthony. 1998. *The End of the Terraces: The Transformation of English Football in the 1990s.* London: Books International.

LaFlamme, Alan. 1977. "The Role of Sport in the Development of Ethnicity." *Sport Sociology Bulletin* 6 (1): 47–51.

Lanfranchi, Pierre, and Matthew Taylor. 2001. *Moving with the Ball: The Migration of Professional Footballers.* Oxford: Berg.

Lefebvre, Henri. [1973] 1991. *The Production of Space.* London: Blackwell.

Lever, Janet. 1983. *Soccer Madness.* Chicago: University of Chicago Press.

Levinsky, Sergio. 1995. *El negocio del fútbol.* Buenos Aires: Ediciones Corregidor.

Leyenaar, Ted. 1978. *Ulama: The Perpetuation in Mexico of the Pre-Spanish Ball Game Ullamaliztli.* Leiden: Rijksmusuem voor Volkenkunde.

Llistosella, Jorge. 1977. *Los Pumas.* Buenos Aires: Ediciones Match.

Lopes, José Leite. 1995. *Esporte, emoção e conflito social.* Rio de Janeiro: n.p.

Low, Setha. 2000. *On the Plaza: The Politics of Public Space and Culture*. Austin: University of Texas Press.

Lowry, Philip. 1992. *Green Cathedrals: The Ultimate Celebration of All 271 Major League and Negro League Ballparks Past and Present*. Reading, MA: Addison-Wesley.

Lucena, Ricardo de Figueiredo. 2000. *O esporte na cidade*. Campinas, Brazil: Editora Autores Associados.

Lynch, Kevin. 1964. *The Image of the City*. Cambridge, MA: MIT Press.

———. 1972. *What Time Is This Place?* Cambridge, MA: MIT Press.

MacAloon, John. 1981. *This Great Symbol: Pierre de Coubertin and the Origins of the Modern Olympic Games*. Chicago: University of Chicago Press.

———. 1984. *Rite, Drama, Festival, Spectacle*. Philadelphia: Institute for the Study of Human Issues.

Malhano, Clara, and Hamilton Malhano. 2002. *Memoria social dos esportes: São Januário—Arquitetura e historia*. Rio de Janeiro: MAUAD.

Mangan, J., A. Lamartine, and P. DaCosta, eds. 2001. *Sport in Latin American Society: Past and Present*. London: Frank Cass.

Mascarenhas de Jesus, Gilmar. 2000. "Construindo a cidade moderna: A introdução dos esportes na vida urbana do Rio de Janeiro." *Estudos Históricos* 23 (1): 17–37.

———. 2002a. "A geografia ineditada do futebol no Brasil." Universidade do São Paulo, 2002.

———. 2002b. "Varzeas, operarios e futebol: Uma outra geografia." *GEOgraphia* 4 (8): 115–129.

Mason, Colin, and Andrew Moncrief. 1993. "The Effect of Relocation on the Externality Fields of Football Stadia: The Case of St Jonstone FC." *Scottish Geographical Magazine* 109 (2): 96–105.

Mason, Colin, and Richard Robbins. 1991. "The Spatial Externality Fields of Football Stadiums: The Effects of Football and Non-Football Uses at Kenilworth Road, Luton." *Applied Geography* 11: 251–266.

Mason, Tony. 1995. *Passion of the People? Football in South America*. New York: Verso.

Massey, Dolores. 1994. *Space, Place, and Gender*. Minneapolis: University of Minnesota Press.

Mayochi, Enrique Mario. 1992. "El primer gol que les hicimos a los ingleses." *La Nación*, no. 1184 (Mar. 15), 15.

Meade, Teresa. 1997. *"Civilizing" Rio: Reform and Resistance in a Brazilian City, 1889–1930*. University Park: Pennsylvania State University Press.

Melo, Victor, and J. A. Mangan. 1997. "A Web of the Wealthy: Modern Sports in the Nineteenth-Century Culture of Rio de Janeiro." *International Journal of the History of Sport* 14 (1): 168–173.

Menschell, Robert. 2002. *Markets, Mobs and Mayhem: A Modern Look at the Madness of Crowds.* Hoboken, NJ: John Wiley and Sons.

Miller, Stephen, William Coulson, and Helmut Kyrieleis. 1988. "The Stadium at Nemea and the Nemean Games." Paper presented at the International Symposium on the Olympic Games, Athens.

Moore, A. B., P. Whigham, A. Holt, C. Aldridge, and K. Hodge. 2003. "A Time Geography Approach to the Visualization of Sport." Paper presented at the 7th International Conference on Geocomputation, 18.

Morales, Franklin. 2000. *Maracanã: Los laberintos del carácter.* Montevideo, Uruguay: Ediciones Santillana.

Moura, Gisella de Araujo. 1998. *O rio corre para o Maracanã.* Rio de Janeiro: Fundação Getulio Vargas.

Mumford, Lewis. 1961. *The City in History: Its Origins, Transformations, and Its Prospects.* New York: MJF Books.

Murad, Mauricio. 1996. *Dos pes a cabeça: Elementos básicos de sociologia do futebol.* Rio de Janeiro: Irradiação Cultural.

Needell, Jeffrey. 1995. "Rio de Janeiro and Buenos Aires: Public Space and Public Consciousness in Fin-de-Siècle Latin America." *Comparative Studies in Society and History* 37 (3): 519–540.

Negreiros, Plínio Jose. 1997. "O estádio do Pacaembú." In *Coletanea do V Encontro de História do Esporte, Lazer e Educação Física.* Ijuí: Editoria da Unijuí.

Noll, Roger, and Andrew Zimbalist, eds. 1997. *Sports, Jobs, and Taxes: The Economic Impact of Sports Teams and Taxes.* Washington, DC: Brookings Institution.

Olivova, Vera. 1984. *Sports and Games in the Ancient World.* New York: St. Martin's Press.

Outtes, Joel. 2003. "Disciplining Society through the City: The Genesis of City Planning in Brazil and Argentina (1894–1945)." *Bulletin of Latin American Research* 22 (2): 137–164.

Paoli, Maria Celia, Maria Victoria Benevides, Paulo Sergio Pinheiro, and Roberto DaMatta. 1982. *Violencia brasileira.* São Paulo: Editora Brasiliense.

Parker, Richard. 1990. *Bodies, Pleasures and Passions: Sexual Culture in Contemporary Brazil.* Boston: Beacon Press.

Parrilli, Marcelo. 1997. *Barrabrava de boca: El juicio.* Buenos Aires: Ediciones La Montana.

Pereira, Leonardo Addonso de Miranda. 2000. *Footballmania: Uma his-*

toria social do futebol no Rio de Janeiro, 1902–1938. Rio de Janeiro: Nova Fronteira.

Perlman, Janice. 1976. *The Myth of Marginality: Urban Poverty and Politics in Rio de Janeiro.* Berkeley: University of California Press.

Pimenta, Carlos Alberto Maximo. 1995. *Futebol e violencia.* São Paulo: Pontifícia Universidade Católica do São Paulo.

———. 2003. "Torcidas organizadas de futebol: Identidade e identificações, dimensões cotidianas." In *Futbológicas: Fútbol, identidad y violencia en América Latina,* edited by Pablo Alabarces. Buenos Aires: CLASCO.

Pineto, Carlos. 1997. *Torcidas organizadas de futebol.* Tabate: Vogal.

Prebish, Charles. 1993. *Religion and Sport: The Meeting of the Sacred and the Profane.* New Haven, CT: Greenwood Press.

Pred, Allan. 1984. "Place as Historically Contingent Process: Structuration and the Time-Geography of Becoming Places." *Annals of the Association of American Geographers* 74 (2): 179–297.

Pronger, Brian. 1990. *The Arena of Masculinity: Sports, Homosexuality and the Meaning of Sex.* New York: St. Martin's Press.

Quadros, Raymundo. 2004. *Chuva de glorias: A trajetoria do São Cristóvão de futebol e regatas.* Rio de Janeiro: Pontes.

Quirarte, Jacinto. 1970. *Juego de pelota en Mesoamerica: Su desarrollo arquitecnico.* Austin: Institute of Latin American Studies, University of Texas.

Radcliffe, Sarah. 1993. "Women's Place / El Lugar de Mujeres: Latin America and the Politics of Gender Identity." In *Place and the Politics of Identity,* edited by Michael Keith and Steve Pile. London: Routledge.

Raitz, Karl. 1995. *The Theatre of Sport: A Landscape Perspective.* Baltimore, MD: Johns Hopkins University Press.

Ramos, Roberto. 1984. *Futebol: Ideologia do poder.* Petropolis, Brazil: Vozes.

———. 1990. *A palavra e futebol.* São Paulo: Scipione.

Relph, Edward. 1976. *Place and Placelessness.* London: Pion.

———. 1987. *The Modern Urban Landscape.* Baltimore, MD: Johns Hopkins University Press.

Rodgers, Dennis. 1999. *Youth Gangs and Violence in Latin America and the Caribbean: A Literature Survey.* New York: World Bank, Latin America and the Caribbean Region.

Rodrigues, Mario, Jr. (Mario Filho). 1964. *O negro no futebol brasileiro.* Rio de Janeiro: Editora Civilização Brasileira.

Romero, Amilcar. 1986. *Muerte en la cancha.* Buenos Aires: Editorial Nueva América.

Rosenthal, Anton. 2000. "Spectacle, Fear, and Protest: A Guide to the History of Urban Public Space in Latin America." *Social Science History* 24 (1): 33–73.

Sabugo, Mario. 1983. *Las canchas: Monumentos bohemios.* Buenos Aires: CEPA.

Sands, Robert. 1987. *Anthropology, Sport and Culture.* Bridgeport, CT: Bergin and Garvey.

Santos, Tarcyanie Cajueiro. 2003. "O lado 'hard' da cultura 'cool': As torcidas e a violencia no futebol." In *Futbológicas: Fútbol, identidad y violencia en América Latina,* edited by Pablo Alabarces. Buenos Aires: CLASCO.

Scarpaci, Joseph. 2004. "Changing Public Spaces in the Spanish American Plaza and Barrio: Commodifying and Conviviality as Simultaneous Processes." Paper presented at the conference "The End of Public Space in the Latin American City?" Austin, TX, Mar. 4–5.

———. 2005. *Plazas and Barrios: Heritage Tourism and Globalization in the Latin America Centro Histórico.* Tucson: University of Arizona Press.

Scheffler, Lilian. 1985. *El juego de pelota prehispánico y sus supervivencias actuales.* Tlahuapan, Mexico: Premia Editora.

Scher, Ariel. 1996. *La patria deportista.* Buenos Aires: Planeta.

Scher, Ariel, and Hector Palomino. 1988. *Fútbol: Pasión de multitudes y de élites.* Buenos Aires: CLASCO.

Schumway, Nicholas. 1991. *The Invention of Argentina.* Berkeley: University of California Press.

Scobie, James R. 1974. *Buenos Aires: Plaza to Suburb, 1870–1910.* New York: Oxford University Press.

Sebreli, Juan José. 1983. *La era de fútbol.* Buenos Aires: Editorial Sudamericana.

Sheard, Rod. 2001. *Sports Architecture.* London: Spon.

———. 2005. *The Stadium: Architecture for the New Global Culture.* North Clarendon, VT: Periplus Editions.

Sibley, D. 1995. *Geographies of Exclusion: Society and Difference in the West.* London: Routledge.

Smith, Neil. 1998. "Antinomies of Space and Nature in Henri Lefebvre's the Production of Space." In *The Production of Space,* edited by Andrew Light and Jonathan Smith. Lanham, MD: Rowman and Littlefield.

Soares, Antonio. 2000. "Historia e a invenção de tradicoes no futebol brasileiro." In *Peligro del gol,* edited by Pablo Alabarces. Buenos Aires: CLASCO.

Soares, Antonio, and Hugo Lovisolo. 2003. "O caso do 'po-de-arroz': O rigor necessario." *Polemica* 11 (1).

Solina, Ubitatan. 2007. *Journal do Casaca!* 4 (26). 222.casaca.com.br.

Spinetto, Horacio. 1992. "Ciento veinte años de rugby argentino." *Revista Todo es Historia,* no. 295: 8–36.

Stein, Steven. 1988. "The Case of Soccer in Early 20th Century Lima." In *Sport and Society in Latin America: Diffusion, Dependency and the Rise of Mass Culture,* edited by Joesph Arbena. New York: Greenwood Press.

Swaddling, Judith. 1999. *The Ancient Olympic Games.* Austin: University of Texas Press.

Taylor, Chris. 1998. *The Beautiful Game: A Journey through Latin American Football.* London: Phoenix Press.

Thrift, Nigel. 1999. "The Making of a Capitalist Time-Consciousness, 1300–1880." In *Human Geography,* edited by John Agnew, David Livingstone, and Alisdair Rogers. London: Routledge.

Tilley, Christopher. 1994. *The Phenomenology of Landscape: Places, Paths and Monuments.* Providence, RI: Berg.

Tranter, Neil. 1998. *Sport, Economy and Society in Britain, 1750–1914.* Cambridge: Cambridge University Press.

Tuan, Yi-Fu. 1974. *Topophilia: A Study of Environmental Perception, Attitudes and Values.* Englewood Cliffs, NJ: Prentice-Hall.

———. 1977. *Space and Place: The Perspective of Experience.* Minneapolis: University of Minnesota Press.

———. 1978. "Sacred Space: Explorations of an Idea." In *Dimensions of Human Geography: Essays on Some Familiar and Neglected Themes,* edited by Karl Butzer. Chicago: University of Chicago, Department of Geography.

Turner, Victor. 1969. *The Ritual Process.* Chicago: University of Chicago Press.

———. 1973. "The Center out There: Pilgrim's Goal." *History of Religions* 12 (3): 191–230.

Urruita, Miguel. 1991. *Long-Term Trends in Latin American Economic Development.* Washington, DC: Inter-American Development Bank.

Vieira, Claudio. 2000. *Maracanã: Templo dos deuses brasileiros.* Rio de Janeiro: Construtora Varca Scatena.

Vinnai, Gerhard. 1977. *Futebol como ideología.* Buenos Aires: Siglo Veintiuno, 1975.

Voigt, David. 1976. *America through Baseball.* Chicago: Nelson-Hall.

Wallerstein, Immanuel. 1984. *The Politics of the World-Economy.* Cambridge: Cambridge University Press.

Weiner, Jay. 2000. *Stadium Games: Fifty Years of Big League Greed and Bush League Boondoggles*. Minneapolis: University of Minnesota Press.

Zirin, Dave. 2005. *What's My Name Fool? Sports and Resistance in the United States*. Chicago: Haymarket Books.

Zukin, Sharon. 1991. *Landscapes of Power: From Detroit to Disney World*. Berkeley: University of California Press.

Index

Page numbers in italics refer to photos, maps, and figures.